ON THE CLOCK: EDMONTON OILERS

ON THE CLOCK: EDMONTON OILERS

Behind the Scenes
with the Edmonton Oilers
at the NHL Draft

ALLAN MITCHELL

TRIUMPH
B O O K S

Library of Congress Cataloging-in-Publication Data available upon request.

This book is available in quantity at special discounts for your group or organization. For further information, contact:

Triumph Books LLC
814 North Franklin Street
Chicago, Illinois 60610
(312) 337-0747
www.triumphbooks.com

Printed in U.S.A.
ISBN: 978-1-62937-894-7
Design by Preston Pisellini
Page production by Patricia Frey

This book is dedicated to my mom, Lois Mitchell; my wife, Jo-Anne; and my children, Michael and Chelsea. Having supportive people all my life has made difficult things possible. I am forever grateful for each of them.

CONTENTS

Foreword by Frank Seravalli   ix

Introduction   xi

1 A Dynasty Is Formed 1

2 Stanley Cup Champions! 27

3 Champions in the NHL; Pipeline Begins
to Fade. 68

4 A Fifth Stanley and a Draft Shutout. 115

5 From the Penthouse to the Middle of
Nowhere—a Quick Fall. 124

6 Nadir's Raiders 1.0: Oilers Reach a New
Low, but the Draft Picks Improve 155

7 Oilers Are Back! 188

8 A Brand-New Day: Kevin Prendergast
Replaces a Legend 232

9 The Decade of Darkness Begins 285

10 A False Spring. 313

11 The Hockey Gods Shine a Light, Again 365

12 Ball of Confusion. 376

13 A Measured Approach. 399

14 Final Summary 418

Appendix: Oilers Draft List   426

Sources   449

FOREWORD

THE LIFEBLOOD OF an NHL organization is amateur procurement. Period. End of story.

Perhaps no franchise exemplifies that statement more than the Edmonton Oilers. Oil Country has experienced the highest of highs and the lowest of lows—from City of Champions to the Decade of Darkness—as a result of the ebbs and flows, the finds and follies of the annual NHL Entry Draft. No matter the era, converting picks into productive NHL players is central to sustained success. Scouting staffs that hit repeatedly, particularly in later rounds, often wind up with their names etched on Lord Stanley's mug.

My good friend Allan Mitchell has been a keen observer of the NHL Draft—not just over the years, but particularly throughout the Oilers' history. Over the following pages, he will succinctly outline the correlation between drafting and on-ice success. There are no details missed, no trend that he did not discover.

He will take modern analytics tools and apply them to the draft beginning in 1979 to uncover fascinating draft facts, including a three-year run in 1979–81 by Oilers scouting director Barry Fraser that perfectly married drafting skill with future success. Those drafts were a textbook template for success in the modern game. But Fraser and his staff merely stumbled into the results by accident—and never embraced mathematical formulas as a draft tool. They relied solely on the eye test. It was a different time.

For years after its initial success, Edmonton abandoned its focus on skill and paid a heavy price. Only in the last decade has the organization returned to its brilliant, if not unintentional, roots.

Allan will take you through 40-plus seasons of the draft, with specific attention paid to the 2014 draft and beyond, noting the improvements made in Edmonton's draft template.

His book serves as both a fascinating read and a great reference piece—truly essential reading for both the die-hard or casual Oilers fan, as well as any hockey draft aficionado.

Enjoy!

Frank Seravalli is a hockey insider and president of hockey content at Daily Faceoff. He was previously a hockey insider for Canadian sports network TSN. In 2019, he was elected president of the Professional Hockey Writers' Association.

INTRODUCTION

BEGINNING IN JUNE 1979, the first summer of the Edmonton Oilers' NHL existence, and running through the 1980 and 1981 drafts, director of scouting Barry Fraser delivered the heart of a hockey dynasty with just 23 picks.

Much of this book will focus on the math of the draft—what can be learned from statistical analysis. Anyone observing Fraser and his scouting staff in the early years might have guessed the club valued "saw him good" scouting reports supplemented with a credible reading of the player's scoring numbers.

A scouting report from the era would have included birth date, height, weight, and scoring numbers over the last two seasons. That would have been followed by remarks and grades on skating, scoring, shooting, passing, puck control, positional play, use of body, checking, size and strength, aggressiveness, desire, and hockey sense. Then a final grade.

There was very little math in the scouting reports, despite how much the math liked Edmonton's 1979 selections.

By the fall of 1981, the NHL roster and pipeline were teeming with impact players. If Fraser continued to draft as he had in 1979–81, the mind boggles at the script that could have been written.

Looking back, management must have been betting Edmonton's elite young players would play for the team for a decade or more, under affordable contracts. It would prove to be a grievous error, as the 1980s would see massive salary increases annually. Eventually, the Oilers' elite talents required incredible salaries to keep pace with the rest of the league, and Edmonton's contract costs spiraled out of control.

What actually happened did not resemble the clarity of 1979–81. The team drafted as if the skill positions would be filled in perpetuity by the brilliant stars who dominated from 1980 to '87.

The organization abandoned the Fraser "skill" draft formula. Having procured several of the best players in the game, the scouts (one assumes with management's blessing) turned their attention to shutdown prospects with complementary talents.

By the time Edmonton spent most of the 1982–90 drafts on players who displayed a wide range of skills (but were not elite offensive talents), the bill came due on the elite talents drafted between 1979 and '81.

Glen Sather, the manager, was caught between a rock and a hard place.

By 1988, when Gretzky was traded to the Los Angeles Kings, Sather badly needed to acquire elite talents in return for his stars. He was often successful, but the talent bleed took the Oilers from the top of the NHL to mid-level quickly before a crash to the bottom in the early 1990s.

The nucleus of the Oilers dynasty came from eight names among those first 23 selections, plus the acquisition of under-age superstar Wayne Gretzky in 1978, during the dying days of the WHA. That upstart league, no longer acknowledged in any meaningful way by the club or the NHL, breathed life into the Oilers organization and gifted it the best player in the history of the game.

What happened after that, beginning with the 1979 draft, gives us the foundation for this book and the belief the draft is the king of procurement tools.

The early Oilers would bring five Stanley Cups over a stunning seven-year period, 1984–90.

It was followed by a long period of struggle and erosion, with a brief period of glory in 2006.

And then, beginning in 2010, the scouting department once again began discovering the "skill" formula. After some fits and starts, and some incredible luck, the organization began the climb that may one day lead to a sixth Stanley Cup.

Because this book went to print prior to the 2022 NHL Draft, that is the only edition that is not included herein.

SOME DRAFT HISTORY

The universal draft, as it currently exists, began in 1969, one full decade before the NHL arrived in Edmonton. It changed everything.

Since the universal draft was introduced, teams who can beat the average—even over a small period of years—will win often and have a great chance to win championships.

Over many years of assessing draft seasons and individual teams' success, we can conclude the most important element in drafting well is luck (which includes avoiding injury). Due diligence, a keen eye, and increasingly an acknowledgment of the math of the draft are essential, but teams still need to get lucky to beat the odds. Draft skill, avoid injury.

Fraser would spend most of 20 years trying to recreate the magic of 1979–81, but luck abandoned him, and Edmonton's scouting staff was unable to get the Oilers back to the Stanley Cup Final.

Five seasons after Fraser retired, Edmonton would return to the Final.

The draft is even more important now than during Fraser's time. Why? Since the salary cap's arrival in 2006, maintaining a pipeline of young, inexpensive talent has become a vital aspect of the general manager's job.

1

A DYNASTY IS FORMED

THE 1979 DRAFT

SUCCESS AND FAILURE for the Edmonton Oilers franchise over 40-plus years can be directly connected to their fortunes at the draft table.

The 1979 draft was special in several ways. The NHL merged with the WHA that summer, meaning players were changing teams at a dizzying rate via the expansion draft and reclaims. (NHL teams had a right to WHA players if they had been drafted in the regular amateur draft.)

Before 1979, the NHL, with few exceptions, drafted players in the summer they turned 20. The rival WHA had been raiding junior leagues for years, taking the best teenage hockey players available to feed star power into the upstart league.

Gretzky was the greatest theft, and because he was not yet 20, no NHL team had drafted him. That little window—under-20 superstar vital to the success of a team's future—had a population of one. Oilers owner Peter Pocklington made retaining Gretzky for the Oilers a condition of the NHL-WHA merger, and the NHL allowed it.

Why? My own opinion is the establishment (league owners, managers) felt Gretzky wouldn't make a massive difference. If Gretzky had the frame of Eric Lindros or Mario Lemieux—bigger, stronger men—it's likely there would have been a helluva fight.

Gretzky's brilliance was more brains than brawn, and so there was no fight for him from the older league during the merger. In a way, he was the ultimate example of what this book is about: recognizing production by properly assessing scoring numbers.

The NHL view at the time was reflected in an anecdote attributed to Dick Beddoes of the *Toronto Star*. He said Gretzky wouldn't make the great Maple Leafs of the late 1940s. That was a team that boasted an amazing one-two-three punch at centre (Ted Kennedy, Max Bentley, and Syl Apps).

As good as those throwback-era Leafs were, and as smart as the NHL wise men of the time were purported to be, Gretzky and the Oilers set them all ablaze for a decade.

The other kids playing in the WHA who were not yet 20 did not receive the Gretzky treatment. Those young men would be accounted for at the 1979 draft.

The players couldn't be sent back to junior, having already played pro. They couldn't be awarded to teams, as the NHL clubs had no claim and the WHA teams had no say.

So the solution from the NHL gave the 1979 draft a massive pool of talent. It was decided players under 20 who were already playing pro could be placed in the amateur draft pool. With those players added to the group who were turning 20—the "traditional" NHL pool—1979 was basically two drafts in one.

Not every team benefitted, but all these years later, the 1979 draft results for the Oilers franchise are reflected in three plaques at the Hockey Hall of Fame.

The WHA teams received no favours from the established NHL teams, with the new clubs drafting at the end of each round. For Edmonton, that meant picking No. 21 and last in the first round, due to retaining Gretzky.

Edmonton entered the draft with picks No. 21, 42, 63, 84, 105, and 126. The team would make six picks, but there were a couple of trades during the proceedings.

PROSPECT SPOTLIGHT
NO. 21 OVERALL: D KEVIN LOWE, QUEBEC REMPARTS (QMJHL)

Kevin Lowe was ranked No. 11 on Edmonton's list, and in Lowe's book with Stan Fischler, *Champions: The Making of the Edmonton Oilers*, Fraser was quoted as saying, "We liked his composure on the ice and he never seemed to get into too much trouble. When his name came up, we didn't think about it for a minute."

Lowe would make the big club in the fall of 1979, score the first goal in the team's NHL history, and play 1,254 games in the league. To this day, he is No. 1 in games played in franchise history (1,037).

Lowe was named Edmonton's head coach in 1999 and its general manager in 2000, and he has been associated with the organization for most of the last 40 years. He was named to the Hockey Hall of Fame in 2020, the crowning achievement in a career that is aligned with the franchise more than any other.

Scouting Report and Legacy: Lowe was 6'2", 200 pounds and played a rugged style for 19 seasons. In Edmonton in the 1980s, a team famous for high-octane offence, beautiful passes, and end-to-end rushes, Lowe's button-down, two-way style could have been easily overlooked. In the team's early years, defensive play was sporadic, but Lowe was a mainstay on the blue line. His attention to detail, willingness to sacrifice his body to make plays, and lack of fear set the tone for the team and reflected a physical, punishing style inspired by his first defensive partner in Edmonton (Lee Fogolin). Lowe played the game to the very edge physically, and at times beyond. He could pass and carry the puck, and his career highs (10 goals one season, 46 points in another) confirm his two-way ability. He could help offensively, jump into the rush, and finish a play a few times a season.

The enduring image of Kevin Lowe for Oilers fans: in a physical, net-front battle with a giant opposition winger, protecting the house. By the time Edmonton won its first Stanley Cup in 1984, much of the roster had learned to play the defensive game after having broken scoring records in the early years.

Lowe arrived with the defensive tool kit, substantial ability, and a great deal of desire. As he gained experience, he became an on-ice leader, and by the middle of his career it was easy to project him as a future coach or general manager. He accomplished both with the Edmonton Oilers.

PROSPECT SPOTLIGHT
NO. 48 OVERALL: C MARK MESSIER, CINCINNATI STINGERS (WHA)

Messier was described as "raw-boned" on his draft day, an old-time reference seldom used today. Messier had good size (6'1", 205 pounds), could skate like the wind, and showed offensive ability in Tier 2 junior (25 goals for the St. Albert Saints in 1977–78 at age 16).

On draft day, Jim Matheson of the *Edmonton Journal* quoted Oilers coach Glen Sather as saying "he has unlimited potential," which sounded hyperbolic when placed against his output (one goal in 47 games) for Cincinnati.

Sather coached against Messier's Stingers in 1978–79, getting a view of the youngster few NHL scouts would have seen. Messier and Edmonton's top centre, Dennis Sobchuk, got into a fight during a game. Sobchuk was 24, with man strength, and Messier just 17, but the younger man had a slight edge in punches landed, 12–0.

Legend has it Sather was a loud voice in the Oilers' landing Messier at No. 48 overall.

Scouting report and legacy: Messier was a classic version of the modern power forward before the term existed. He had enormous determination, no fear, and the ability to intimidate even brave men. He was big, fast, fierce, and skilled, developing several patented moves (off the rush, right side, lifting his right leg and sending a hard, heavy wrister that often beat the goalie clean) that led to goals.

It's almost impossible to describe his impact these decades later, but one fact reflects his value perfectly.

Glen Sather moved Messier to centre permanently on February 15, 1984. The Oilers won the first of five Stanley Cups 63 days later.

Messier won the Conn Smythe Trophy with eight goals and 26 points in 19 games.

Peter Gzowski, the gifted writer who chronicled Canada's culture in the last half of the 20th century, wrote a book on the early Oilers, *The Game of Our Lives*. His words on Messier ring true 40 years later: "Of all the factors that have turned the Oilers around in the last few weeks—from the trades to the midnight raids in Hartford—none have been more important than Mark's decision to apply himself. The wreckless [sic] abandon of the early months has now turned into a controlled fury on the ice, and in many games he has been the Oilers' most exciting player. He kills penalties and adds zest to the powerplay. No one knows for sure what has turned Messier around, although it appears more than coincidence that he began his new dedicated approach about the time his cousin Don Murdoch was banished to the minors. So many of the other youngsters take their moves from him that there are those who believe he will one day be captain of the Oilers."

PROSPECT SPOTLIGHT
NO. 69 OVERALL: RW GLENN ANDERSON, UNIVERSITY OF DENVER (NCAA)

The third Hall of Famer drafted by Edmonton in 1979 was the free spirit in the group. Barry Fraser liked him, saying, "He's very quick, probably the second-best player there [Olympics training camp in Calgary]."

Lorne Davis, Edmonton's western Canadian scout for forever and the man credited with finding Anderson, said, "He's got the speed of Guy Lafleur. But the thing about Anderson is he's powerful, too. Sometimes he'll skate right over a guy. I'd say he was the best player on either the Canadian or U.S. Olympic teams."

Anderson created an enormous amount of chaos during his shifts. Although average in size (5'11", 175 pounds) for the era, he was a royal pain for opponents. The major asset in his game was foot speed, made doubly effective because of his playing style. Anderson with the puck on his stick in the offensive zone was driving to the net about 90 percent of the time. He was a world-class finisher.

He also had an ability to linger at the end of a play, leaning on an opponent or losing his balance and falling with his opposite number along for the ride. His stick would nick an opponent at times—whether it was accidental would cause another stir.

Anderson scored goals in bunches, mostly on the power play, and earned a reputation for scoring big goals in big games.

Scouting report and legacy: Anderson was a dynamic winger, dangerous on every shift and capable of making great passes in shooting situations to confuse the enemy.

He was often on a line with Messier, their signature move a "criss-cross" at centre ice that sometimes confused the opposing defenceman. Norm Lacombe, who played for a time with Messier and Anderson, tried to criss-cross with the duo early in his time with Edmonton with almost disastrous results.

Centre Mark Messier, selected No. 48 overall in 1979, was awarded the Conn Smythe Trophy as Stanley Cup MVP in Edmonton in 1984. *(AP Photo/Dave Buston, CP)*

NO. 84 OVERALL: LW MAX KOSTOVICH
Portland Winterhawks (WHL)

The first player drafted from the WHL in what would become a franchise obsession, Kostovich was a good junior scorer who could play a physical game despite his average size. He turned pro in 1979 but played just 20 games for the Oilers' main farm team (Houston Apollos) and was out of pro hockey quickly. He was the only Oilers draft pick from 1979 who did not play in the NHL. He was regarded as a hard-working player.

NO. 105 OVERALL: C MIKE TOAL
Portland Winterhawks (WHL)

Toal was a strong pick this late in the draft and played in three NHL games during the 1979–80 season. He hung around for three seasons on Edmonton's top farm teams, scoring a point per game in his rookie season in the CHL with the Apollos. He was out of hockey after three pro seasons.

NO. 126 OVERALL: RW BLAIR BARNES
Windsor Spitfires (OHA)

The final pick in the draft, Barnes would play one NHL game (for the Los Angeles Kings in 1982–83). In junior he was both a quality scorer and an enforcer, despite his average size (5'11", 190 pounds). Barnes would hit the ground running in pro hockey and built up enough value to be traded for an NHL player (Paul Mulvey) in June 1982.

Cluster Draft and Other Procurement

If a team is brilliant at scouting—and lucky—picking three talents like Kevin Lowe, Mark Messier, and Glenn Anderson in a decade would be considered fine work. Three Hall of Famers in five years would be the foundation of a championship team.

Three in one season? Historic, once-in-a-lifetime success.

There are a dozen roster spots that are vital for a franchise:

- Top two lines
- No. 3 centre
- Top two defensive pairings
- Starting goaltender

Barry Fraser and the Oilers delivered three of the 12, or 25 percent of a championship roster, in one draft. It remains a singular feat, the highest peak in Oilers draft history—and NHL draft history, full stop.

Along with Wayne Gretzky, protected in the expansion draft, the major pieces of the Stanley Cup teams were being put in place.

1979 Draft Summary

We can state one true thing about Barry Fraser's first draft for the NHL Oilers: he selected impact offensive players. He said at the time he was in pursuit of "heart," but there's no doubt he also landed every time on skill.

That is reflected in each player's 1978–79 totals. (Number in parentheses is points per game.)

- Kevin Lowe (QMJHL), age 19: 68 games, 26–60–86 (1.26)
- Mark Messier (AJHL), age 17: 17 games, 15–18–33 (1.94)

- Glenn Anderson (NCAA), age 17: 41 games, 26–29–55 (1.34)
- Max Kostovich (WHL), age 19: 64 games, 29–27–56 (0.88)
- Mike Toal (WHL), age 19: 71 games, 38–83–111 (1.56)
- Blair Barnes (OHA), age 18: 66 games, 63–67–130 (1.97)

One fact this 40-plus-year look at the NHL draft will prove: even the NHL checkers and shutdown NHL players were impact offensive players in junior. Kevin Lowe was an offensive leader on his QMJHL team, but power-play time waned in the NHL and his defensive ability became his calling card. There's a lesson there, and it will be driven home time and time again throughout this book.

NHL Career Games Played

1. Mark Messier: 1,756
2. Kevin Lowe: 1,254
3. Glenn Anderson: 1,129
4. Mike Toal: 3
5. Blair Barnes: 1

In all, Fraser's six draft picks from 1979 played in 4,143 NHL games, the equivalent of 50.5 seasons in the NHL.

One Final Note on 1979

Due to the merger and the large number of underage picks, the NHL packaged two years together (19- and 20-year-olds) in the 1979 drafts.

The league also shortened the draft from 22 rounds to six rounds. It sounds drastic, but the last several rounds in previous seasons were just the Montreal Canadiens fishing.

In 1978, 234 players were drafted; the number a year later (126) was just over half that.

That left a large number of unsigned players as full free agents. I've spoken to several over the years, and all of them hoped not to be drafted because the bonus money would be better in free agency.

On September 14, 1979, the Oilers signed two-way defender Charlie Huddy. He was left-handed but could play either side and made a massive impression on the NHL beginning in 1980. He would play in 1,017 NHL games and was part of all five Stanley Cup teams in Edmonton.

Other signings that first year:

- Cal Roadhouse, a big, tough winger signed from the Billings Bighorns (WHL). He played five pro seasons but fell short of the NHL.
- Mike Kouwenhoven, another winger from Billings. He was less talented than Roadhouse and exited pro hockey quickly.

Trades That Involved Draft Picks

On June 9, 1979, the Oilers made a trade with the Minnesota North Stars. In exchange for not making Paul Shmyr one of its priority selections in the expansion draft, Edmonton received the No. 69 pick in the 1979 draft (Glenn Anderson). It was a great deal for the Oilers.

On August 9, 1979, the Oilers traded a 1979 second-round pick (No. 42, Neal Broten) and a 1979 third-round pick (No. 63,

Kevin Maxwell) to the Minnesota North Stars for the rights to Dave Semenko and a 1979 third-round pick (No. 48, Mark Messier).

Edmonton's first NHL general manager was Larry Gordon, who arrived in time for the acquisition of Gretzky and helped the transition from WHA to NHL roster through a dizzying dispersal draft, engineering the first draft-day trade in franchise history.

In the summer of 1979, Glen Sather, who was the driving force behind the team for its first 20 NHL seasons, was head coach but had a large amount of control over personnel and the day-to-day handling of the team.

Sather was very interested in reacquiring enforcer Semenko. He played for the WHA Oilers in 1977–78 and 1978–79, gaining a reputation for being a fearsome fighter and policeman. The Minnesota North Stars claimed him in the dispersal draft, having selected him in the second round of the 1977 amateur draft.

Gordon made a deal with the North Stars, as described earlier.

Semenko would play with the Oilers until his trade to the Hartford Whalers in December of 1986. He would be part of two Stanley Cup–winning teams (1984, 1985) with Edmonton and returned to the organization after retirement. (That will become a theme throughout this book.) He spent time as a scout, as an assistant coach, and as part of the radio broadcast team. Broten and Messier would enjoy substantial careers.

THE 1980 DRAFT

The Oilers' first NHL season was a success. The team's record (28–39–13) was good enough to make the playoffs, and its goal differential (301–322) was second best among expansion teams (Hartford Whalers: 303–312).

The Philadelphia Flyers made quick work of the upstart Edmonton kids in the first round of the playoffs. The Oilers lost 4–3 on April 8, 5–1 on April 9, and then in double overtime 3–2 on April 11, the Flyers sweeping the best-of-five series in three straight games.

Youth was served, with three players from the 1979 draft making their NHL debut:

- Mark Messier: 75 games, 12–21–33
- Kevin Lowe: 64 games, 2–19–21
- Mike Toal: 3 games, 0–0–0

Added to Wayne Gretzky (79 games, 51–86–137), Edmonton had three stunning talents to build on. As the 1980s began, the Oilers, along with the Minnesota North Stars, were correctly regarded as the next big threat to dominant teams like the New York Islanders, Montreal Canadiens, and Boston Bruins.

No one expected 1980 to be another monster draft by Barry Fraser.

PROSPECT SPOTLIGHT
NO. 6 OVERALL: D PAUL COFFEY, KITCHENER RANGERS (OHL)

Coffey was a bit of a surprise selection. *The Hockey News* ranked him No. 20 overall, and the Oilers took him much earlier.

Coffey was a converted forward playing defence, and there was chaos to his coverage in junior and in the NHL.

He was a brilliant skater, smooth as silk and capable of changing gears in a heartbeat. Coffey's ability to transport the puck, deke an opponent defender, and then score made him a complete offensive player from the back line. He also had great vision and passing ability.

Defensively, he had issues; there were run-ins with his coaches due to coverage lapses throughout Coffey's long and impressive NHL career.

In Coffey's first training camp and preseason, Coach Glen Sather was on the first-round pick to play a more controlled game.

In one preseason contest, Coffey was paired with another (undrafted) junior graduate named Jim Crosson.

Crosson was a tough WHL defender (256 PIM) with some offensive ability (69 games played, 16-60-76) on a very good Calgary Wranglers team.

Early in the game they were paired together, Coffey carried the puck into the opposition zone, deep in the corner, and then behind the net. A quick scrum ensued and the puck was turned over, with Coffey falling. In one of those quick tape-to-tape passes, it was suddenly jailbreak the other way.

Crosson knew Coffey was dead in the water and the play turned over so quickly that he turned, took two strong strides to get some clearance on the oncoming rush, and then turned around to face the (he assumed) 3-on-1.

Except, when he turned around, Paul Coffey was there, beside him. And that, in his words, was the day he knew what Paul Coffey was in the game of hockey.

Scouting report and legacy: Coffey's speed was breathtaking. He could pass even good NHL skaters easily. That skill was less useful to him defensively than it should have been, as Coffey's mindset was never a match for the grueling, rugged work of an NHL defenceman.

He owns several records, including most goals by a defenceman in a single season (48 in 1985–86) and most consecutive games by a defenceman with at least one point (28 with the Oilers from November 1985 to January 1986).

Right winger Jari Kurri, drafted No. 69 overall in 1980, won five Stanley Cups in his NHL career, all with Edmonton (1984, 1985, 1987, 1988, and 1990). The Oilers retired his No. 17 jersey on October 6, 2001. *(AP Photo/Adrian Wyld)*

He was one of the first of the great Oilers from the 1980s to be traded, as a 1987 training-camp holdout turned bitter when owner Peter Pocklington got involved.

It was left to general manager Sather to deal his gifted defender to the Pittsburgh Penguins in a massive deal that saw winger Craig Simpson return as the key piece for Edmonton.

NO. 48 OVERALL: RW SHAWN BABCOCK
Windsor Spitfires (OHL)

Babcock was young for the 1980 draft, as his birth date (July 24, 1962) was fairly close to the cutoff date (September 15).

Babcock had average size (5'10", 180 pounds), had good speed, and played a rugged style, posting 241 PIM in 51 games (scoring 12–13–25).

He was shy offensively compared to other Oilers picks in 1980 and did not progress during his two post-draft seasons, meaning he had a limited pro upside:

- Draft Year (OHL): 51 games, 12–13–25 (.490 points per game)
- Draft +1 (OHL): 62 games, 10–18–28 (.451 points per game)
- Draft +2 (OHL): 56 games, 17–18–35 (.625 points per game)

He would turn pro in 1982 and spend two seasons in the AHL, playing a depth role before heading back home and finding his calling as a firefighter with the Kingston Fire Department.

PROSPECT SPOTLIGHT
NO. 69 OVERALL: RW JARI KURRI, HELSINKI (FINLAND)

If it's possible for a player to be in the Hall of Fame and underrated at the same time, surely Jari Kurri is that man.

Drafted in the fourth round, partly due to a rumour he would stay in Finland to play in the 1982 World Hockey Championships in his hometown, Kurri arrived in Edmonton in the fall of 1980 with a full skill set.

After the draft, Barry Fraser told Jim Matheson of the *Edmonton Journal*, "He was the best player out of Europe, aside from Vladimir Krutov. In our opinion he was a first-round draft pick. I had him rated around No. 10."

Kurri was NHL-ready the moment he arrived in Edmonton. He was born in May 1960, meaning he was 20 when drafted and fully equipped for the world's best league.

During the Oilers' glory years, Kurri was noted as being the second half of "Gretzky to Kurri," the bookend piece to the greatest player in history.

At the peak of their careers, observing the two men in action on an ongoing basis, Kurri's defensive acumen, fantastic passing, and intuition could be seen as a vital part of a virtuoso performance by the duo.

Gretzky to Kurri dismantled opposition.

This selection, along with the Messier pick in the third round in 1979, represented Barry Fraser's high point as a scouting director. Getting these men as depth picks in back-to-back seasons had the effect of making Fraser "scouting director for life," even though many lean seasons were to come.

Looking back on the 1980s Oilers, one thing stands out more than any other. Kurri, who scored 601 NHL goals and played a brilliant two-way game every night, was the winner of just one major award: the 1984–85 Lady Byng Trophy. He led the league in goals (68) during the 1985–86 season; a Rocket Richard Trophy awarded retroactively might help make up for the hardware shortfall.

Scouting report and legacy: Offensively, Kurri had great vision. He could skate well, he was an excellent passer, and his quick release was death for goalies. Defensively, his awareness and anticipation gave him the ability to impact the game at a veteran's level soon after he arrived.

The status of Kurri's military commitment (two years in Finland) reportedly contributed to his falling in the draft. Legend has it that Fraser was the only man in the NHL who knew Kurri did not plan on entering the army for a two-year stint but would instead serve during offseasons.

His plan was to play one or two seasons in the NHL and then return to Finland. Plans changed, partly because Glen Sather stated at the beginning of training camp, "I've got to get Gretzky someone to play with," and Kurri won the day.

Peter Gzowski's book *The Glory of Our Times* sheds some light on the adjustment Kurri had to go through in coming to North America: "Much of the credit for his new extroversion belongs to his roommate, Paul Coffey, who night after night plays cards with him and painstakingly works on vocabulary skills. The Oilers publicity department would have people believe that Kurri has been learning his English from *Happy Days*, but both he and Coffey prefer game shows."

NO. 90 OVERALL: LW WALT PODDUBNY
Kingston Canadians (OHL)

Poddubny was born in 1960, so, like Kurri, he was drafted at age 20 and immediately entered pro hockey.

Although he played just four games with the Oilers, Poddubny showed he had NHL potential as a raw rookie with the Wichita Wind in 1980. Here are his two minor league seasons, the first showing his potential and the second showing he had outgrown the league:

- Age 20: 70 games, 21–29–50 (.714 points per game)
- Age 21: 60 games, 35–46–81 (1.35 points per game)

Poddubny was ready at the end of the 1981–82 season, but the Oilers had three fantastic young wingers (Messier, Anderson, and Kurri) who had established themselves as NHL players.

Poddubny was dispatched to the Toronto Maple Leafs with Phil Drouillard in exchange for centre Laurie Boschman on March 9, 1982. Although Poddubny would play some centre in his NHL career, Sather wanted an established pivot and Boschman fit the description.

Scouting report and legacy: Poddubny had good size for the era (6'1", 205 pounds) and good speed. His shot was the big reason Poddubny reached the NHL and had success. His play away from the puck was the subject of consternation on draft day and at times during a productive career.

Poddubny would play in 468 NHL games and score 184 goals. He endured some knee injuries over the years and had his career cut short because of it.

Poddubny died on March 22, 2009, at his sister's house in Thunder Bay, Ontario. After retiring from hockey (injuries forced him to retire at 34) he tried his hand at coaching, but with limited success.

After that, Poddubny found it difficult to find a living in the game and was unable to transition to another career.

At the time of his passing, he had not worked in the game for several years.

NO. 111 OVERALL: C MIKE WINTHER
Brandon Wheat Kings (WHL)

Winther played two full seasons in the WHL before being drafted, scoring 36 goals both times. He scored 38 goals for three WHL teams in his draft-plus-one season, turning pro the following year (1981–82). He played just four games for Kalamazoo (IHL) and that was the end of his hockey career.

NO. 132 OVERALL: G ANDY MOOG
Billing Bighorns (WHL)

The first goalie drafted by the Oilers was a late-round gem who won the hearts of the fans with a brilliant performance in the spring of 1981. He was called up to the Oilers early in his pro career (December 19) to back up Eddie Mio. A few short months later, he backstopped the Oilers to a thrilling playoff series win over the Montreal Canadiens. It was the first indication that Sather and Fraser were building something special in Edmonton. Moog was brilliant in the victory.

Scouting report and legacy: Moog was listed at 5'9" and 170 pounds. (Author's note: I'm that height and he was shorter than me when I met him in 1980.) His fantastic reflexes and lightning glove hand were keys to his success, and he was extremely competitive in the net.

In the summer of 1981, after the Canadiens series, Moog was wildly popular in Edmonton. Fans were surprised when the Oilers chose a goalie (Grant Fuhr) in the first round of that summer's draft, as Moog was just 21 and seemed to have a major future.

As Fuhr and Moog found their way in the NHL under coach Glen Sather, both performed well, but the coach showed a preference for Fuhr in the playoffs.

The Oilers won Stanley Cups in 1984, 1985, and 1987 with the tandem, before Moog became embroiled in a contract dispute and bolted for the Canadian Olympic team. (He would play in the 1988 Olympics.)

Moog was eventually traded to the Boston Bruins in March 1988 for Bill Ranford and Geoff Courtnall. To this day, it's easy to find Oilers fans who are still mad about Moog's handling after Fuhr arrived. Some fans never got past it.

NO. 153 OVERALL: G ROB POLMAN-TUIN
Michigan Tech (NCAA)

The second goalie drafted by Edmonton in 1980, Polman-Tuin built a solid résumé in the late 1970s playing for the BCJHL's Merritt Centennials. He was voted best goalie in the league in 1978 and 1979, before heading to Michigan Tech.

Polman-Tuin played three seasons in college and then turned pro, playing sparingly for the Milwaukee Admirals (IHL) for two seasons. He represented the Netherlands at the 1979 World Hockey Championships, the team placing first in Pool C.

NO. 174 OVERALL:
C LARS-GUNNAR PETTERSSON
Lulea (Sweden Div. I)

Pettersson would make his mark on hockey in the top Swedish league, the SEL (now the SHL). He was a highly skilled centre who broke league scoring records during a career that saw him deliver offence consistently. He was part of a Swedish team that won silver in the 1986 World Hockey Championship and gold in 1987 at Worlds. He also played on SEL champion Umea in 1987.

The Oilers sent him to the Vancouver Canucks in March 1981, along with Blair MacDonald in a deal for Gary Lariviere and Ken Berry.

There's no doubt he had NHL ability, but European players in this era often stayed at home and played in front of fans in their own nation.

1980 Draft Summary

The concentration on skill in 1979 continued with the picks of 1980. (Number in parentheses is points per game.)

- Paul Coffey (OHA), age 18: 75 games, 29–73–102 (1.36)
- Shawn Babcock (OHA), age 17: 51 games, 12–13–25 (0.49)
- Jari Kurri (Liiga), age 19: 33 games, 23–16–39 (1.18)
- Walt Poddubny (OHA), age 19: 62 games, 33–26–59 (0.95)
- Mike Winther (WHL), age 18: 69 games, 36–54–90 (1.30)
- Andy Moog (WHL), age 19: 46 games, 3.67 goals-against average, .892 save percentage

- Rob Polman-Tuin (NCAA), age 18: 13 games, 3.72 goals-against average, .894 save percentage
- Lars-Gunnar Pettersson (Swe-I), age 19: 26 games, 35–10–45 (1.73)

Coffey was a year younger than Lowe in his draft year and posted better numbers. Kurri was 19 and scoring more than a point per game in a good pro league. There were 12 skaters chosen in the first two drafts. Only Babcock posted low offensive numbers in his draft year.

It was an amazing run that netted 14 picks and five Hall of Famers over two draft summers.

NHL Career Games Played

1. Paul Coffey: 1,409
2. Jari Kurri: 1,251
3. Andy Moog: 713
4. Walt Poddubny: 468

Coffey looked like he was gliding above the ice, his stride was so effortless. In more than 40 years of watching hockey, I'd never seen anyone like Coffey on skates, until Connor McDavid arrived in 2015.

Kurri had a fantastic shot, quick and accurate, and yet my lasting memory of him is hunting down pucks and finding Gretzky with a pass. He was a supreme two-way forward.

Moog was a small goalie with cat-quick reflexes. The image in the brain of Oilers fans is Moog backstopping an upstart bunch to that dream series win over the Montreal Canadiens in the spring of 1981. Unforgettable. He finished No. 3 in WHL save percentage in his draft year, with the No. 1 man destined to have an impact on his career.

Poddubny was the first of the Oilers' draft picks to be clearly NHL quality while also not being able to break into the nightly lineup. He had a fine career after leaving the Oilers, shortened by injury. He had consecutive seasons of 40, 38, and 38 goals mid-career that reflected his real ability, but he was fading by the end of the 1980s.

One Final Note on 1980

After the 1979 draft, the Oilers signed several free agents to contracts among the pool that did not get drafted. Charlie Huddy was among them.

In 1980, Edmonton did it again, along with other NHL teams. Players were hoping not to get drafted after the first couple of rounds, as the bonus money for undrafted free agents was more than was being offered for being a mid-round selection.

Jim Crosson, a high-scoring defenceman for the Calgary Wranglers in 1979–80, signed with the Oilers and split the 1980–81 season between the Oilers' two minor league teams that year (Wichita Wind of the CHL and Milwaukee Admirals of the AHL).

Gord Stafford was another. He played for the Billing Bighorns (WHL) in 1979–80 and worked in both Milwaukee and Wichita in 1980–81. Stafford would hang around with the Milwaukee team through most of the 1980s. Crosson suffered a broken back in his second pro season, which ended his playing career.

An NHL team has 12 "foundation" positions on the roster: the top two forward lines, the No. 3 centre, the top two defensive pairings, and the starting goaltender.

At the end of the 1980–81 season, the Oilers had seven impact foundation pieces, all but one (Gretzky, No. 1 centre) via the draft.

Trades That Involved Draft Picks

On June 13, 1979, the Oilers traded their 1980 second-round selection, No. 27 overall. The Canadiens drafted defenceman Ric Nattress, who would play 536 NHL games. Edmonton acquired then minor league winger Dave Lumley (who would come right to the NHL in 1979–80 and score 20 goals for Edmonton) and Dan Newman (who played 1978–79 on the same minor league team as Lumley, the Nova Scotia Voyageurs).

On June 11, 1980, the Oilers dealt forward Ron Areshenkoff (picked by the Oilers in the expansion draft) and selection No. 195 (used on defenceman Bob O'Brien, who would not play in the NHL) to the Philadelphia Flyers for power forward Barry Dean.

2

STANLEY CUP CHAMPIONS!

THE 1981 DRAFT

The Oilers' second season (1980–81) built on the strong showing in year one. The team's regular season record improved only slightly, to 29–35–16 (one more victory), but the club won a playoff round (against the Montreal Canadiens).

Bryan Watson was named coach, allowing Sather to concentrate on general manager duties, but it didn't work out and Sather went behind the bench again after 18 games.

Although the 1979 draft was stronger than the 1980 edition, the rookies in 1980–81 were more impressive because Glenn Anderson (from the 1979 draft) finally signed and began his pro career. Here are the rookie numbers for the Oilers' 1980–81 crop:

- Jari Kurri: 75 games, 32–43–75
- Glenn Anderson: 58 games, 30–23–53

- Paul Coffey: 74 games, 9–23–32
- Charlie Huddy: 12 games, 2–5–7
- Andy Moog: 7 games, 3.82 goals-against average, .882 save percentage

The peak of Fraser's career as an amateur scouting director was in the past, but he remained exceptional at his job. The 1981 draft would push the franchise closer to glory and its first Stanley Cup.

PROSPECT SPOTLIGHT
NO. 8 OVERALL: G GRANT FUHR, VICTORIA COUGARS (WHL)

Fuhr was the No. 10 prospect for the 1981 draft, according to *The Hockey News*, but the Oilers didn't need a goalie. Andy Moog, chosen the year before, appeared to be the goalie of the future.

For Fraser, picking Fuhr was a case of taking the best player available. For Glen Sather, he had a good problem with two young, quality goaltenders. Fuhr showed himself to be the better goalie, with the proof coming in the playoffs. He became the goaltender of record for the Oilers during the playoffs from 1984 to '88: 61 wins, 18 losses. Four Stanley Cups. It's hard to argue with that kind of success.

Fuhr didn't give the usual hockey answer during interviews. Even in the 1980s, responses by players were often a cliché built out of another cliché and repeated many times.

Peter Gzowski described Fuhr's style early in his career in his book *The Game of Our Lives*: "With broadcasters and the press, Fuhr showed a still more remarkable facet of his personality. He would answer questions as if he had never learned the art of the 'interview'—the ritual by which hockey players would phrase wordy and predictable answers to wordy and predictable questions. Fuhr answered what was asked of him, no less but certainly no more."

Scouting report and legacy: Fuhr was an acrobat and a showman, meaning that playing goal was a perfect fit for his skills and personality.

He was 5'10", 185 pounds—not big for a goalie, so he needed to use quickness (both glove and feet) to his advantage. Fuhr played in front of a run-and-gun group of players in Edmonton in the early years, so he became accustomed to several breakaways per game.

Fuhr was famous in a heartbeat, owing to his style and success. He was a brilliant athlete and had been mentored by Hall of Fame goalie Glenn Hall as a youngster growing up in the Edmonton area.

As a rookie, he lost his first game and then went on a long unbeaten streak. Although Edmonton is far from a media centre, the Oilers play across North America and Fuhr gained fame for being a rising star who also happened to be a Black man. He gained lots of recognition and helped break down barriers, combining brilliant on-ice performance with a laid-back style that had appeal. Later players, including Fred Brathwaite and Jarome Iginla, would say Fuhr was their idol and inspiration growing up.

The enduring legend of Fuhr is as the last line of defence, making spectacular saves and leading the high-flying Oilers to victory.

Fuhr ended his career with 868 games (No. 12 all time) and 403 wins (No. 12 all time). He was a major player in four Stanley Cup victories (1984, 1985, 1987, and 1988). He won the Vezina Trophy in 1988 and owns a 74–32 career postseason win-loss record.

NO. 29 OVERALL: LW TODD STRUEBY
Regina Pats (WHL)

Strueby was the No. 7 WHL prospect in the 1981 draft, according to *The Hockey News*.

He was a rugged winger, shy offensively in his draft year, and the trend continued. At 20, in the AHL, he scored 17–25–42 in 72 games, and he would play just five NHL games during his hockey career.

He had good size (6'1", 185 pounds) but was never in danger of becoming an NHL regular with the Oilers. He left training camp in October 1985 and was traded a couple of months later. Edmonton would deal him in December 1985 with Larry Melnyk for Mike Rogers.

NO. 71 OVERALL: RW PAUL HOUCK
Kelowna Buckaroos (BCJHL)

Barely eligible for the 1981 draft, Houck was born August 1963 (cutoff September 15, 1983). He had big numbers in the BCHL and had a strong offensive season as a sophomore at Wisconsin (NCAA), scoring 38 goals and 71 points to lead the 1982–83 Badgers in scoring.

Over the summer of 1983, Wisconsin lost Pat Flatley, Bruce Driver, and Chris Chelios to the NHL, the Canadian national team, and the U.S. national team, respectively, and Houck's scoring fell badly (20–20–40 in 37 games).

Houck would never play for the Oilers, but he had value. He was dealt to the Minnesota North Stars on May 31, 1985, for goalie Gilles Meloche.

Meloche would be dealt in September of 1985 before he ever played for the Oilers. The Pittsburgh Penguins acquired Meloche for enforcer Marty McSorley and left winger Tim Hrynewich. That deal ranks among Sather's better transactions.

NO. 92 OVERALL: LW PHIL DROUILLARD
Niagara Falls Flyers (OHL)

Drouillard was the third player born in 1963 drafted by Fraser (Fuhr was September 1962). He was a strong skater, but offence didn't come naturally to him. He scored more than a point per game at 19 in the OHL but didn't play pro hockey. Edmonton dealt him in March 1982 in the deal for Laurie Boschman (with Walt Poddubny also heading to the Toronto Maple Leafs). There was never a time, even on his draft day, when Drouillard's offence projected him as a possible NHL player.

NO. 111 OVERALL: D STEVE SMITH
London Knights (OHL)

Smith was not highly rated on draft day and his junior numbers (62 games, 4–12–16 with 141 PIM) suggested a rugged shutdown defender, not the rock-solid two-way blueliner who would play in more than 800 NHL games.

Smith grew an inch after he was drafted and blossomed offensively with London in his draft-plus-one season (58 games, 10–36–46). Fraser doesn't get credit for the increased height, but this is an example of a teenager (born in 1963) spiking a little late, and credit is due to the scouting staff for finding him in the sixth round.

Scouting report and legacy: A rugged two-way defender who tended to have painful-sounding injuries (specifically his left shoulder, an ongoing issue), Smith had a wide range of skills and could contribute at both ends of the ice. He was a big defender for the era (6'4", 215 pounds) and exceeded 50 points twice during his time in Edmonton.

A lifetime of fine play and good works cannot erase the pain of a single event in a vital 1986 game against the Calgary Flames. It was Game 7 of the Smythe Division Final series between the two Alberta teams, and Smith's 23rd birthday.

Early in the third period, with the score tied 2–2, Smith retreated into his own end to pick up the puck as Calgary changed lines. Grant Fuhr was in net, and Smith ventured forth from behind the net to Fuhr's left and sent an errant pass meant for a breaking forward. The puck glanced off Fuhr and into the net, a young Smith collapsing where he stood, overwhelmed with emotion.

Although Smith is blamed to this day for the mistake, two things have always stuck with me about the event. First, the 3–2 goal for the Flames was scored at 5:14 of the third period, meaning the Oilers, winners of two Stanley Cups in a row, had almost 15 minutes to tie things up.

That didn't happen, and that's not on Smith. He didn't play the rest of the game, which is the other thing that has always struck me as curious. Instead of throwing the young defender back out immediately, Sather sat him all game, which became all spring, then into summer.

The bookend to the story is the moment when Wayne Gretzky, after the Oilers won the 1987 Stanley Cup, handed the Cup to Smith first. It was, in my opinion, the ultimate moment for the

'80s Oilers, with the 1987 club representing peak Oilers, then and now.

Smith was traded in the fall of 1991 to the Chicago Blackhawks and enjoyed a long and productive career.

NO. 113 OVERALL: C MARC HABSCHEID
Saskatoon Blades (WHL)

Two spots after the Smith selection, Fraser went back to the WHL for the third time in the 1981 draft with skill centre Habscheid. He was an exceptional junior and a key player for Canada in 1982 when the nation won its first World Junior Hockey Championships title.

Habscheid had a lot of positives when he was drafted, but he was a little shy as a skater. As a 1983-born player, he had more room to develop than an older player. He posted 97 points in 72 WHL games for the Blades in 1980–81 and scored 151 points in 55 games in his draft-plus-one season. He finished top 10 in league scoring and earned an NHL recall as a teenager (1–3–4 in seven games during 1981–82).

The following year, his age 19 season in 1982–83, Habscheid played junior hockey, but not for long. In just six games with the Kamloops Oilers (WHL), he scored 7–16–23 and earned another recall to Edmonton. In 32 games with the big club, he scored 3–10–13, playing less than he would have in a lesser league.

Habscheid turned 20 in March of 1983, making him eligible for the AHL (junior players had to be returned to their teams if they didn't play with the NHL club). He scored well, going 19–37–56 (.789 points per game) in 71 games.

Habscheid, like Poddubny before him, had little room to grow with the Oilers. By the time he arrived in pro hockey in the fall of 1983, Edmonton's centre depth chart was elite, and when Mark Messier moved into the middle, it was over for minor league centres in the Oilers system. During the 1984 Stanley Cup playoffs, Edmonton's four centres were Wayne Gretzky, Mark Messier, veteran Ken Linseman, and giant checker/enforcer Kevin McClelland.

It's little wonder, then, Habscheid was dispatched via trade in December of 1985 in a deal that saw Edmonton reacquire Gord Sherven.

NO. 155 OVERALL: D MIKE STURGEON
Kelowna Buckaroos (BCJHL)

In Sturgeon, Fraser grabbed another Tier 2 junior player from Kelowna (he had chosen Paul Houck earlier in the 1981 draft). Sturgeon was a big defender (6'4", 180 pounds) who moved up to the WHL in his draft-plus-one season but did not play pro hockey.

NO. 176 OVERALL: D MILOSLAV HORAVA
Kladno (Czech)

Horava was a solid two-way defenceman who played in the Czech league and in many international tournaments. Horava played in the 1981 World Junior Championships and then in April 1981 he was on the bronze-medal-winning Czech team at the World Hockey Championships. Fraser and the Oilers drafted him, but he didn't come over until Sather dealt his rights to the New York Rangers in 1986 in a major trade that returned Finn defender Reijo Routsalainen. The major piece sent by the Oilers was Don Jackson, but Horava would play in parts of three seasons for the Rangers.

NO. 197 OVERALL: C GORD SHERVEN
Weyburn Beavers (SJHL)

Sherven was headed for the fine North Dakota (WCHA) college program in the U.S. and had played for Notre Dame College (high school). Drafted this late, NHL expectations were low, but Sherven signed in the spring of 1984 and got into two NHL games. He spent half the year in Edmonton in 1984–85, then was traded to the Minnesota North Stars in a substantial deal for winger Mark Napier. His 1984–85 NHL stats, for two teams: 69 games, 11–19–30. That was good production, but Sherven was dealt back to the Oilers in December of 1985. It was another significant deal, with Edmonton sending away Marc Habscheid, Don Barber, and Emmanuel Viveiros. He would spend most of the rest of the season in the AHL and was claimed on waivers during preseason 1986. In all, Sherven would play in five NHL seasons, but only 97 games. He enjoyed a long international playing career, spending his final season (1999–2000) with Rosenheim in the German League.

1981 Draft Summary
Although the draft haul by Barry Fraser and the Oilers in 1981 can't compete with the 1979 and 1980 editions, the 1981 draft did yield one Hall of Fame talent (Grant Fuhr) and another long and productive career (Steve Smith). Skill was still prevalent in 1981. (Number in parentheses is points per game.)

- Grant Fuhr (WHL), age 17: 59 games, 2.78 goals-against average, .908 save percentage
- Todd Strueby (WHL), age 17: 71 games, 18–27–45 (0.63)
- Paul Houck (BCHL), age 17: 56 games, 65–53–118 (2.11)

- Phil Drouillard (OHL), age 17: 62 games, 14–10–24 (0.39)
- Steve Smith (OHL), age 17: 62 games, 4–12–16 (0.26)
- Marc Habsheid (WHL), age 17: 72 games, 34–63–97 (1.35)
- Mike Sturgeon (BCHL), age 17: 50 games, 6–20–26 (0.52)
- Miloslav Horava (Czech), age 19: 44 games, 13–15–28 (0.64)
- Gord Sherven (SJHL), age 17: 44 games, 35–34–69 (1.57)

Fuhr was an inspired pick. He led the WHL in save percentage the year *before* Edmonton drafted him. Strueby (along with Babcock in 1980) foreshadowed the trend Edmonton developed in not selecting high skill with early picks. Houck, Habscheid, Horava, and Sherven were promising offensive players and all made the NHL. Smith wasn't an offensive defenceman, but he grew as a player after he was drafted. No quarrel with taking Smith at No. 111 overall; the high-end players are usually gone by then.

The 1981 draft wasn't at the same level as 1979 and 1980, and the Strueby pick was out of time with Fraser's previous drafts, but Edmonton once again got quality players (and a Hall of Fame goalie) in the draft.

NHL Career Games Played

1. Grant Fuhr: 868
2. Steve Smith: 804
3. Marc Habscheid: 345
4. Gord Sherven: 97
5. Miloslav Horava: 80

6. Paul Houck: 16
7. Todd Strueby: 5

Edmonton signed one undrafted player of note, Ray Cote. He graduated from the Calgary Wranglers (WHL) and arrived in the NHL with the Oilers to play a regular role in the 1983 playoffs. He played sparingly in the following two seasons.

Trades That Involved Draft Picks

On August 22, 1979, during the post–expansion draft chaos, Edmonton dealt winger Reg Thomas to the Toronto Maple Leafs for the 1981 No. 111 overall pick (Steve Smith).

On March 11, 1980, Edmonton traded veteran winger Cam Connor and a 1981 third-round pick (Peter Sundstrom) to the New York Rangers for winger Don Murdoch.

On March 10, 1981, Edmonton traded a seventh-round pick (Craig Hurley) to the Los Angeles Kings for centre Garry Unger.

THE 1982 DRAFT

The 1981–82 season was a memorable one in Edmonton. The first two seasons saw the Oilers win 28 and 29 games, with the playoff chase lasting much or all of the season.

In 1981–82, the win total jumped to 48, the club finished first in the Smythe Division, and Wayne Gretzky scored 92 goals and 212 points. Mark Messier scored 50 goals, Glenn Anderson passed 100 points, Paul Coffey posted 89 points (a monster total for a defenceman), and Jari Kurri exceeded 50 assists for the first time.

Grant Fuhr played 48 games as a rookie, winning 28, losing five, and posting 14 ties. His .898 save percentage tied for second among NHL regulars.

It was a dream season for a newly famous group of impact talents, but the upstart Oilers were victims of looking past the opening round opponents just one year after the Montreal Canadiens committed the same sin against Edmonton. The Los Angeles Kings beat Edmonton three games to two, the third game as wild as anything seen before or since. It would be a bitter pill for Sather.

Rookies in 1981–82 were led by the impressive goalies:

- Grant Fuhr: 48 games, 3.31 goals-against average, .898 save percentage
- Andy Moog: 8 games, 4.82 goals-against average, .841 save percentage
- Charlie Huddy: 41 games, 4–11–15
- Tom Roulstovin: 35 games, 11–3–14
- Ken Berry: 15 games, 3–2–5

Added to Gretkzy, Kevin Lowe, Messier, Anderson, Coffey, and Kurri, the final foundation pieces were in place for the first Stanley Cup run, which was two years away by the time the 1982 draft arrived.

The pool of talent in the 1982 draft was not close to the previous three seasons, and that is reflected by Edmonton's draft haul. Barry Fraser would use 12 picks in 1982, double the 1979 total and well clear of both 1980 (eight) and 1981 (nine).

The 1982 draft was Fraser's first failure. In making that claim, it's important to put the performance in perspective. Hockeydb .com shows us the percentage of overall picks making the NHL fell (as a percentage) drastically through the Oilers' first four drafts, partly a reflection of four expansion teams as well as the strength of the 1979 draft. However, note the average career games played:

- 1979 draft: 126 drafted, 103 made the NHL (81.7 percent); average NHL games: 479
- 1980 draft: 210 drafted, 132 made the NHL (62.9 percent); average NHL games: 363
- 1981 draft: 211 drafted, 114 made the NHL (54.0 percent); average NHL games: 310
- 1982 draft: 252 drafted, 109 made the NHL (43.4 percent); average NHL games: 374

In 1979, Edmonton drafted three men who exceeded 479 games. In 1980, four men played more than 363 games. In 1981, three men finished with more than 310 career games.

In 1982? No Oilers player was close.

Edmonton's first three drafts would carry the organization to the highest levels in the game, but 1982 would contribute just one unique player to the cause. For the first time in its history, the organization was losing ground to the competition at the draft table.

NO. 20 OVERALL: D JIM PLAYFAIR
Portland Winterhawks (WHL)

Playfair was a safe pick, as brother Larry had been in the NHL for more than three years on draft day. Both were rugged, shutdown types, but Jim Playfair weighed 30 pounds less (6'3", 185 pounds) than his brother. His body could not endure the style he played. He finished his junior career, got a cup of coffee (scored a goal and an assist in his first game), and then began his AHL audition. In the minors, Playfair suffered several injuries, including a severe liver injury in February 1987. He moved on to the Chicago

Blackhawks as a free agent and finished his playing career with 21 NHL games, playing just two for Edmonton.

NO. 41 OVERALL: LW STEVE GRAVES
Sault Ste. Marie Greyhounds (OHL)

Graves had a pedestrian draft season for the Greyhounds but caught fire in the playoffs, scoring eight goals in 13 postseason games. He was a high pick in the OHL draft, and Edmonton grabbed him in the second round of the NHL draft a year later. A good measure for pro prospects is AHL performance at age 20, and Graves (80 games, 17–15–32, .4 points per game in 1984–85) was well below what a future NHL player might deliver. (Marc Habscheid posted .789 points per game at age 20 in 1983–84.) Graves spent parts of three seasons with Edmonton but couldn't win a job over a veteran. He finished with 35 NHL games and then headed to Europe.

NO. 62 OVERALL: LW BRENT LONEY
Cornwall Royals (OHL)

Loney was a typical Oilers winger in the Sather era, a tough player who could score some and fight as required. Edmonton drafted Loney in June 1982 and traded him in August with Risto Siltanen in a major trade for centre Ken Linseman. Loney would play a couple of AHL seasons but did not make the NHL.

NO. 83 OVERALL: LW JAROSLAV POUZAR
Ceske Budejovice (Czech)

Pouzar, a substantial European player who had already performed in two Olympics (1976 and 1980) and two Canada Cups (1976 and 1981), was 30 when the Oilers drafted him. His draft status was somewhat controversial. Per Hockey Draft Central, "[Pouzar] was released to NHL by Czechoslovakian authorities after 1981–82 season, making him a strong prospect for the 1982 draft despite his advanced age. The NHL ruled he would have to enter the league through the 1982 Entry Draft rather than through a special draft for Czechoslovakian players as had been the case with two players released to the NHL one year earlier."

Pouzar was listed at 6'0", 200 pounds, but he hit like a freight train and had more skill than one would expect from such a physical player. He was smart and defensively responsible and often played on a line with Gretzky and Kurri in his time with Edmonton.

Pouzar was not fast and drew the ire of fans at times, but he contributed to the 1984, 1985, and 1987 Stanley Cups, providing a unique and valuable skill set. He would play in just 186 NHL games but made the most of them.

NO. 104 OVERALL: D DWAYNE BOETTGER
Toronto Marlboros (OHL)

Boettger was a defender who played a rugged style despite being average in size (6'0", 190 pounds). He is one of the few Oilers prospects of the era who played three AHL seasons in the organization without getting an NHL game.

NO. 125 OVERALL: LW RAIMO SUMMANEN
Kiekkoreipas Lahti (Liiga)

A talented winger with speed and the ability to score goals, Summanen was the first Finnish player Fraser drafted after the massive success Jari Kurri enjoyed in the NHL. Summanen was 20, so an older prospect in the draft, and he arrived in Edmonton in time for the 1983–84 Stanley Cup run, scoring five points in five playoff games. He didn't become a regular until 1985–86, scoring 19 goals in 73 games for the Oilers. He was traded in March 1987 to the Vancouver Canucks for Moe Lemay.

NO. 146 OVERALL: RW BRIAN SMALL
Ottawa 67's (OHL)

Small was a 1964-born prospect, meaning he was one of the younger players in the 1982 draft. He scored 18–24–42 in 66 OHL games at 17. It meant he had plenty of room to grow, but he did not progress offensively and did not turn pro.

NO. 167 OVERALL: D DEAN CLARK
St. Albert Saints (AJHL)

Drafted as a defenceman but moved to left wing soon after, Clark played in the WHL (Kamloops Oilers) and NCAA (Ferris State) in 1982–83. His physical style was more suited to the WHL, and he flourished during three seasons in the league but did not turn pro despite promising numbers. He would go on to coach in the WHL for more than a decade.

NO. 188 OVERALL: G IAN WOOD
Penticton Knights (BCJHL)

Wood had a strong run over two seasons with Penticton and played one game with Portland (WHL) before he was drafted. A small (5'10", 160 pounds) goaltender, he was just average in two WHL seasons post-draft. Wood signed with Edmonton and attended training camp but did not play pro in the Oilers organization. Wood did play in Germany for several years.

NO. 209 OVERALL: D GRANT DION
Cowichan Valley Capitals (BCJHL)

Another 1964-born player, Dion had a big season in the BCJHL (11–35–46 in 44 games) before heading to the University of Denver (NCAA) for four years. He improved every year and signed with the Oilers but would play just 107 minor league games to complete his career.

NO. 230 OVERALL: G CHRIS SMITH
Regina Pats (WHL)

Smith had an unusual draft year. He began 1981–82 playing for the Oshawa Generals (OHL) but was released in January 1982, finding his way west to Regina (WHL), where he completed the season. After Edmonton drafted him, Smith signed that summer with the Oilers and played two AHL seasons with the farm club (Moncton Alpines). He was blocked by Grant Fuhr, Andy Moog, Mike Zanier, and others, and his playing career ended in 1984.

NO. 251 OVERALL: RW JEFF CRAWFORD
Regina Pats (WHL)

Crawford is one of the biggest players ever drafted by the Oilers at 6'5", 221 pounds. He was an effective junior enforcer, aged 20 on draft day, and he played part of the following season with the Pats. He played portions of two seasons in the AHL before retiring from the game.

1982 Draft Summary

(Number in parentheses is points per game.)

- Jim Playfair (WHL) age 17: 70 games, 4–13–17 (0.24)
- Steve Graves (OHL) age 17: 66 games, 12–15–27 (0.41)
- Brent Loney (OHL) age 17: 65 games, 13–12–25 (0.38)
- Jaroslav Pouzar (Czech) age 30: 34 games, 19–17–36 (1.06)
- Dwayne Boettger (OHL) age 18: 66 games, 4–21–25 (0.38)
- Raimo Summanen (Liiga) age 20: 36 games, 15–6–21 (0.58)
- Brian Small (OHL) age 17: 66 games, 18–24–42 (0.64)
- Dean Clark (AJHL) age 17: 59 games, 21–32–53 (0.90)
- Ian Wood (BCHL) age 17: 2.19 goals-against average
- Grant Dion (BCHL) age 17: 44 games, 11–35–46 (1.05)
- Chris Smith (WHL) age 19: 10 games, 4.33 goals-against average; .853 save percentage
- Jeff Crawford (WHL) age 19: 63 games, 15–22–37 (0.59)

The 1982 draft ran completely counter to the Fraser template from 1979–81. The quality of the draft was not as high as previous years, but it's also true Edmonton left skill on the board at every turn. After Fraser picked Playfair at No. 20, the Stanley Cup champion New York Islanders chose Patrick Flatley, who, at 17, had posted more than one point per game for the University of Wisconsin. The Oilers had established a successful formula in 1979–81 and then ventured in a new, less productive direction in 1982.

None of the forwards drafted came close to 1.25 points per game in 1982.

Fraser didn't get enough from the 1982 draft, but Jaroslav Pouzar was a useful player during multiple Stanley Cup runs, and Raimo Summanen brought back value in trade after a productive campaign with the team. Some bad luck with injuries cut several careers short and curtailed Jim Playfair's trajectory.

NHL Career Games Played

- Jaroslav Pouzar: 186
- Raimo Summanen: 151
- Steve Graves: 35
- Jim Playfair: 21
- Dean Clark: 1

The total games (394) from the 1982 draft represents a massive fall from each of the first three Edmonton drafts: 1979 (4,143 games), 1980 (3,841), and 1981 (2,215). There are no Hall of Famers, no one playing 500-plus games.

Trades That Involved Draft Picks

On February 2, 1981, Edmonton acquired goalie Gary Edwards for future considerations.

On August 21, 1981, Edmonton traded Don Murdoch and a third-round pick in the 1982 draft (Wally Chapman) to the Minnesota North Stars for defenceman Don Jackson (and Gary Edwards' rights).

THE 1983 DRAFT

The 1982–83 season built on the previous year, with another strong regular season allowing the Oilers to win the Smythe Division for the second year in a row. Edmonton's 47 wins and 106 points were just shy of the 1981–82 totals, but fans were focused on the playoffs after the 1981 disappointment against the Los Angeles Kings.

The Oilers rolled over the Winnipeg Jets in three straight games early in April, then dispatched the Calgary Flames in five games mid-month. Edmonton's scoring edge (35–13) in that series was breathtaking, with the skill on display a match for the goal differential. By early May, Edmonton defeated the Chicago Blackhawks in four straight and then set its sights on the three-time defending champion New York Islanders.

The Oilers lost four straight. Although the newcomers played well, the healthy, veteran Islanders completed a fantastic four-year Stanley Cup run by outscoring Edmonton 17–6.

Rookies in 1982–83 were:

- LW Jaroslav Pouzar: 74 games, 15–18–33
- D Randy Gregg: 80 games, 6–22–28
- C Marc Habscheid: 32 games, 3–10–13

Gregg was another of Sather's free-agent signings, this time via Canadian college (University of Alberta Golden Bears), the Canadian Olympic team, and Kokudo of the Japanese League. Gregg signed in October 1982 and played quality two-way defence with the Oilers through the end of the decade. His NHL career counted 474 games and five Stanley Cups before he was claimed on waivers by the Vancouver Canucks in the fall of 1990.

The 1983 draft was a strong recovery year for Fraser and the Oilers. Although a little shy of 1981 in terms of NHL career games, Edmonton's scouting staff produced two men who would go on to play long and productive careers in the NHL. Fraser and staff found quality in Finnish junior and Tier 2 Canadian leagues as well as the usual pipelines in what was an innovative draft.

NO. 19 OVERALL: D JEFF BEUKEBOOM
Soo Greyhounds (OHL)

The first thing you noticed about Jeff Beukeboom was his size. At 6'5", 230 pounds, he was an actual mountain on skates. There was never a doubt about what he would bring to the NHL, and it was reflected in his draft year offence: 70 games, no goals, 25 assists, and 143 PIM.

He was an outstanding junior defender, with OHL first-team honours in 1984–85. He was involved in a lot of altercations and extracurricular activities, meaning multiple injuries, many half-seasons, and some rather long suspensions.

Beukeboom and Steve Smith emerged in the second half of the 1980s as the new generation of Oilers defencemen. Until that point, the club's top defencemen had been stable for years (Paul Coffey, Charlie Huddy, Kevin Lowe, Lee Fogolin, Randy Gregg).

Scouting Report and Legacy: Beukeboom was an enforcer, a nuclear deterrent against any opponent who had an idea about creating mischief around Wayne Gretzky and the high-flying Oilers. He was also a strong defender who could clear the front of the net and win battles along the wall—something the Oilers also needed in abundance.

Beukeboom got suspended several times and was injured dozens of times. He was suspended 10 games by the NHL at the start of the 1988–89 season for coming off the bench to fight.

He lost his career on a vicious sucker punch by Los Angeles Kings enforcer Matt Johnson in November of 1998. Johnson punched an unsuspecting Beukeboom from behind and knocked him out. It was a severe injury, but Beukeboom did return, taking another far less dangerous hit. Still, the concussion from the Johnson punch was too much to overcome. His career ended after 804 rugged NHL games.

Edmonton traded Beukeboom on November 12, 1991, to the New York Rangers in exchange for defender David Shaw. It was a future considerations deal that landed after the blockbuster trade of October 4, 1991. It was a trade that would alter the future of two franchises and mark the end of the Stanley Cup runs for the brilliant cluster.

NO. 40 OVERALL: C MIKE GOLDEN
Reading High School (USHS, Massachusetts)

The first U.S. high school draft pick by the Oilers, Golden had talent and size (6'1", 190 pounds). His late birthday (June 1965) meant there would be more development time for him than older players in the same draft. He was an exceptional offensive player at the high school level.

Golden attended the University of New Hampshire (NCAA) in his draft-plus-one season but played in just seven games (1-1-2) before joining Stratford (OHA Jr. B), a Tier 2 junior team in Ontario. He then transferred to Maine, meaning he had to sit out the 1984-85 season.

Edmonton traded Golden in October 1986 in a deal for defenceman Reijo Ruotsalainen, and Golden would not play in the NHL. He did play three seasons in the IHL after his college career and showed some offensive ability.

His career highlight came when he was a finalist for the Hobey Baker Award in 1987–88, the same year Maine made it to the Frozen Four.

At the time, Golden was the highest-ranked high school player drafted by the Oilers. (Edmonton would pick a U.S. high school player in the first round of the 1992 draft.)

NO. 60 OVERALL: D MIKE FLANAGAN
Acton-Boxborough High School (USHS, Massachusetts)

A huge (6'5", 220 pounds) defenceman, Flanagan was named all-league after his outstanding senior season in high school. He was an impressive offensive defenceman in his draft year, scoring 17

Left winger Esa Tikkanen (right), drafted No. 80 overall in 1983, won the Stanley Cup five times in his career, including four with the Oilers in 1985, 1987, 1988, and 1990. (AP Photo/Rusty Kennedy)

goals and 48 points in 23 games to win the all-league honour. He attended Providence College, played a depth role in all four seasons of his college career, and did not turn pro.

PROSPECT SPOTLIGHT
NO. 80 OVERALL: LW ESA TIKKANEN, HELSINKI (JR. LIIGA)

From the time he arrived in April 1985 (his first game took place in the postseason) through his retirement on April 19, 2001, Esa Tikkanen was a unique and bewildering force of nature.

Tikkanen was the third player Fraser drafted from Finland. All three would play with the Oilers. Tikkanen joined Kurri as a Stanley Cup winner (four times) and won another with the New York Rangers in 1994. He was an outstanding scorer in junior during his draft year.

Scouting Report and Legacy: Tikkanen was an excellent two-way winger, tough as nails and fantastic at forechecking and on the penalty kill. He could skate well and possessed a quick release, and his shot was heavy. He scored 23 or more goals in each of his first five full seasons.

Tikkanen played on a line with Wayne Gretzky and Jari Kurri and was quite possibly the most skilled left winger in the history of that line.

Describing Tikkanen's on-ice presence is difficult. He talked all the time, in a half-English, half-Finnish language that no one understood. (It was called "Tikkanese" when he played in Edmonton.) He played at the outer edge of the rules, often using his stick to impede progress, and played hard every shift.

He would often get the tough checking assignments, facing the opposition's best for much of the game.

Tikkanen did not win any major awards but was a strong contender annually for the Selke Trophy, awarded to the league's best defensive forward.

When he was traded, the Oilers had been dismantling the great 1980s team for some time. But Tikkanen had enough left in the tank for Sather to acquire Doug Weight, a brilliant centre who would lead the Oilers through the 1990s, in exchange.

Tikkanen played a feature role on the Oilers for the final three Stanley Cups. I define a feature role as any player who plays one of the following vital positions: starting goalie, first pairing defence (left and right), second pairing defence (left and right), top-line forward (left wing, centre, right wing), second-line forward (left wing, centre, right wing), or No. 3 centre.

Tikkanen spent his Oilers career on the top two lines (left wing), killed penalties, and spent time on the power play. He was the final player drafted by Barry Fraser who would play a foundation role on the Stanley Cup–winning Oilers team. He was drafted in 1983, the fifth NHL draft of Fraser's career.

NO. 120 OVERALL: RW DON BARBER
Kelowna Buckaroos (BCJHL)

Barber was an impressive scorer in the BCJHL (26–31–57 in 36 games) and had another strong year in the AJHL with the St. Albert Saints in his draft-plus-one season. Barber took his skills to Bowling Green University in 1984 and scored 83 goals in four seasons. By the time he left college, the Oilers had sent him (in December 1985) to the Minnesota North Stars in the trade that brought Gord Sherven back to Edmonton. Barber would play 115

NHL games and score 25 goals with Minnesota, the Winnipeg Jets, the Quebec Nordiques, and the San Jose Sharks.

NO. 140 OVERALL: C DALE DERKATCH
Regina Pats (WHL)

At 5'5", 145 pounds, it is a reflection of his exceptional skill that Derkatch got drafted at all. His draft year in the WHL showed stunning offence (84–95–179 in 67 games) as he led the entire league in scoring despite being a draft-eligible player. He followed it up with another ridiculous offensive season, then began a hockey career that took him to Italy, Finland, Great Britain, Switzerland, and Germany. If he were in a modern draft, Derkatch would get an NHL contract and a full shot at making the league. In 1983, that opportunity did not exist for players his size.

NO. 160 OVERALL: LW RALPH VOS
Abbottsford Flyers (BCJHL)

A big (6'2", 185 pounds) winger, Vos scored a bunch of points in the BCJHL (53 games, 39–100–139) in his draft year. He went to Northern Michigan (NCAA) the fall after he was drafted and spent a productive four years there. He turned pro, playing one year in the Edmonton system with the Nova Scotia Oilers (AHL) and Milwaukee Admirals (IHL). He would then head to the Netherlands and later Germany to continue his playing career.

NO. 180 OVERALL: G DAVE ROACH
New Westminster Royals (BCJHL)

One of the few 1965-born prospects drafted by Edmonton in 1983 (most were overagers or born in 1964), Roach had a solid year (33 games, 3.60 goals-against average, .900 save percentage) in his draft year. He spent four productive years with Michigan Tech, including winning a team MVP award for 1986–87. He turned pro in 1987–88, tended goal for two years in the AHL, and moved along.

NO. 200 OVERALL: C WARREN YADLOWSKI
Calgary Wranglers (WHL)

Yadlowski was shy offensively in his draft year (65 games, 3–11–14) but had delivered impressive results in Edmonton minor hockey. In his first year after the draft, he started slowly in Calgary, was traded to the Prince Albert Raiders, and eventually moved to the Tier 2 St. Albert Saints. He dominated at that level but did not turn pro with the Oilers.

NO. 220 OVERALL: D JOHN MINER
Regina Pats (WHL)

Miner was a productive pick this late. Modern drafting knowledge (he was born in August 1965, meaning he was among the youngest players in the draft pool) would have had him in the top four rounds of the draft. Miner was a tough, productive two-way defenceman in junior and signed with Edmonton. He spent three seasons in the AHL, getting 14 solid NHL games (2–3–5) in 1987–88. In August 1988, Sather dealt Miner to the Los Angeles for defender Craig Redmond, but he never played for the Kings. After playing in the Kings' system for two seasons, Miner embarked on a European playing career and was active forever. He was last tracked playing pro hockey in 2007–08, in France, at the age of 42. An impressive career.

NO. 240 OVERALL: D STEVE WOODBURN
Verdun Jr. (QMJHL)

A tough defenceman who could pass the puck had completed three seasons in the QMJHL by the time he was drafted. (1963 born, he turned 20 in October of his draft season.) The fact he passed through the draft in 1982 and he was drafted so late a year later was an indication he would not receive an NHL contract. Woodburn spent an extra season in junior and then played pro hockey for years in France and then Germany.

1983 Draft Summary

Barry Fraser and his scouting staff recovered from the startling lack of success in the 1982 draft with two gems in 1983. Fraser scored in the first round (Beukeboom) and fourth round (Tikkanen), and the 1983 draft now ranks as the best one between 1981 and the end of the decade. (Number in parentheses is points per game.)

- Jeff Beukeboom (OHL) age 17: 70 games, 0–25–25 (0.36)
- Mike Golden (USHS) age 17: 23 games, 22–41–63 (2.74)
- Mike Flanagan (USHS) age 17: 23 games, 17–31–48 (2.09)
- Esa Tikkanen (Jr. Liiga) age 17: 30 games, 34–31–65 (2.17)
- Don Barber (BCHL) age 17: 36 games, 26–31–57 (1.58)
- Dale Derkatch (WHL) age 17: 67 games, 84–95–179 (2.67)
- Ralph Vos (BCHL) age 18: 53 games, 39–100–139 (2.62)
- Dave Roach (BCHL) age 17: 33 games, 3.60 goals-against average, .900 save percentage
- Warren Yadlowski (WHL) age 17: 65 games, 3–11–14 (0.22)

- John Miner (WHL) age 17: 71, 11–23–34 (0.48)
- Steve Woodburn (QMJHL) age 18: 69 games, 5–28–33 (0.48)

The Oilers grabbed an enforcer defenceman in the first round, passing on lots of skill. It worked out, as Beukeboom delivered a strong career. After that, the club went to U.S. high schools, Finnish junior, and the BCHL, finding skill (the points-per-game totals are outstanding) everywhere.

Only Tikkanen worked out from the secondary leagues, but the bets were strong. Derkatch would likely have had a career if he had been drafted in the 2010s.

NHL Career Games Played
1. Esa Tikkanen: 877
2. Jeff Beukeboom: 804
3. Don Barber: 115
4. John Miner: 14

The 1983 draft was the final one before Edmonton would win the Stanley Cup for the first time. There would be no top-10 overall selections until 1993.

Here's how the 1983 draft class ranked in terms of total NHL games played:
1. 1979 (4,143 games)
2. 1980 (3,841 games)
3. 1981 (2,215 games)
4. **1983 (1,810 games)**
5. 1982 (394 games)

There were no Hall of Fame talents, but Tikkanen built a solid résumé before falling short (he would have needed stronger career numbers, but injuries curtailed his career). Beukeboom's career, although it was a significant length, was cut short by several years due to two devastating injuries.

Trades That Involved Draft Picks

On August 10, 1981, Edmonton traded a fifth-round pick in the 1983 draft (Garry Galley) to the Los Angeles Kings for defenceman Jay McFarlane from the Los Angeles Kings.

THE 1984 DRAFT

The 1983–84 season was one of glory for the Edmonton Oilers. Owner Peter Pocklington and general manager Glen Sather and his staff, including Fraser and the scouts, all had massive impact on a roster that was formed from unproven kids, veterans who had been cast off, and a couple of astute trades.

Five years. Five years to win the Stanley Cup. For Fraser and the procurement staff, there was great pride in the team's success.

Here are the 10 names Fraser and staff drafted or were influential in signing as undrafted free agents: Glenn Anderson, Paul Coffey, Grant Fuhr, Randy Gregg, Charlie Huddy, Jari Kurri, Kevin Lowe, Mark Messier, Andy Moog, and Jaroslav Pouzar.

Fraser and his staff accomplished more in five drafts than most staffs do in a lifetime. As much satisfaction as the club gained from the fast track to Stanley, and as much pride as Fraser must have felt through the rest of the 1980s watching his players win five Cups, doing it again was going to prove to be difficult.

Impossible, as it turned out.

NHL rookies in the championship season were many, but only a couple of names played more than a few games, and few were draft picks by Edmonton:

- Pat Conacher: 45 games, 2–8–10
- Ken Berry: 13 games, 2–3–5
- Raimo Summanen: 2 games, 1–4–5
- Jim Playfair: 2 games, 1–1–2
- Gord Sherven: 2 games, 1–0–1
- John Blum: 4 games, 0–1–1
- Todd Strueby: 1 game, 1–0–1
- Ray Cote: 13 games, 0–0–0
- Kari Jalonen: 3 games, 0–0–0
- Steve Graves: 2 games, 0–0–0
- Dean Clark: 1 game, 0–0–0

Conacher was signed as a minor league free agent out of the New York Rangers system. He landed in Edmonton in time for the first Stanley Cup run and hung around the league for more than a decade in a support role.

Summanen began his career in Edmonton with such hope and would play a productive role in the playoffs as a part-time option, but he would not join fellow Finn Kurri as a feature player on the Oilers' destiny teams.

Among undrafted free agents, Mike Zanier completed his junior career by playing for four teams in 1981–82 (Calgary Wranglers, Spokane Flyers, Medicine Hat Tigers, and Billing Bighorns). In 1982–83, he played for the Trail Smoke Eaters (WIHL), where he saw a lot of minutes and had success. Signed by the Oilers, he went to the Moncton Alpines in 1983–84 and played well (31 games, 3.30 goals-against average, .885 save percentage).

He played in three games for the Oilers in 1984–85 and was on the Oilers bench when the team won its first Stanley Cup in 1984. He would play four seasons in the minors for the organization before heading to Europe, where he enjoyed a long playing career, mostly in Italy. He settled in Sweden, where he became a successful radio analyst on SHL hockey broadcasts.

The 1984 draft was disappointing, but the scouts were less to blame than injuries. The early years of Oilers drafting saw prospects develop, arrive in the NHL, and flourish with very little derailment due to injuries, but 1984 was the season that bad luck arrived at Edmonton's doorstep, beginning in the first round.

NO. 21 OVERALL: D SELMAR ODELEIN
Regina Pats (WHL)

Odelein was an impressive prospect, drafted from the WHL after a strong first year in the league. He was ranked as the No. 11 overall prospect by *The Hockey News* and fell to the Oilers (who had him valued at No. 16, according to the *Edmonton Journal*), who were drafting last in the first round due to winning the Stanley Cup.

He continued his junior career after he was drafted and scored an impressive 24 goals with the Pats in 1984–85. He turned pro in the fall of 1986, but suffered a substantial knee injury on October 11, 1986, and missed the rest of the season.

It would have a major impact on his career.

Odelein played 43 games in the minors in 1987–88 and another 12 after being recalled to the Oilers. Edmonton would win the Stanley Cup that season, but Odelein didn't play a game in the playoffs. His time in the organization ended after the 1988–89 season, and Odelein finished his playing career with one season with the Canadian national team and then four years in Europe.

His career highlight was playing for the gold medal–winning Canadian team at the 1985 World Junior Championships.

Odelein had all the elements to be a solid NHL defenceman—he could skate, defend, pass, and shoot, and he was aggressive. In the long history of the Oilers at the draft, the team would have several stories like Odelein's, but his was the first.

NO. 42 OVERALL: G DARRYL REAUGH
Kamloops Oilers (WHL)

In 1984, the idea of the Oilers drafting another goaltender seemed farfetched. Fuhr and Moog were still on the Oilers, with many years to go in the NHL. But Reaugh was the No. 2–ranked goaltender in the entire draft, so Fraser took him at the very end of the second round.

In 55 games with Kamloops, he boasted a 4.34 goals-against average and an .864 save percentage, and he followed it up with an even better year in 1984–85, eventually earning a one-game look with Edmonton.

Reaugh would spend the next two seasons in the minors before getting another NHL look in 1987–88. He played with the organization through the end of the 1988–89 season and became a free agent. He would play several more seasons in the minors and got into 20 more games in the NHL with the Hartford Whalers in 1990–91.

He is now one of the most respected hockey television broadcasters in the industry as part of the Dallas Stars broadcast team.

NO. 63 OVERALL: C TODD NORMAN
Hill-Murray High School (USHS, Minnesota)

Norman was a heralded high school centre, making the All-State first team in 1983–84 and breaking all school scoring records. He scored 35 goals in 24 games in his draft season and had a strong freshman season at North Dakota in his draft-plus-one campaign (42 games, 10–6–16).

In January 1986, in his sophomore season with North Dakota, Norman suffered a severe knee injury that required surgery, ending his season and derailing his career. He would reappear in the ECHL in 1990, but his pro career was short and far from the NHL.

Two of Fraser's first three picks in 1984 did not reach their peak due to injury (Odelein and Norman). That's a big blow to any draft class.

NO. 84 OVERALL: RW RICHARD NOVAK
Richmond Sockeyes (BCJHL)

A scoring winger with size (6'1", 170 pounds), Novak went 20–29–49 in 40 games during his draft year. He attended Michigan Tech beginning fall 1984 and received several scholastic awards while in college.

Novak missed much of 1986–87 and was allowed to redshirt, meaning he played his four college seasons of eligibility over five years. He turned pro and played one season, split between the ECHL and IHL.

NO. 105 OVERALL: LW RICK LAMBERT
Henry Carr Crusaders (Metro Junior B Hockey League, MJBHL)

Lambert played junior hockey in Rexdale, Ontario (Tier 2), and filled the net (22–29–51 in 42 games). He was in the penalty box (172 minutes) when he wasn't scoring. At 6'1" and 200 pounds, he was a load and had skill, but scored just 17 goals in four years of college (University of New Hampshire, NCAA). He played one year pro in 1988–89 but did not win an Oilers contract.

NO. 106 OVERALL: D EMANUEL VIVEIROS
Prince Albert Raiders (WHL)

In terms of pure talent, Viveiros was NHL calibre for certain. In his draft season with the Raiders, he had 94 assists in 67 games— an absolutely stunning total for any defenceman in a major junior league. His two seasons after the draft were also impressive, but in December 1985 the Oilers sent him to the Minnesota North Stars in a trade for Gord Sherven.

He played three seasons in the Minnesota minor league system, getting into 29 NHL games (12 points) and showing brilliant puck-moving ability. He followed that up with two more AHL seasons.

Viveiros headed to Europe in 1991, starring in Austria, Germany, Italy, and Austria again.

After his playing career ended, Viveiros began coaching first in Austria, then back in Canada with the WHL's Swift Current Broncos. The Oilers hired him as an assistant coach in 2018, but the job lasted just one season. He is currently coaching the Spokane Chiefs of the WHL and building an impressive résumé. His Swift Current club won the WHL championship in 2017–18.

NO. 126 OVERALL: LW IVAN DORNIC
Trencin (Czech)

After the success of drafting overage Czech Jaroslav Pouzar in 1982, Fraser and his staff tried again two years later with Dornic. He was already established (22 at the time of his draft) as a quality winger internationally, having played on the 1982 silver-medal Czech team at the World Junior Championships.

Dornic scored 20 goals in 42 Czech league games in 1983–84; he was 22 that season. Despite being a solid player in Europe and being named to several Czech teams who played in international tournaments during the mid-80s, Dornic never signed with the Oilers and did not play in the NHL. The numbers suggest he would have been less than a lock to have an NHL career if he had chosen to come over. His scoring rates in the Czech league weren't at Pouzar levels, but they were competitive:

- Pouzar in the Czech league: 461 games, 278–159–437 (0.948 points per game)
- Dornic in the Czech league: 385 games, 147–112–259 (0.673 points per game)

We'll never know, but it was an astute selection by Fraser at this point in the draft.

NO. 147 OVERALL: D HEIKKI RIIHIJARVI
Karpat Oulu (Finland Div. I)

Riihijarvi was a big (6'4", 205 pounds) defensive prospect drafted from a league lower than the Liiga (Finland's top league), but he quickly moved up to the top league and established himself as a regular. After playing on two championship teams in Finland, he moved to France and won three more championships. Despite having NHL size, he never came to North America. It's difficult to be overly critical of a scouting department for not getting an NHL player when the résumé suggests he might have been able to play at the level but didn't sign.

NO. 168 OVERALL: RW TODD EWEN
New Westminster Bruins (WHL)

Ewen was an enforcer, an excellent fighter who was able to endure pain and stay in the lineup. The things that made him a useful player would later contribute to his demise. Edmonton drafted him out of the WHL, where he had quickly established himself as a forward who could play a regular shift (11–13–24 in 68 games) and a willing pugilist (176 PIM). In his final junior season, he scored 28 goals (289 PIM) and was clearly on a trajectory for an NHL career. The Oilers had plenty of help in the enforcer category in the fall of 1986, with Dave Semenko and Kevin McClelland as the incumbent forwards. Sather dealt Ewen to the St. Louis Blues for robust defenceman Shawn Evans. Ironically, Semenko would be traded in December 1986.

Ewen would play in more than 500 NHL games and endure countless injuries (and later surgeries).

Per Hockey Draft Central, Ewen "wrote a guest column in the [December] 14, 2004, issue of *The Hockey News* in which he recounted his own career, noting that he 'broke every finger on both hands at least twice' and had to have two of his right fingers wired together to preserve them. He also noted that he had 15 operations, including his career-ending double-knee reconstruction in October 1997."

Ewn passed away on September 19, 2015.

NO. 209 OVERALL: LW JOEL CURTIS
Oshawa Generals (OHL)

Curtis was average in size (6'1", 180 pounds) and did not deliver a big offensive season in his draft year (8–12–20 in 67 games). He did not have a late birthday (teams sometimes draft and follow August and early-September birthdays, as they have more development time). Curtis did play centre before hitting junior and would play centre at times during his junior career after he was drafted. Curtis did not progress offensively and did not sign a pro contract.

NO. 229 OVERALL: C SIMON WHEELDON
Victoria Cougars (WHL)

Wheeldon possessed similar talent to Curtis, the previous selection. Wheeldon's offence was shy (56 games, 14–24–38), but the pool of talent had been picked clean by this point in the draft.

Wheeldon had a late birthday (August 1966) and exploded in the year after his draft, scoring 126 points in 67 games for the Cougars. He had an even better season in year two, scoring 157 points in 70 games.

Wheeldon did not sign with Edmonton, instead re-entering the draft. No NHL teams drafted him, but Wheeldon signed as an unrestricted free agent with the New York Rangers in the spring of 1987. He would play 15 games with the Rangers and Winnipeg Jets.

NO. 250 OVERALL: D DARREN GANI
Belleville Bulls (OHL)

Gani delivered a strong offensive season in his draft year (16–40–56 in 67 games), and Edmonton selected him with the final pick in the 1984 draft. He had another solid offensive season in year one after the draft but faded and did not sign a pro contract.

1984 Draft Summary

The 1984 draft featured some promising two-way prospects and some high-octane players too. Injuries would have an impact, but the draft-year numbers held promise. (Number in parentheses is points per game.)

- Selmar Odelein (WHL) age 17: 71 games, 9–42–51 (0.72)
- Darryl Reaugh (WHL) age 18: 55 games, 4.34 .864
- Todd Norman (USHS) age 17: 24 games, 35–32–67 (2.79)
- Richard Novak (BCHL) age 17: 40 games, 20–29–49 (1.23)
- Rick Lambert (Ontario HS) age 17: 42 games, 22–29–51 (1.21)
- Emanuel Viveiros (WHL) age 17: 67 games, 15–94–109 (1.63)
- Ivan Dornic (Slovak) age 22: 42 games, 20–12–32 (0.76)
- Heikki Riihijarvi (Finland Jr.) age 17: numbers are unavailable
- Todd Ewen (WHL) age 17: 68 games, 11–13–24 (0.35)
- Joel Curtis (OHL) age 17: 67 games, 8–12–20 (0.29)
- Simon Wheeldon (WHL) age 17: 56 games, 14–24–38 (0.68)
- Darren Gani (OHL) age 17: 67 games, 16–40–56 (0.84)

Odelein was a two-way defenceman who brought enough offence to be considered a candidate for one of the top two pairings. He was shy of Lowe and Coffey offensively, but he was also younger (17) on draft day. Norman was a highly touted talent who suffered a knee injury in college. Viveiros was a slick puck mover born 20 years too early; his high-octane offence from the blue line would have made him a strong candidate for NHL success in the 2010s.

NHL Career Games Played

The 1984 draft showed lots of focus on skill, but injuries to two high picks in 1984 (Selmar Odelein, Todd Norman) give this year's group a different feel. Here is the final tally of NHL games played by 1984 Oilers picks:

1. Todd Ewen: 518
2. Emanuel Viveiros: 29
3. Darryl Reaugh: 27
4. Selmar Odelein: 18
5. Simon Wheeldon: 15

The 1984 draft came in the days that followed Edmonton's first Stanley Cup victory, so there was a general euphoria surrounding the franchise. There was a sense that the good times were just starting and that there would be many more championships to come. The drafting, as it was in 1979, would be central to the team's future success.

Unlike 1979, the 1984 group was shy of success when it came to NHL games played:

1. 1979 (4,143 games)
2. 1980 (3,841 games)

3. 1981 (2,215 games)
4. 1983 (1,810 games)
5. **1984 (607 games)**
6. 1982 (394 games)

The best player drafted was Ewen, who had a significant career in other NHL cities. As Edmonton celebrated the 1984 Stanley Cup, cracks were forming in the prospect pipeline.

Trades That Involved Draft Picks

On December 5, 1983, the Oilers dealt right winger Tom Roulson to the Pittsburgh Penguins for centre Kevin McClelland and the No. 106 pick in the 1984 draft (Emanuel Viveiros).

The trade worked out very well for Edmonton, as McLelland emerged as a first-class centre on the fourth line. He was an enforcer who could fight and check while also scoring what might be the biggest goal in Oilers history (in Game 1 of the 1984 Stanley Cup Final against the New York Islanders).

On January 20, 1984, Edmonton traded its ninth-round pick in the 1984 draft to the New York Rangers for veteran defenceman Rick Chartraw.

Chartraw played 24 games (2–6–8) on defence down the stretch after the trade but was insurance only in the playoffs (playing one game).

The draft pick, Heinz Ehlers, was the first Danish player to be selected by an NHL team. He did not make the NHL.

3

CHAMPIONS IN THE NHL; PIPELINE BEGINS TO FADE

THE 1985 DRAFT

EDMONTON WON ITS second Stanley Cup (and second in a row) in 1984–85. The team's record (49–20–11) was a far cry from 1983–84 (57–18–5) and the goals were down markedly from 446 in 1983–84 to 401 in 1984–85. Coach Glen Sather also shaved off 16 goals against (314–298), so the net decrease in goal differential was less severe. It was Edmonton's fourth time finishing on top of the Smythe Division, dating back to 1981–82.

The names inscribed on the Stanley Cup in 1985 who were procured via the draft or first pro contract—Glenn Anderson, Paul Coffey, Grant Fuhr, Randy Gregg, Charlie Huddy, Jari Kurri, Kevin Lowe, Mark Messier, Andy Moog, and Jaroslav Pouzar—all won their second Stanley Cup, joined by new arrival Esa Tikkanen. That's 11 players, half of the team, brought into the system through strong scouting and drafting by the amateur scouting staff.

NHL rookies in 1984–85:

Gord Sherven: 37 games, 9-7-16. He was traded in the middle of the season (to Minnesota, for Mark Napier) and finished 11-19-30 in 69 games for the two teams.

- Raimo Summanen: 9 games, 0-4-4
- Ray Cote: 2 games, 0-0-0
- Steve Smith: 2 games, 0-0-0
- Mike Zanier: 3 games, 3.89 goals-against average, .880 save percentage
- Darryl Reaugh: 1 game, 5.04 goals-against average, .857 save percentage

NO. 20 OVERALL: C SCOTT METCALFE
Kingston Canadians (OHL)

Through seven drafts for the Oilers, Metcalfe was the first forward the team selected in the first round of an NHL draft. Fraser liked Metcalfe because "he's something like Dave Hunter was coming out of junior."

Metcalfe was typical of the player type Edmonton chose among forwards in this era: he was aggressive, could score some goals, and was a willing combatant, leading up to and including fighting.

Metcalfe's 1984–85 scoring totals (58 games, 27-33-60, 1.03 points per game) in the OHL probably gave Fraser the impression Metcalfe was a good bet for a checking line with the hope he would develop into something more.

He didn't get much of a chance in Edmonton, as Sather dealt Metcalfe in his rookie pro season (1987–88) in a deadline trade for veteran defenceman Steve Dykstra. Metcalfe would play in 19 NHL games, just two with the Oilers.

NO. 41 OVERALL: D TODD CARNELLEY
Kamloops Blazers (WHL)

As happened often during the Fraser years, the Oilers double-dipped when choosing Carnelley in 1985. Edmonton had selected goaltender Darryl Reaugh from Kamloops the previous season and must have seen Carnelley do some good things.

At the time of the draft, Fraser said, "We had him rated 21st overall. He's not flashy, but a good, sound player."

An offensive defender who was overshadowed by fellow puck movers Greg Hawgood and Mark Ferner, Carnelley's draft year offence (18–29–47 in 56 games) was outstanding but zoomed because he was playing for an outstanding team. The 1984–85 Blazers scored 423 goals under head coach Ken Hitchcock.

Carnelley turned pro in 1986, playing for two IHL teams in his one season in the league. He later played for the Canadian national team.

NO. 62 OVERALL: RW MIKE WARE
Hamilton Steelhawks (OHL)

The Oilers were not alone in their pursuit of enforcers, but nevertheless the club drafted its fair share. A big man (6'5", 215 pounds) who didn't score much (4–14–18 in 57 games), Ware spent several hours in his draft year (225 minutes) in the penalty box. Fraser said he was "very tough" and Edmonton had a lot just like him in the system during the 1980s.

As a pro, Ware played in five NHL games and performed well in four minor league seasons but was never a threat to play as an NHL regular. He finished his career with several seasons in Britain.

NO. 104 OVERALL: C TOMAS KAPUSTA
Gottwaldov (Czech)

Fraser drafted another Czech forward in 1985, this time not an overager. Kapusta had good size and some scoring touch and came over to North America in 1989 (aged 22).

Kapusta scored well in the AHL (49 points in 55 games as a rookie with the Cape Breton Oilers in 1989–90) but didn't get an NHL look with Edmonton. He returned to Europe in 1992 and played the rest of the decade playing in high European leagues.

Based on his scoring totals in Europe and North America, Kapusta had NHL talent.

NO 125 OVERALL: G BRIAN TESSIER
North Bay Centennials (OHL)

Beginning in 1980 with Andy Moog and continuing through 1988, the Oilers took at least one goaltender in every draft. This was despite the fact the NHL club had Grant Fuhr and Moog as a brilliant (and young) tandem for most of that time. Tessier didn't progress in junior after his draft day, did not sign with Edmonton, and didn't have a pro career.

NO. 146 OVERALL: RW SHAWN TYERS
Kitchener Rangers (OHL)

Tyers played for three different teams in his draft year, posting 13–26–39 in 57 games. He had good size, and his rookie season in the OHL showed some promise. He played only 26 games in the season after he was drafted, and that was the extent of his recorded hockey career.

NO. 167 OVERALL: RW TONY FAIRFIELD
St. Albert Saints (AJHL)

Fairfield was a big, physical winger with enough skill to get noticed in Tier 2. Fraser mentioned at the draft that Fairfield might attend the University of Alberta in the fall of 1985. As it turned out, he went to Northern Arizona University for a year and then landed at the University of Calgary in the late 1980s, where his playing career ended.

PROSPECT SPOTLIGHT
NO. 188 OVERALL: RW KELLY BUCHBERGER, MOOSE JAW WARRIORS (WHL)

Buchberger played 1,182 games in the NHL. He scored 105 goals and 309 points and posted a whopping 2,297 penalty minutes.

Buchberger was not an offensively talented forward, but he played a rugged game and was tireless on the forecheck. In his first pro season, he scored 12–20–32 in 70 games and finished ninth among forwards in team scoring. He would play longer than any of them.

He was a crowd favourite for years in Edmonton. His signature move involved trying to go wide on a defender as he rushed down the ice. Although he tried it hundreds of times, it was a rare success. Oilers fans adopted him as an everyman early in his career and would scream, "Take 'em wide, Bucky!" during those sojourns down the ice.

Scouting report and legacy: Buchberger emerged as a gritty fourth-line forward who would do any chore to help his team win. Blocking shots, killing penalties, and moving up the depth chart only as required, he played from 1986 to 1999 with the team, eventually leaving via the Atlanta Thrashers in their expansion draft.

He retired in 2004 and a year later was assistant coach of Edmonton's farm team (the Roadrunners). He would be an assistant coach for the Oilers for six seasons beginning in 2008–09 and spent 2019–20 coaching the WHL's Tri-City Americans.

NO. 209 OVERALL: D MARIO BARBE
Chicoutimi Sagueneens (QMJHL)

Barbe was a tough defender who had 211 penalty minutes in 64 games in his draft year. The offensive side of his game improved in his draft-plus-one season after a trade to the Granby Bisons.

Barbe played well enough to earn a pro contract and was a regular in each of his three AHL seasons (all spent with the Cape Breton Oilers). He final pro season was 1990–91.

NO. 230 OVERALL: C PETER HEADON
Notre Dame High School, Wilcox (Saskatchewan)

Headon had good size for the position (6'1", 190 pounds) and came from a well-respected program in Wilcox, Saskatchewan. Headon went to Boston University in the fall of 1985, spending three years there in a secondary role (he played a total of 37 games, posting eight points). He did not sign with Edmonton and did not play pro hockey.

NO. 251 OVERALL: G JOHN HALEY
Hull High School (USHS, Massachusetts)

Haley was drafted out of U.S. high school and went to RPI, where he played sparingly for two seasons. He transferred to UMass-Boston. Haley did not sign with the Oilers but did play in the ECHL for two seasons beginning in 1989.

1985 Draft Summary

The 1985 draft amounted to one player who made the NHL for any length of time. One NHL player out of 11 draft picks is a poor result, but to give credit where credit is due, the Oilers got a long-term solution on the checking line in Kelly Buchberger. (Number in parentheses is points per game.)

- Scott Metcalfe (OHL) age 17: 58 games, 27–33–60 (1.03)
- Todd Carnelley (WHL) age 17: 56 games, 18–29–47 (0.84)
- Mike Ware (OHL) age 17: 57 games, 4–14–18 (0.32)
- Tomas Kapusta (Czech) age 17: 36 games, 5–7–12 (0.33)
- Brian Tessier (OHL) age 17: 5 games, 3.30
- Shawn Tyers (OHL) age 17: 35 games, 8–12–20 (0.57)

- Tony Fairfield (AJHL) age 17: numbers are unavailable
- Kelly Buchberger (WHL) age 17: 51 games, 12–17–29 (0.57)
- Mario Barbe (QMJHL) age 17: 64 games, 2–13–15 (0.23)
- Peter Headon (SK HS) age 17: numbers are unavailable
- John Haley (USHS) age 17: numbers are unavailable

The selection of Metcalfe represented less than full value. Joe Nieuwendyk was available and was posting 1.55 points per game at Cornell (NCAA).

NHL Career Games Played
1. Kelly Buchberger: 1,182
2. Scott Metcalfe: 19
3. Mike Ware: 5

One quick note on a player who never stepped onto NHL ice (Tomas Kapusta)—Fraser drafted a winner in Kapusta; he just didn't come to North America. You can't blame a scouting department for that outcome.

The total NHL games played by the 1985 draft, courtesy of Buchberger, performed well compared to other mid-80s drafts:
1. 1979 (4,143 games)
2. 1980 (3,841 games)
3. 1981 (2,215 games)
4. 1983 (1,810 games)
5. **1985 (1,206 games)**
6. 1984 (607 games)
7. 1982 (394 games)

Looking back, a draft like 1985's haul was predictable. Fraser and his crew had drafted so many skill spots in the first three drafts it was difficult for players to break through. Esa Tikkanen, selected in the 1983 draft, worked his way up the depth chart to play on a line with Wayne Gretzky and Jari Kurri. A player like Kapusta might have been enticed to sign an NHL deal if he wasn't blocked by young Oilers who were having an impact in the NHL.

That may also be a reason why Fraser drafted a checking forward in the first round of the 1985 draft. The team had been focused on a skill centre (Jeff Wenaas) until changing course at the last minute when Metcalfe remained available at the end of the first round.

It's also true that Fraser's evaluation ability was no longer as sharp as it had been. Nieuwendyk was chosen by the Calgary Flames in the second round. Fraser and his scouts would have seen him multiple times. They did not put a high enough grade on Nieuwendyk, and the rival Flames landed him. He would finish with 564 NHL goals in a long and impressive career.

Trades That Involved Draft Picks

On March 6, 1984, Sather dealt the No. 83 selection in the 1985 draft for talented forward Risto Jalo, whose rights were acquired from the Washington Capitals.

Jalo had been drafted in 1981, and by 1984 he was the top playmaking forward for Ilves Tampere of the top Finnish league (Liiga). His winger, Raimo Summanen, had been drafted by Edmonton in 1982, and this was another example of Sather looking to add a piece before the price got too high.

Jalo played just three NHL games, assisting on three goals, for the 1985–86 Oilers. Washington used the selection on defenceman Larry Shaw, who did not play in the NHL.

THE 1986 DRAFT

The 1985–86 Oilers season was the most frustrating year imaginable. The team rolled through the regular season, winning 56 games and finishing with 119 points. Edmonton beat the second-place Calgary Flames by 30 points in the standings, and the runaway included Jari Kurri leading the league with 68 goals and Wayne Gretzky winning another scoring title.

It was complete domination…until the Oilers met Calgary in the second round of the 1986 playoffs. The series went seven games. The Flames won the goal differential in those seven games 25–24 and won Game 7 due to a momentary lapse by young defenceman Steve Smith that put the Oilers down a goal with most of the third period to go.

It was devastating. The loss would light a fire under Sather no one had seen before, as trades rained down on the roster from summer to the trade deadline. It was a time of great upheaval for a great hockey club.

NHL rookies in 1985–86:

- Raimo Summanen: 73 games, 19–18–37
- Steve Smith: 55 games, 4–20–24
- Esa Tikkanen: 35 games, 7–6–13
- Risto Jalo: 3 games, 0–3–3
- Selmar Odelein: 4 games, 0–0–0

I've always wondered if Summanen's quick departure from the team after a solid rookie season was a matter of bad timing.

Sather rarely sent away talented players at such a young age, but Summanen's rookie campaign landed in the wrong year. Smith and Tikkanen would go on to long and productive careers.

NO. 21 OVERALL: RW KIM ISSEL
Prince Albert Raiders (WHL)

Issel was a big winger (6'4", 200 pounds) who had some offensive talent (68 games, 29–39–68 in his draft year) and played on a Memorial Cup winner as a junior.

His problem came during each training camp in Edmonton—the parent club's depth chart was too strong for him to find any room. He played four games with Edmonton in 1988–89, a year when the right wing depth chart featured Jari Kurri, Glenn Anderson, Norm Lacombe, and Kelly Buchberger as regulars.

He was traded in 1991 to the Pittsburgh Penguins for Brad Aitken but did not play again in the NHL. He would play in Austria, Italy, Germany, and Slovenia after leaving North America.

Issel scored well as a rookie pro and improved each season. His bad luck was getting drafted by the 1980s Oilers. These are solid AHL numbers:

- 1987–88: 68 games, 20–25–45 (.662 points per game)
- 1988–89: 65 games, 34–28–62 (.954 points per game)
- 1989–90: 62 games, 36–32–68 (1.10 points per game)

These numbers show a player who was sent down and told to improve his game, and he did each season. He had the kind of size Edmonton liked and posted two seasons of 30-plus goals in the minors. He ranks high among Oilers picks who earned a shot but did not receive it.

NO. 42 OVERALL: RW JAMIE NICOLLS
Portland Winterhawks (WHL)

Nicolls was a good bet in the second round. He was chosen in his first year of eligibility and scored well enough (65 games, 15–37–52) to be considered a legit NHL draft prospect on his draft day.

He improved offensively in his draft-plus-one season but fell off in the final year of junior. He did sign a pro contract but was stuck in the minors behind Issel and others. He did not play in the NHL but played in France for a time before retiring in the early 1990s.

NO. 63 OVERALL: D RON SHUDRA
Kamloops Blazers (WHL)

Shudra was a big (6'2", 195 pounds) defenceman with real offensive ability (72 games, 10–40–50) in his draft year. He played for the Kamloops Blazers, who were a powerhouse in those years, so Shudra's offensive ability was overstated in his numbers.

That was especially true in his draft-plus-one season (71 games, 49–70–119), when he was one of five Blazers to finish with more than 100 points.

Shudra signed with the Oilers and scored five points in 10 NHL games as a rookie pro in 1987–88. He played the rest of his rookie year in the AHL, and Edmonton traded him early in 1988–89, his second pro campaign. The Oilers received two-way defenceman Jeff Crossman from the New York Rangers in return, neither man seeing the NHL with his new team.

NO. 84 OVERALL: LW DAN CURRIE
Soo Greyhounds (OHL)

Currie was 6'2", 195 pounds, and emerged as a substantial AHL scorer for the Oilers system but didn't establish himself as an NHL player. Currie did get several chances (22 career NHL games, 17 with the Oilers) but most of his work was done for Oilers farm teams.

He was an OHL regular in his draft year (66 games, 21–22–43) before he exploded offensively in his draft-plus-one season (66 games, 31–52–83) and his final junior season (57 games, 50–50–109).

When he hit pro hockey, Currie kept posting good numbers. His first pro season at age 20 (77 games, 29–36–65, .844 points per game) signaled he was a real talent.

Currie gained a reputation for being a player who needed to be pushed by his coach, but even making allowances for unseen factors, he looks like a player from here. He backed up his AHL rookie season with four more tremendous seasons in the minors, but couldn't crack the Oilers lineup, which by 1992–93 was in a period of transition.

He eventually landed in the Los Angeles Kings organization. He played in the high minors through 2001 before heading to Europe.

Currie had the talent to play in the NHL.

NO. 105 OVERALL: LW DAVID HAAS
London Knights (OHL)

Haas was yet another big winger (6'2", 196 pounds) who had an enforcer's approach to the game and enough skill to be draft-worthy for the Oilers. Haas also had some offensive ability and has a place in Oilers minor league history. He delivered a hat trick for the Cape Breton Oilers in 1993 as the team won the AHL Championship (the Calder Cup). It's the only championship by an Oilers minor league team. Haas had an outstanding playoff run along with Bill McDougall, who scored 26 goals in 16 playoff games that spring. He would play five games with the Oilers and two with the Calgary Flames in a brief NHL career.

NO. 126 OVERALL: D JIM ENNIS
Boston University (NCAA)

The Oilers drafted many prospects from Tier 2 hockey who attended U.S. colleges, but Ennis was just the third player drafted from an NCAA team (Glenn Anderson in 1979, Rob Polman-Tuin in 1980).

He played hockey near Edmonton (Sherwood Park), and the Oilers would have known about him before his freshman season in college. After he was drafted, Ennis played one more year in college and turned pro.

In the AHL, he played a consistent two-way game that earned him a five-game look in the NHL with the Oilers. In October 1989, he was traded to the Hartford Whalers for Norm MacIver, a trade that worked out very well for Edmonton.

Ennis would play one more season in the minors before retiring and getting a head start on a business career.

MacIver grew from a minor league puck mover to an NHL offensive defenceman and would play most of the 1990s in the big leagues with the Oilers, Ottawa Senators, Pittsburgh Penguins, Winnipeg Jets, and Phoenix Coyotes.

NO. 147 OVERALL: RW IVAN MATULIK
Bratislava Slovan (Slovakia)

Matulik was a big winger who was shy offensively but hung around the Oilers' AHL farm team for his entry deal and played six seasons in the minors before heading to Europe to continue his playing career.

NO. 168 OVERALL: LW NICK BEAULIEU
Drummondville Voltigeurs (QMJHL)

Another tough winger from the Quebec league, Beaulieu scored 39 goals in his final season of junior and 10 goals in his only AHL season. He hung around the IHL and other North American leagues for several seasons.

NO. 189 OVERALL: G MIKE GREENLAY
Calgary Midgets AAA

Greenlay was ahead of his time in that his size (6'3", 200 pounds) was unusual at the time but is vital for modern goaltending.

He played for the Calgary Midgets and briefly for the Penticton Knights of the BCJHL before being drafted. His next stop was Lake Superior State (CCHA), where he played well but didn't get much work. He moved to the Saskatoon Blades in his second season after the draft and backstopped that club to a Memorial Cup berth (he was named best goalie at the tournament).

Greenlay peaked early as a pro, appearing in two games with the Oilers in 1989–90 and winning the starting role with the AHL Cape Breton Oilers.

He did not progress from that point but played several years in the minors before retiring. He is currently the Minnesota Wild colour analyst, an area of the hockey industry he shares with fellow Oilers draft picks Darryl Reaugh and Mike Zanier. All are goalies.

NO. 210 OVERALL: D MATT LANZA
Winthrop High School (USHS, Massachusetts)

Oilers took Lanza out of U.S. high school, and he had the kind of size (6'4", 215 pounds) Fraser valued in defencemen. He played for RPI (NCAA) in his draft-plus-one season and did not play again.

NO. 231 OVERALL: D MOJMIR BOZIK
Kosice (Czech)

Bozik was an undersized, puck-moving defender who played for years in the Czech league but didn't come to North America.

NO. 252 OVERALL: RW TONY HAND
Murrayfield Racers (BHL)

Hand is a fascinating story in the history of the Oilers' drafting. He played for the Murrayfield Racers of the BHL (British Hockey League) in '81–82. He was 14 years old.

Hand was really good—not just good for Great Britain, but actually good. He was drafted by the Oilers in 1986, came to North America, and had a terrific camp. He became a sort of celebrity; I remember very well play-by-play broadaster Rod Phillips calling preseason games on 1260 CFRN and raving about him.

Legend has it Hand was offered a contract but was homesick. He did play three WHL games with the Victoria Cougars, where he scored 4–4–8, before going home.

There, he beat the living daylights out of the competition. In 86–87, Hand scored 19 short-handed goals and had 22 hat tricks during the regular season. His stats for that year? 35 games, 105–111–216.

Among his feats:

- First British-trained player in NHL draft
- Young Player of the Year (November 1985)
- Scottish National League Champion (1985–86 Edinburgh Racers)
- British Premier League Champion (1986–87 Murrayfield Racers, 1987–88 Murrayfield Racers)
- Best forward (WC D 1990, WC C 1992)
- Named to All-British All-Star team (1990–91)
- FBNL points scorer (2001–02, '02–03 Dundee Stars, '03–04 Edinburgh Capitals)
- All-Star team ('90–91, '91–92, 2001–02, '03–04, '04–05)
- Powerplay Player of the Month (Oct 2003)
- FBNL Most League Assists (2003–04 Edinburgh Capitals)
- FBNL Most Assists Playoffs (2003–04 Edinburgh Capitals)
- British Ice Hockey Writers Association Player of the Year (2003–04, '04–05)
- Scored his 1000th point February 18, 1989, at Whitley Bay
- Had one eight-goal game, three nine-assist games, and one 14-point game (March 19, 1988)

Hand didn't play in the NHL, but he was clearly good enough to have been considered a substantial prospect as a teenager. It was an opportunity missed for Hand, and the Oilers.

1986 Draft Summary

Fraser and the Oilers scouting staff drafted some talented players in 1986, but none in the group scored well above one point per game, and none in the group had an NHL impact. (Number in parentheses is points per game.)

- Kim Issel (WHL) age 17: 68 games, 29–39–68 (1.00)
- Jamie Nicolls (WHL) age 17: 65 games, 15–37–52 (0.80)
- Ron Shudra (WHL) age 17: 72 games, 10–40–50 (0.69)
- Dan Currie (OHL) age 17: 66, games 21–22–43 (0.65)
- David Haas (OHL) age 17: 62 games, 4–13–17 (0.27)
- Jim Ennis (NCAA) age 18: 40 games, 1–4–5 (0.13)
- Ivan Matulik (Slovak) age 17: numbers are unavailable
- Nick Beaulieu (QMJHL) age 17: 70 games, 11–20–31 (0.44)
- Mike Greenlay (Calgary Midgets) age 17: numbers are unavailable
- Matt Lanza (USHS) age 17: numbers are unavailable
- Mojmir Bozik (Czech) age 24: 46 games, 6–20–26 (0.57)
- Tony Hand (BHL) age 18: 32 games, 79–85–164 (5.13)

Were they all "tweeners," or was it a matter of being drafted by a team with enormous talent playing ahead of them in the NHL? These years later, you could make a case for both theories.

NHL Career Games Played

1. Dan Currie: 22
2. Ron Shudra: 10
3. David Haas: 7
4. Jim Ennis: 5
5. Kim Issel: 4
6. Mike Greenlay: 2

Currie and Issel earn some acknowledgement for building on their success each season after being drafted and, in both cases, well into pro hockey. I'm less inclined to be critical of the scouting staff, although Fraser did seem to pursue players who matched Dave Hunter's talents as if Gretzky, Messier, Kurri, Anderson, and the others would be on the Edmonton roster forever.

The 1986 draft was easily the least successful of all drafts by Edmonton in the first decade of the team's existence in terms of total NHL games played:

1. 1979 (4,143 games)
2. 1980 (3,841 games)
3. 1981 (2,215 games)
4. 1983 (1,810 games)
5. 1985 (1,206 games)
6. 1984 (607 games)
7. 1982 (394 games)
8. **1986 (50 games)**

The success of four of the first five drafts becomes increasingly clear, with the 1979–81 cluster soaring higher with each year evaluated. The 1986 draft isn't the worst in Oilers history, but it's close. I'm not certain it should be viewed as a complete failure, however; there were good players chosen. Luck is part of success, and the 1986 draft had very little of that.

THE 1987 DRAFT

The 1986–87 season saw the Oilers return to 50 wins (for the final time), post 106 points, and claim the No. 1 spot in the Smythe Division. Edmonton won its third Stanley Cup on a team that featured 14 players procured by Fraser and the scouting staff:

Glenn Anderson, Jeff Beukeboom, Kelly Buchberger, Paul Coffey, Grant Fuhr, Randy Gregg, Charlie Huddy, Jari Kurri, Kevin Lowe, Mark Messier, Andy Moog, Jaroslav Pouzar, Steve Smith, and Esa Tikkanen.

Sather, determined to return to the Stanley Cup Final and win it, took no prisoners. He traded or released trusted veterans Lee Fogolin, Dave Semenko, and Dave Lumley and young scorer Raimo Summanen during the season.

NHL rookies in 1986–87:

- Jeff Beukeboom: 44 games, 3–8–11
- Stu Kulak: 23 games, 3–1–4
- Steve Graves: 12 games, 2–0–2
- Wayne Van Dorp: 3 games, 0–0–0

Beukeboom was a strong defensive defenceman who also served in an enforcer role. He was a punishing player who would enjoy a solid NHL career.

Sather made a number of midseason moves involving draft picks; there is a detailed account of these at the end of the chapter.

NO. 21 OVERALL: LW PETER SOBERLAK
Swift Current Broncos (WHL)

There was a lot to like about Soberlak on his draft day: his skill, speed, size, and a midseason spike in offence after being traded to the Broncos suggested a strong career ahead.

Edmonton drafted Soberlak in the first round, just six spots after Broncos centre Joe Sakic. Sakic drove results even in his draft season, scoring 133 points in 72 games.

Soberlak's remaining junior seasons were solid, if unspectacular (68 goals in 104 games in those two years), but he didn't have the same kind of support when turning pro.

He scored 15 goals in 60 games as an AHL rookie and followed it up with 18 goals in 70 games the following year. He was finished with pro hockey at the end of his entry deal.

NO. 42 OVERALL: D BRAD WERENKA
Northern Michigan University (NCAA)

Werenka displayed grit and skill as part of the Sherwood Park Crusaders in 1983–84 and continued to show two-way ability at Northern Michigan.

He spent five seasons in college, turning pro in 1991 and showing well in his AHL debut. The following year he spent 27 games with the Oilers and some time in the minors and with the Canadian national team.

Sather traded Werenka in 1994 for a goalie the organization liked a lot (Steve Passmore). Werenka would play effective hockey for the Quebec Nordiques, Chicago Blackhawks, Pittsburgh Penguins, and Calgary Flames for the rest of the decade. He would finish with 320 career NHL games. A concussion in 2001 would end his career.

NO. 63 OVERALL: D GEOFF SMITH
St. Albert Saints (AJHL)

Smith was the final player drafted by Edmonton who also played on a Stanley Cup winner for the Oilers.

He played a defensive game and despite having size (6'2", 200 pounds), he didn't take a lot of penalties. Smith made simple, effective plays and got the puck to forwards quickly.

He arrived in Edmonton with the Oilers in 1989–90, making the team out of camp (a difficult feat in the 1980s). His steady play was effective on a team that would lose much of its identity during his time with the team.

Edmonton dealt him to the Florida Panthers in December of 1993. He would play in 462 career NHL games.

NO. 64 OVERALL: LW PETER ERIKSSON
Jonkoping (SEL)

Eriksson was the second player Edmonton drafted out of Sweden (after Lars-Gunnar Pettersson) and the first Oilers draft pick to play in the NHL. It would be 14 years before the club drafted another.

On his draft day, he was almost 22, so the Oilers had a more mature player in Eriksson than most of the players chosen in 1987. He scored 10–14–24 in 36 games with a mid-quality team at age 21 and would be in the NHL by 1989.

Eriksson came over for the 1989–90 season and played in both the AHL (21 games, 5–12–17) and the NHL (20 games, 3–3–6) before heading back to Sweden for several more seasons with Jonkoping.

NO. 105 OVERALL: C SHAUN VAN ALLEN
Saskatoon Blades (WHL)

The Oilers returned to the Saskatoon Blades for another centre after having success choosing Marc Habscheid in the sixth round in 1981.

Van Allen was almost 20 on draft day 1987 and signed plus turned pro that fall. He was an impressive offensive centre in his final year of junior, but in pro hockey spent most of his entry deal in the minors learning how to play the two-way game.

While the Oilers were winning the Stanley Cup in 1990, Van Allen was emerging as a quality centre in the AHL (69 points in 61 games) and was ready for the NHL.

In 1990–91, Edmonton's NHL checking centres included veterans Craig MacTavish and Ken Linseman, as well as Mark Lamb, who played a significant role in Edmonton's 1990 Stanley Cup victory.

In 1991–92, he led the AHL in points, and the following year played an integral role in the Cape Breton Oilers winning the AHL Championship (Calder Cup).

After the 1992–93 campaign and spending just 23 games with the Oilers over six seasons, Edmonton released Van Allen.

It was the best thing that ever happened to him. Van Allen caught on with the expansion Anaheim Mighty Ducks, where he established himself as a solid two-way centre.

After three years with the Ducks, he landed with the Ottawa Senators, where he filled a similar role for four seasons. He would make stops with the Dallas Stars, Montreal Canadiens, and Ottawa again before ending his career.

Van Allen played 794 career NHL games. He couldn't break into the Oilers lineup in the months after the team won its final Stanley and hung around for six minor league seasons knocking on the door.

His career after Edmonton proved he could play in the NHL.

NO. 126 OVERALL: C RADEK TOUPAL

Ceske Budejovice HC (Czech)

Toupal was playing in the top Czech league by age 16 and scored 16 goals (aged 20) in 1986–87.

That was enough to draw the attention of the Oilers, who by 1987 had a steady parade of young Czech players (Miloslav Horava in 1981, Jaroslav Pouzar in 1982, Tomas Kapusta in 1985, and Mojmir Bozik in 1986).

Although Edmonton drafted Toupal, and Oilers management would see him winning the 1992 Olympic and 1993 World Championships bronze medals with the Czechs, he never signed or came over to North America. He enjoyed a long career, playing at a high level through 2001.

NO. 147 OVERALL: LW TOMAS SRSEN

Brno (Czech)

Srsen was an overage pick (he would turn 21 the summer Edmonton drafted him) who was a bona fide scorer at the pro level.

Edmonton brought him over in 1990, the fall after the team's fifth Stanley Cup win. At that point in franchise history, the Oilers had real swagger with enough pull to attract top-quality players to North America.

Srsen played in two NHL games and scored 32 goals for the Cape Breton Oilers in 1990–91, showing impressive skill. He was less effective in his second season and went back to Europe, where he played pro hockey until 2003.

NO. 168 OVERALL: D AGE ELLINGSEN
Storhammer (Norway)

Ellingsen was the first player from Norway drafted by Edmonton, and the third Norwegian all-time to be drafted by an NHL team.

He was 24 at the time of his draft and played in Sweden the year after his draft. In all other seasons, from 1979 to 1994, he played in various leagues in Norway.

Ellingsen was a big (6'4", 209 pounds) defender who was an impact player in Norway, less so in Sweden. Ellingsen was a mainstay on the Norwegian national team, and a reasonable draft bet in an era when gems could be found in obscure places, but never a real threat to play in the NHL.

NO. 189 OVERALL: G GAVIN ARMSTRONG
RPI (NCAA)

Armstrong was drafted out of RPI (U.S. collegiate hockey) after his freshman season (26 games, 3.42 goals-against average, .889 save percentage), but he played in just four games the following season and found himself playing for the SJHL Nipawin Hawks by the end of that season.

Armstrong would attend the University of Alberta in Edmonton and play for the Golden Bears for the following two seasons. He played pro hockey in the BNL, or British National League, for several seasons.

NO. 210 OVERALL: C MIKE TINKHAM
Newburyport High School (USHS, Massachusetts)

Tinkham was a prolific scorer on his hometown high school team, and Massachusetts has produced some NHL players via the high school system (the most notable being Bob Corkum).

Tinkham attended UMass-Lowell briefly and then played in various lower pro leagues (ECHL, Sunshine League, CHL) after college.

NO. 231 OVERALL: D JEFF PAULETTI
University of Minnesota (NCAA)

Edmonton drafted Pauletti from college, but he gained traction in high school as a prospect. He attended Minnesota but played little while he was there and didn't turn pro. Pauletti became a successful hockey coach in Minnesota before losing his job in what became a famous court case, as reported in the *Washington Post*.

NO. 241 OVERALL: D JESPER DUUS
Rodovre (Denmark)

Duus was a big, two-way defenceman drafted out of Denmark who found his ceiling in Sweden and the SHL. Although he never signed with Edmonton, Duus played in the SHL from 1987 to 2001.

NO. 252 OVERALL: LW IGOR VYAZMIKIN
CSKA Moscow (RSL)

NHL teams stayed away from Russian players for a long time, but by the mid-80s there were a few names each season. Barry Fraser chose Vyazmikin with the final pick in the 1987 draft, knowing he was NHL calibre and that Russian players would have an impact.

Vyazmikin arrived in North America in time for the 1990–91 season. Edmonton had just won the Stanley Cup that spring and was still set to deploy a strong contender that season. He had close to a point per game in the AHL (12–19–31 in 33 games with the Cape Breton Oilers) and had one goal in four NHL games with Edmonton.

That represented the sum of his NHL career. Vyazmikin finished his playing career back in Russia in 1998–99.

1987 Draft Summary

The 1987 draft saw Fraser's scouting staff identify several NHL players of note, all outside the first round. (Number in parentheses is points per game.)

- Peter Soberlak (WHL) age 17: 68 games, 33–42–75 (1.10)
- Brad Werenka (NCAA) age 17: 30 games, 4–4–8 (0.27)
- Geoff Smith (AJHL) age 17: 57 games, 7–28–35 (0.61)
- Peter Eriksson (SEL) age 22: 36 games, 10–14–24 (0.67)
- Shaun Van Allen (WHL) age 19: 72 games, 38–59–97 (1.35)
- Radek Toupal (Czech) age 20: 35 games, 16–14–30 (0.86)
- Tomas Srsen (Czech) age 20: 40 games, 15–8–23 (0.58)
- Age Ellingsen (Norway) age 23: 36 games, 22–24–46 (1.28)
- Gavin Armstrong (NCAA) age 18: 26 games, 3.42 goals-against average, .889 save percentage
- Mike Tinkham (USHS) age 18: numbers are unavailable
- Jeff Pauletti (NCAA) age 18: 4 games, 0–1–1 (0.25)
- Jesper Duus (Denmark) age 18: 30 games, 7–17–24 (0.80)
- Igor Vyazmikin (RSL) age 21: 4 games, 0–0–0

Soberlak's numbers in his draft year put him about equal with Scott Metcalfe and Kim Issel as NHL prospects, meaning Edmonton was aiming too low (tweeners) but would wait a few years to find out. Van Allen was a couple of years older but more promising offensively. Among defencemen, both Werenka and Smith projected as two-way types, well clear of Playfair and Beukeboom.

After several disappointing drafts from 1984 to '86, Fraser and his scouting staff delivered an impressive number of NHL players in 1987. Only Geoff Smith contributed to a Stanley Cup, and Shaun Van Allen would succeed elsewhere, but the scouts did a good job on draft day.

NHL Career Games Played
1. Shaun Van Allen: 794
2. Geoff Smith: 462
3. Brad Werenka: 320
4. Peter Eriksson: 20
5. Igor Vyazmikin: 4
6. Tomas Srsen: 2

The early years of success skew a draft like this one, but an NHL team drafting late in each round should consider this a success. Three men had NHL careers from this draft; that's a solid number.

One area for concern in Edmonton by 1987: the first-round picks (Odelein, Metcalfe, Issel, Soberlak) were not developing as quickly or having the same impact as Edmonton's picks in the past. Fraser's wand was broken.

Here's how the 1987 draft class ranked in terms of total NHL games played:
1. 1979 (4,143 games)
2. 1980 (3,841 games)

3. 1981 (2,215 games)
4. 1983 (1,810 games)
5. **1987 (1,602 games)**
6. 1985 (1,206 games)
7. 1984 (607 games)
8. 1982 (394 games)
9. 1986 (50 games)

The 1987 draft isn't considered an especially strong one and didn't produce an impact player (or more) like the 1979–81 and 1983 editions did.

But it was a success, and that was progress in 1987.

Trades That Involved Draft Picks

On March 6, 1987, the Oilers traded Mark Napier, Lee Fogolin, and a 1987 fourth-round pick (John Bradley) to the Buffalo Sabres for Norm Lacombe, the rights to Wayne Van Dorp, and a 1987 fourth-round pick (Peter Eriksson).

Jesper Duus was drafted using the New York Rangers' pick in Round 12 of the 1987 draft. No record of a transaction is available.

THE 1988 DRAFT

The 1987–88 season saw the great Oilers team fade to second place in the Smythe Division and fall from 50 to 44 wins. The team's 363 goals trailed the division champion Calgary Flames by 34, but Edmonton would march to the fourth Stanley Cup in team history by defeating the Winnipeg Jets in five games, the Flames in four straight, the Detroit Red Wings in five, and the Boston Bruins in four straight.

It would be a stunning summer marked by Wayne Gretzky's move to Los Angeles (it was a sale, not a trade) and other massive changes in the team. The 1987–88 list of players who won the Stanley Cup via Fraser's procurement numbered 10: Glenn Anderson, Jeff Beukeboom, Grant Fuhr, Randy Gregg, Charlie Huddy, Jari Kurri, Kevin Lowe, Mark Messier, Steve Smith, and Esa Tikkanen.

NHL rookies in 1987–88:

- Steve Graves: 21 games, 3–4–7
- John Miner: 14 games, 2–3–5
- Ron Shudra: 10 games, 0–5–5
- Chris Joseph: 7 games, 0–4–4
- Selmar Odelein: 12 games, 0–2–2
- Kelly Buchberger: 19 games, 1–0–1
- Jim Ennis: 5 games, 1–0–1
- Scott Metcalfe: 2 games, 0–0–0
- Mark Lamb: 2 games, 0–0–0

Buchberger got his name on the Stanley Cup in 1987 but didn't play in postseason games in 1988. Steve Graves had some promise, and Chris Joseph looked like an NHL player in brief exposure. Mark Lamb played two games with the Oilers, but he would be a key performer for Edmonton in the days to come.

NO. 19 OVERALL: D FRANCOIS LEROUX
St. Jean Castors (QMJHL)

The Oilers went back to the QMJHL in the first round for the first time since 1979 in selecting Leroux.

Leroux was a big (6'6", 247 pounds) shutdown defender who played a physical game. He was also a step slow (that's not unusual for big men) and a raw defenceman.

The risk with a player like Leroux is how much he'll develop in the two or three years after the draft. Leroux developed enough to make the NHL and played as an NHL regular for four seasons. Edmonton lost him on waivers to the Ottawa Senators.

NO. 39 OVERALL: RW PETRO KOIVUNEN
Kiekko-Espoo (Finland Jr.)

Koivunen played centre and wing, had good size and skill, and posted huge numbers in Finland's junior league in his draft season (31 games, 27–31–58).

He enjoyed a solid career in Finland's top league (Liiga), playing 385 games and posting 218 points. He then moved on to coaching and remains a successful coach in Finland's II Divisioona league. He never came to North America.

NO. 53 OVERALL: C TREVOR SIM
Seattle Thunderbirds (WHL)

The selection used on Sim was acquired from the Hartford Whalers in December 1986 in exchange for LW Dave Semenko.

Sim was a centre with good size (6'2", 192 pounds) who scored well at 16 in the AJHL (38–50–88 in 57 games with the Calgary Spurs).

He moved up to the WHL in his draft year and delivered average offence (17–18–35 in 67 games).

During the four decades Edmonton has been drafting, a CHL forward with those numbers in his draft year has not proved to be a good bet for an NHL career.

Sim turned pro in 1989–90 and played three NHL games (they would be the only games of his career) and scored 20 goals in the AHL (in 62 games). He joined the Canadian national team at the end of his entry deal and then moved on to the IHL and ECHL for the rest of the decade.

NO. 61 OVERALL: D COLLIN BAUER
Saskatoon Blades (WHL)

Bauer was an impressive puck mover whose numbers spiked in his draft year (70 games, 9–53–62). He had NHL size (6'1", 190 pounds) and performed well at the 1989 Memorial Cup for the Blades (0–4–4 in four games).

He turned pro in 1990 and played 95 AHL games over two seasons and spent several seasons in the IHL but did not appear in the National Hockey League.

NO. 82 OVERALL: D CAM BRAUER
RPI (NCAA)

A big shutdown defenceman from Calgary, Brauer was drafted out of college hockey and immediately moved to the WHL (Regina Pats).

Over the years, Edmonton has drafted college kids and moved them to Canadian leagues because their style is a better fit for the CHL. Brauer was an early example of this.

He was completing his final junior season when Edmonton traded him to the Hartford Whalers for defenceman Marc Laforge.

NO. 103 OVERALL: D DON MARTIN
London Knights (OHL)

Martin was drafted a few months after he turned 20, his numbers blossoming in his final two seasons of junior. Edmonton turned him pro right away, but Martin played just three games in the AHL before being sent to the IHL. He would play in various minor leagues through 2003.

NO. 124 OVERALL: C LEN BARRIE
Victoria Cougars (WHL)

Barrie was the third Victoria Cougars player drafted by Edmonton (Grant Fuhr, Simon Wheeldon) in the team's first decade in the NHL.

Barrie was an overager (19 on his draft day) who spiked offensively (37–49–86 in 70 games) and served notice he was a legit NHL prospect. His size (6'1", 200 pounds) and skill made him an interesting player.

Barrie is a member of a rare group—players who spent their age 20 seasons in junior hockey and then played in the NHL.

He never played with the Oilers, signing out of junior at the end of his final season with the Kamloops Blazers.

In his post-playing career, Barrie was co-owner of the Tampa Bay Lightning for a time. He is also the father of NHL defenceman Tyson Barrie, who signed with the Oilers in the 2020 offseason and again in the 2021 offseason.

NO. 145 OVERALL: RW MIKE GLOVER
Soo Greyhounds (OHL)

Like Martin earlier in the same year, Edmonton drafted a pro-ready winger who was already 20 in Glover. A rugged winger, he also scored 41–42–83 in 63 games (along with 130 PIM).

Glover scored reasonably well in pro, posting 9–11–20 in 61 games for the Cape Breton Oilers. He played just one IHL game the following year and that represented the end of his pro career.

He is currently a scout for the Windsor Spitfires of the OHL.

NO. 166 OVERALL: LW SHJON PODEIN
Minnesota-Duluth (NCAA)

Podein's numbers in his draft year were pedestrian (30, 4–4–8) and he was already 20 when Fraser drafted him. He played a gritty game (48 PIM in those 30 games) and blossomed in his third (junior) season with Minnesota-Duluth.

Podein played a throwback style on left wing, grinding out every shift and chipping in offensively enough to stay in the lineup.

He turned pro with the Cape Breton Oilers in 1990–91, scoring 14–15–29 in 63 games, and then blossoming in year two (30–24–54 in 80 games) with Cape Breton.

In 1992–93, he made the NHL and scored 13 goals in 40 games, playing on Edmonton's only AHL championship team, the 1992–93 Cape Breton Oilers.

He was on the Edmonton roster in 1993–94, but a dropoff in offence led the Oilers to cut him loose that summer.

In August 1994, Podein signed on with the Philadelpha Flyers. Before he left the NHL, he would play on a Stanley Cup champion and score 100 goals in 699 games.

NO. 187 OVERALL: G TOM COLE
Woburn High School (USHS, Massachusetts)

Edmonton drafted Cole out of high school with the knowledge it would get four seasons to watch him play for Northeastern University (NCAA).

Cole didn't play much as a freshman but emerged as the starter in his sophomore season. He held the job for the final three seasons of his college career but did not sign with Edmonton.

NO. 208 OVERALL: D VLADIMIR ZUBKOV
CSKA Moscow (RSL)

Vubkov was 30 years old when the Oilers drafted him, but he signed in France instead of coming to North America. He would play most of a decade there before retiring. Another big defenceman, two-way type, he was probably too old for the NHL challenge. Speed would have been the issue, not size; he was 6'2", 203 pounds.

NO. 229 OVERALL: LW DARIN MACDONALD
Boston University (NCAA)

Edmonton drafted MacDonald after his freshman college season. He had been used sparingly (1–1–2 in 12 games) but didn't spike offensively in any of the three years that followed, and was not signed.

NO. 250 OVERALL: C TIM TISDALE
Swift Current Broncos (WHL)

Edmonton drafted Tisdale after his 19-year-old junior season. Injuries cut his season in half, but at 20 (in the WHL), Tisdale posted some big numbers (68 games, 57–82–139).

He entered pro hockey and was good enough to play right away, finishing seventh among Cape Breton Oilers scorers. He completed his entry deal with Edmonton, contributing three identical seasons, then spent a few seasons in various North American minor leagues before retiring.

1988 Draft Summary

The Oilers drafted the organization's first player born in 1970 (Francois Leroux) but also selected several players 20 or older in 1988—Don Martin, Mike Glover, Shjon Podein, Vladimir Zubkov, and Tim Tisdale. (Number in parentheses is points per game.)

- Francois Leroux (QMJHL) age 17: 58 games, 3–8–11 (0.19)
- Petro Koivunen (Finland Jr.) age 17: 31 games, 27–31–58 (1.87)
- Trevor Sim (WHL) age 17: 67 games, 17–18–35 (0.52)
- Collin Bauer (WHL) age 17: 70 games, 9–55–64 (0.91)
- Cam Brauer (NCAA) age 17: 18 games, 0–1–1 (0.06)
- Don Martin (OHL) age 20: 57 games, 30–32–62 (1.09)
- Len Barrie (WHL) age 18: 70 games, 37–49–86 (1.23)
- Mike Glover (OHL) age 19: 63 games, 41–42–83 (1.32)
- Shjon Podein (NCAA) age 19: 30 games, 4–4–8 (0.27)
- Tom Cole (USHS) age 18: numbers are unavailable
- Vladimir Zubkov (RSL) age 29: 48 games, 7–3–10 (0.21)

- Darin MacDonald (NCAA) age 17: 12 games, 2–1–3 (0.25)
- Tim Tisdale (WHL) age 19: 32 games, 11–15–26 (0.81)

Leroux is the third in a set of shutdown defencemen taken in the first round of 1980s drafts by Edmonton (Jim Playfair, Jeff Beukeboom). In terms of the math of each draft, this is a poor bet.

One other item about the 1988 selection: when an organization drafts older players, especially those who can come right to pro hockey, it's often to cover from draft disappointments in previous seasons. Fraser was trying to catch up for the misses in 1982, 1984, and 1986.

NHL Career Games Played

1. Shjon Podein: 699
2. Francious Leroux: 249
3. Len Barrie: 184
4. Trevor Sim: 3

Podein had a tough sophomore season in the NHL, and the Oilers were so deep on left wing (Shayne Corson, Zdeno Ciger, Scott Pearson, Dean McAmmond, Kirk Maltby, Louie DeBrusk) that Podein fell through the cracks and the Oilers lost a useful player who would hang around the NHL for some time.

Leroux was much the same story, stifled by a team with better options and nowhere to hide him, so he was lost to waivers from an expansion team.

Still, the scouts found a couple of useful players. There should be no bragging about the haul from 1988, but it gets a passing grade.

Here's how the 1988 draft class ranked in terms of total NHL games played:

1. 1979 (4,143 games)
2. 1980 (3,841 games)
3. 1981 (2,215 games)
4. 1983 (1,810 games)
5. 1987 (1,602 games)
6. 1985 (1,206 games)
7. **1988 (1,135 games)**
8. 1984 (607 games)
9. 1982 (394 games)
10. 1986 (50 games)

This represents the first 10 years of Barry Fraser's career as Oilers NHL scouting director.

Trades That Involved Draft Picks

On December 12, 1986, the Oilers traded Dave Semenko to the Hartford Whalers for a 1988 third-round pick (Trevor Sim).

On March 2, 1987, the Oilers traded their 1988 second-round pick (Link Gaetz) to the Minnesota North Stars for Kent Nilsson. It remains one of the strongest deadline deals in Oilers history, as Nilsson scored 17 points in 27 games for Edmonton in the spring of 1987.

On March 8, 1988, the Oilers traded Andy Moog to the Boston Bruins for Geoff Courtnall, Bill Ranford, and a second-round pick in the 1988 draft (Petro Koivunen). It was a massive trade for both teams, an upgrade for Edmonton because Moog was playing for the Canadian national team at the time. Ranford would have enormous impact for the Oilers in the 1990 Stanley Cup Final— ironically, against the Bruins.

FRASER'S GOLDEN DECADE

No matter how long the Edmonton Oilers franchise exists, no team will be able to duplicate the perfect storm of Wayne Gretzky combined with the 1979–81 drafts of Barry Fraser and his staff.

The 1980s Oilers were an artistic, entertainment, and hockey success, with speed, skill, and swagger in equal parts. For those who lived through those years, nothing since has quite electrified like the five-time Stanley Cup winners from Edmonton.

Fraser's All-Decade Team

Centre: Mark Messier, Walt Poddubny, Shaun Van Allen

Right Wing: Jari Kurri, Glenn Anderson, Kelly Buchberger

Left Wing: Esa Tikkanen, Jaroslav Pouzar, Shjon Podein

Defence: Paul Coffey, Kevin Lowe, Steve Smith, Jeff Beukeboom, Geoff Smith

Goalies: Grant Fuhr, Andy Moog

In a way, Fraser buried himself by over-delivering, leaving any drafts that followed the impossible task of measuring up.

THE 1989 DRAFT

The Edmonton Oilers underwent a major change to the Stanley Cup cluster in the summer of 1988. In mid-July, Sather dealt the rights to Geoff Courtnall to the Washington Capitals for Greg C. Adams (the other Greg Adams was the more talented one).

On August 9, 1988, the world as Oilers fans knew it came to an end. After four Stanley Cups in nine seasons, owner Peter Pocklington sent Wayne Gretzky to the Los Angeles Kings for a pile of cash and some hockey players.

The deal without the money went like this: Gretzky, Mike Krushelnyski, and Marty McSorley to the Kings for Jimmy Carson, Martin Gelinas, and first-round picks in 1989, 1991, and 1993. It was a franchise low point that would be exceeded, but not for several decades.

Edmonton won only 38 games, the lowest total since 1981, and finished third in the division behind eventual Stanley Cup winners the Calgary Flames and Gretzky's Kings. The Oilers would lose in the opening round to Los Angeles in a spirited seven-game series.

Oilers rookies in 1988–89:

- Kelly Buchberger: 66 games, 5–9–14
- Mark Lamb: 20 games, 2–8–10
- Chris Joseph: 44 games, 4–5–9
- Martin Gelinas: 6 games, 1–2–3
- Alan May: 3 games, 1–0–1
- Mike Ware: 2 games, 0–1–1
- Kim Issel: 4 games, 0–0–0
- Francois Leroux: 2 games, 0–0–0
- Selmar Odelein: 2 games

The rookies include Edmonton's draft picks but also players acquired from other organizations before they established themselves in the NHL. Mark Lamb, Martin Gelinas, and Alan May were examples of prospects acquired via trade or waivers by Sather, as he began looking outside the organization more often as draft picks stalled out.

Buchberger would prove to be the only long-term solution in Edmonton from a handsome list of NHL futures.

NO. 15 OVERALL: D JASON SOULES
Niagara Falls Thunder (OHL)

After drafting a defenceman in the first round in five of the first six Oilers drafts, Fraser spent a few years picking forwards. With Leroux in 1988 and Soules in 1989, the parade of rearguards was back again.

Soules had size (6'2", 212 pounds) and was a mobile, shutdown defenceman. He played well positionally and was a good passer, but on draft day he would make his money on the defensive side of the puck.

Edmonton no doubt saw a shy offensive player (57 games, 3–8–11 with 187 PIM) with the kind of rugged toughness men like Jeff Beukeboom and Francois Leroux were drafted to provide.

Soules spent a year in pro hockey but was not impressive in any way with the 1991–92 Cape Breton Oilers. He didn't pursue his pro career, and the Oilers moved on.

NO. 36 OVERALL: RW RICHARD BORGO
Kitchener Rangers (OHL)

Borgo was a smaller winger (5'11", 190 pounds) than the Oilers typically drafted during these years, but he played a physical game and was a fine skater. Much of his offence in junior started with a strong forecheck. He was good along the boards and he scored 20-plus twice before draft day—a solid résumé for a second-round pick.

Like Soules, Borgo did not flourish in the AHL, spending two mediocre seasons with the Cape Breton Oilers before moving on to various North American leagues.

NO. 78 OVERALL: C JOSEF BERANEK
Litvinoc HC (Czech)

Edmonton's first two picks in the 1989 draft failed to develop, but an overager from Fraser's Czech pipeline emerged as an NHL player in the 1990s.

Beranek had good size (6'2", 185 pounds) and more than enough skill to play in the NHL. He lacked consistency but went right to the NHL in 1991–92 when he came to North America.

Edmonton traded him in the middle of his second NHL season (to Philadelphia for Brian Benning), and Beranek would return to the Oilers in 1998 in another deal (sending away Bobby Dollas and Tony Hrkac). In March 2000, Edmonton traded him for a second time, to Pittsburgh for German Titov. It was one of the final trades Sather made as Edmonton's general manager.

Beranek would play more than 500 NHL games. After that, he went back to the Czech Republic and played until 2010.

NO. 92 OVERALL: C PETER WHITE
Michigan State University (NCAA)

White was 20 and had just completed his freshman year at Michigan State when he was drafted. His offensive numbers that year (20–33–53 in 46 games) ranked sixth among Spartans forwards and gave a clear indication about his strengths as a player.

After three more productive seasons, White turned pro and began a long-term assault on AHL goalies (64 games, 12–28–40) that helped the Cape Breton Oilers to the AHL championship in 1993.

White played in the NHL (220 games) but didn't have the dynamic game to play a feature role in the NHL. Edmonton traded him in December of 1995 to the Toronto Maple Leafs in a deal for Kent Manderville. He continued to dominate the AHL for a decade.

NO. 120 OVERALL: C ANATOLI SEMENOV
Moscow Dynamo (RSL)

Semenov was 27 and a regular in Russia's top league by the time Edmonton drafted him. He impressed during the 1987 Canada Cup, as he played centre on a strong two-way line for the Russians. He had been a point-per-game player through his mid-twenties, but in the final two seasons of Semenov's Russia career, his offence was fading.

Semenov began his career in Russia during a time when the idea of playing in the NHL would have been impossible. During his career, a warming of relationships between Russia and the West allowed Semenov and many others to play in the world's best league.

His first full NHL season was 1990–91, although Semenov did play in two playoff games during the 1990 playoffs (Edmonton would win the Stanley Cup that spring).

Semenov was productive immediately, scoring 20 goals in his second NHL season with the Oilers. He was lost to the Tampa Bay Lightning in the 1992 expansion draft and would play in 362 NHL games.

Semenov was the third man drafted from Russia by Edmonton (Vyazmikin in 1987, Zubkov in 1988), but the Oilers would never have major draft success from Russia.

NO. 140 OVERALL: RW DAVIS PAYNE
Michigan Tech (NCAA)

Payne was the second player drafted by Edmonton out of Michigan Tech (Rob Polman-Tuin in 1980). He played a physical style and scored enough as a sophomore and junior to warrant signing consideration.

Payne's performance fell off in his senior season, and the Oilers didn't sign him. He kicked around the minors for a time, then landed with the Boston Bruins and played in 22 games over two seasons.

After his playing career ended, Payne began coaching. He worked his way up to head coach of the St. Louis Blues from 2009 to '12. He has also been an assistant coach with the Los Angeles Kings, Buffalo Sabres, and Ottawa Senators.

NO. 141 OVERALL: LW SERGEI YASHIN
Dynamo Riga (Latvia)

Like Semenov, Yashin was an established player in a league that had previously not allowed access to the NHL. Yashin stayed in Russia for another season and then left for Germany, where he played several more years. He did not sign an NHL contract.

NO. 162 OVERALL: D DARCY MARTINI
Michigan Tech (NCAA)

Martini had size (6'4", 220 pounds) and some offensive ability (35 points in 48 games for the Vernon Lakers of the BCJHL in 1987–88) by his draft day.

He spent much of his four-year college career in the penalty box, but the Oilers signed him to a pro contract. He was a part-time player in 1992–93 but played a feature role the following year (18–38–56 in 65 games). Martini also played two NHL games that season.

Martini left the AHL in 1996, playing in Austria, Germany, and Italy before retiring.

NO. 225 OVERALL: RW ROMAN BOZEK
Ceske Budejovice HC (Czech)

When Bozek was drafted by Edmonton, he was 26 and established as a quality scoring winger in the Czech league. He also had size (6'1", 203 pounds) but didn't come over to North America. Bozek did have one successful season in Finland's Liiga (22 goals in 1990–91) and played in various European leagues through 2002.

1989 Draft Summary

The 1989 draft saw Fraser select another shy offensive player in the first round, but the club started drafting older players in the fourth round (beginning with Beranek) and had success. (Number in parentheses is points per game.)

- Jason Soules (OHL) age 17: 57 games, 3–8–11 (0.19)
- Richard Borgo (OHL) age 17: 66 games, 23–23–46 (0.70)
- Josef Beranek (Czech) age 18: 32 games, 18–10–28 (0.88)
- Peter White (NCAA) age 19: 46 games, 20–33–53 (1.15)
- Anatoli Semenov (RSL) age 26: 31 games, 9–12–21 (0.68)
- Davis Payne (NCAA) age 17: 35 games, 5–3–8 (0.23)
- Sergei Yashin (Latvia) age 26: 44 games, 18–10–28 (0.64)
- Darcy Martini (NCAA) age 19: 37 games, 1–2–3 (0.08)
- Roman Bozek (Czech) age 24: 43 games, 13–19–32 (0.74)

Soules is the big misstep. The odds of his turning into a useful NHL player depended solely on his development as a shutdown defender.

NHL Career Games Played

1. Josef Beranek: 531
2. Anatoli Semenov: 362
3. Peter White: 220
4. Davis Payne: 22
5. Darcy Martini: 2

No long-term Oilers solutions here, but three men spent significant time in the league and all of them brought some offence. Fraser and his team didn't get much done in the first round. It had been six years since Jeff Beukeboom delivered value in the early part of the draft for Edmonton.

Here's how the 1989 draft class ranked in terms of total NHL games played:

1. 1979 (4,143 games)
2. 1980 (3,841 games)
3. 1981 (2,215 games)
4. 1983 (1,810 games)
5. 1987 (1,602 games)
6. 1985 (1,206 games)
7. **1989 (1,137 games)**
8. 1988 (1,135 games)
9. 1984 (607 games)
10. 1982 (394 games)
11. 1986 (50 games)

The 1989 draft gets a passing grade but was somewhat pedestrian. The Oilers were procuring depth pieces who could help for three or four years but no scoring wingers or impact centres and not much in the way of quality defencemen. It had been years since the club drafted a quality goaltender. Just three draft picks aged 17 meant the club wasn't drafting the highest ceiling available.

Trades That Involved Draft Picks

On February 11, 1988, the Oilers traded Scott Metcalfe and the No. 183 pick in 1989 (Donald Audette) to the Buffalo Sabres for Steve Dykstra and No. 140 overall (Davis Payne).

On August 9, 1988, the Oilers traded Wayne Gretzky, Mike Krushelnyski, and Marty McSorley to the Los Angeles Kings for Jimmy Carson, Martin Gelinas, and first-round picks in 1989, 1991, and 1993.

On January 3, 1989, the Oilers traded a 10th-round pick (Rick Judson) to the Detroit Red Wings for Miroslav Frycer.

On January 23, 1989, the Oilers traded a 12th-round pick (Jason Glickman) to the Detroit Red Wings for Doug Halward.

On February 15, 1989, the Oilers traded a fifth-round pick in 1989 (Kevin O'Sullivan) to the New York Islanders for Tomas Jonsson.

On March 7, 1989, the Oilers traded Greg C. Adams and Doug Smith to the Vancouver Canucks for John Leblanc and the No. 92 pick in the 1989 draft (Peter White).

On June 17, 1989, the Oilers traded the 1989 first-round pick acquired in the Gretzky deal (No. 18, Jason Miller) to the New Jersey Devils for Corey Foster.

On June 17, 1989, the Oilers traded a 1989 third-round pick (Wes Walz) to the Boston Bruins for centre Tommy Lehman.

4

A FIFTH STANLEY
AND A DRAFT
SHUTOUT

THE 1990 DRAFT

EACH STANLEY CUP victory by the Oilers had a different feel. The 1984 Cup victory was the end result of a frantic five years of team building, and the bookend to a disappointing Stanley Cup Final loss to the New York Islanders in 1983.

The second Stanley Cup was about the power of the Wayne Gretzky, Mark Messier, Paul Coffey, Jari Kurri, Glenn Anderson, and Grant Fuhr cluster. All of them enjoyed incredible playoff runs.

The 1987 Stanley Cup was about redemption. One of the most famous moments in franchise history came when Gretzky accepted the Cup as captain and handed it to Steve Smith, who had been the author of the famous gaffe that gave Calgary a one-goal lead in the third period of the final game in their series. The Oilers had plenty of time to come back, but they did not, and Smith carried the load for an entire year.

The 1988 Stanley Cup was all business. Edmonton wasn't pushing for any records and finished mid-pack but throttled opponents once the playoffs began.

The 1990 run was unexpected for many reasons, the major one being the fact that Gretzky was in Los Angeles. If you review the names on the 1990 Stanley Cup, it's easy to see the changes from first to last championship. It had been an incredible ride.

Twelve names on the Stanley Cup were drafted or procured as amateurs for the 1990 Oilers: Anderson, Jeff Beukeboom, Kelly Buchberger, Fuhr, Randy Gregg, Charlie Huddy, Kurri, Kevin Lowe, Messier, Geoff Smith, Steve Smith, and Esa Tikkanen.

Oilers rookies in 1989–90:

- Martin Gelinas: 46 games, 17–8–25
- Vladimir Ruzicka: 25 games, 11–6–17
- Geoff Smith: 74 games, 4–11–15
- Peter Eriksson: 20 games, 3–3–6
- Francois Leroux: 3 games, 0–1–1
- Trevor Sim: 3 games, 0–1–1
- Mike Ware: 3 games, 0–0–0
- Mike Greenlay: 2 games, 11.75 goals-against average, .765 save percentage
- Randy Exelby: 1 game, 5.01 goals-against average, .828 save percentage

Smith, drafted in 1987, was the final player Edmonton drafted, developed, and deployed during a Stanley Cup–winning season. It had been a stunning 11 seasons.

A quick note on the 1990 draft—Edmonton chose 11 players, none of whom would play a single NHL game. The mind boggles at the odds it could happen, but all 11 are long retired, and it's a record that remains unmatched.

NO. 17 OVERALL: LW SCOTT ALLISON
Prince Albert Raiders (WHL)

The Oilers drafted out of Prince Albert twice in the 1980s (Manny Viveiros in 1984, Kim Issel in 1986) and were regular shoppers in the WHL (Allison was the 30th player chosen by Edmonton from the league since 1979.)

Allison was typical of a Fraser first-rounder of 1985 and after—a big forward (6'4", 210 pounds) who could intimidate (73 PIM) but was shy offensively (66 games, 22–16–38).

Geoff Sanderson, a superior scorer from the same league, was drafted in the second round by the Hartford Whalers and made a quick trip up the depth chart in time to score 46 goals for the 1992–93 Whalers.

Allison turned pro in 1992–93 and played on the champion Cape Breton Oilers club that season. Here are his three entry seasons and points-per-game totals (number in parentheses is points per game):

- 1992–93: 49 games, 3–5–8 (.163)
- 1993–94: 75 games, 19–14–33 (.440)
- 1994–95: 58 games, 6–14–20 (.344)

Compare these numbers to Kim Issel, Edmonton's 1986 draft pick also out of Prince Albert:

- 1987–88: 68 games, 20–25–45 (.662)
- 1988–89: 65 games, 34–28–62 (.954)
- 1989–90: 62 games, 36–32–68 (1.10)

Fraser and the Oilers scouts, with Sather as their guide, reached their nadir in the 1990 draft.

NO. 38 OVERALL: D ALEXANDER LEGAULT
Boston University (NCAA)

Legault was a defenceman with some size (6'1", 215 pounds) and impressive offence (43 games, 9–21–30). His résumé looked good, but midway through his first post-draft season he left Boston College to play in the QMJHL. He scored well there, but Edmonton didn't sign Legault, and he played a couple of seasons in the ECHL before leaving hockey.

NO. 59 OVERALL: LW JOE CROWLEY
Lawrence Academy (USHS, Massachusetts)

Crowley had good size (6'2", 190 pounds) and some skill, but didn't play much for Boston College in his draft-plus-one season (17 games, 3–0–3). Crowley moved to the QMJHL and played well (41, 11–13–24, 124 PIM) but did not sign an NHL contract.

NO. 67 OVERALL: LW JOEL BLAIN
Hull Olympiques (QMJHL)

Blain is a fairly unusual draft case. He peaked in his draft season, scoring 31–47–78 in 65 games, which represents exceptional value where Edmonton called his name. He fell off in his draft-plus-one season and recovered some in his final junior season. Edmonton passed on signing him.

NO. 101 OVERALL: G GREG LOUDER
Cushing Academy (USHS, Massachusetts)

Louder attended Notre Dame University after high school, playing 33 games and posting an .874 save percentage. As with so many Oilers draft picks in 1990, his career trajectory went down from there and he did not sign with Edmonton.

NO. 122 OVERALL: LW KEIJO SAILYNOJA
Jokerit-Helsinki (Liiga)

Edmonton drafted Sailynoja when he was 20 and an emerging Liiga talent. He boasted NHL size (6'2", 196 pounds) and scored 15–13–28 in 41 games in his draft season (age 19). Although he had a very successful career, including an appearance for Finland in the 1992 Olympic Games, Sailynoja remained in the Liiga for his entire career, retiring after the 2000–01 season.

NO. 143 OVERALL: G MIKE POWER
Western Michigan University (NCAA)

Power was drafted after his freshman season in the NCAA, where he played 24 games amd owned a 4.83 goals-against average and an .847 save percentage. He played just one more game the following season for Western Michigan and saw time in the WHL the season after leaving college. He did not sign with the Oilers.

NO. 164 OVERALL: RW ROMAN MEJZLIK
Dukla Trencin (Czech)

Mejzlik was 22 when Edmonton drafted him; he was emerging in the Czech league (51 games, 11–21–32) at that time. Another winger with size (6'2", 194 pounds), he stayed in the Czech league until 1999, then played a few years in Germany. He has been coaching in the Czech Republic for many years.

NO. 185 OVERALL: LW RICHARD ZEMLICKA
HC Sparta Praha (Czech)

Zemlicka was 26 and an established scorer in the HC Sparta Praha on the day Edmonton picked him. His 1989–90 totals (45 games, 15–14–29) were similar to Mejzlik's. Zemlicka also had some size (6'1", 201 pounds) and did leave the country (for Finland and Germany) before returning home. He did not play in North America.

NO. 206 OVERALL: C PETR KORINEK
Plzen (Czech)

Korinek was the third Czechoslovakian player in a row drafted in 1990, and the 11th drafted by Edmonton since 1979. The big hits (Pouzar, Beranek) made the investment worthwhile, but Korinek (24 when he was drafted) spent his career in Europe.

NO. 248 OVERALL: D SAMI NUUTINEN
Kiekko-Espoo (Finland Div. I)

If Edmonton's success in Czechoslovakia made 11 picks worthwhile, then Finland was made of gold. Nuutinen was the seventh player from Finland chosen by the Oilers since 1979—the successes included Jari Kurri, Raimo Summanen, and Esa Tikkanen. Nuutinen had a fine career in Finland, Sweden, Germany, and Norway, but he didn't play in North America.

1990 Draft Summary

In the first round, Edmonton drafted a forward who delivered just over 0.50 points per game in junior hockey. The Oilers' 1990 draft is infamous, as all their picks missed making the NHL for even a single game. It's the statistical opposite of Edmonton's 1979 entry draft, giving Barry Fraser results on both ends of the draft spectrum. (Number in parentheses is points per game.)

- Scott Allison (WHL) age 17: 66 games, 22–16–38 (0.58)
- Alexander Legault (NCAA) age 17: 43 games, 9–21–30 (0.70)
- Joe Crowley (USHS) age 17: numbers are unavailable
- Joel Blain (QMJHL) age 17: 65 games, 31–47–78 (1.20)
- Greg Louder (USHS) age 17: numbers are unavailable
- Keijo Sailynoja (Liiga) age 19: 41 games, 15–13–28 (0.68)
- Mike Power (NCAA) age 18: 24 games, 4.83 goals-against average, .847 save percentage
- Roman Mejzlik (Czech) age 21: 51 games, 7–16–23 (0.45)
- Richard Zemlicka (Czech) age 25: 45 games, 14–14–28 (0.62)
- Petr Korinek (Czech) age 22: 47 games, 9–19–28 (0.60)
- Sami Nuutinen (Finland Div. I) age 18: 40 games, 8–16–24 (0.60)

The biggest problem for Edmonton was the offensive potential of early selections.

In 1980, Paul Coffey (a defenceman) posted 1.36 points per 60 in the OHL (then the OHA). In 1985, Scott Metcalfe (a forward) posted a 1.03 points-per-game total in the OHL. He was drafted No. 20 overall, but there was a pulse in his offence. In 1990, Scott Allison (a forward) was drafted out of the WHL after scoring 38 points in 66 games (.575 points per game).

The Oilers were going the wrong way.

NHL Career Games Played

The 1990 draft class was the first (and, as of 2020–21, the only) to have no player see NHL game action:

1. 1979 (4,143 games)
2. 1980 (3,841 games)
3. 1981 (2,215 games)
4. 1983 (1,810 games)
5. 1987 (1,602 games)
6. 1985 (1,206 games)
7. 1989 (1,137 games)
8. 1988 (1,135 games)
9. 1984 (607 games)
10. 1982 (394 games)
11. 1986 (50 games)
12. **1990 (0 games)**

A decade before, Fraser's crew found Coffey, Kurri, and Walt Poddubny. In 1990, the Oilers scouting staff couldn't find one player who would go on to play a single NHL game.

At the same time, NHL player salaries skyrocketed and the Oilers, with their bevy of young talent, were a prime target. Sather did his best, trading away veterans for young players under control, but he and the team badly needed the draft to feed continued success.

Consider 1982, 1986, and 1990. When the Oilers crashed, they crashed hard. Fans blamed ownership (and Peter Pocklington's behaviour during the mid-80s ran counter to winning), but the scouts' inability to deliver at previous levels was also a major issue for the organization.

Trades That Involved Draft Picks

On December 21, 1989, the Oilers traded a fourth-round pick (Greg Walters) to the Toronto Maple Leafs for Vladimir Ruzicka.

On January 5, 1990, the Oilers traded right winger Norm Lacombe to the Philadelphia Flyers for a fourth-round pick (No. 67 overall, Joel Blain).

The Oilers attempted to select a player who was not eligible with pick No. 227, and the league ruled it an invalid selection.

5

FROM THE PENTHOUSE TO THE MIDDLE OF NOWHERE—A QUICK FALL

THE 1991 DRAFT

JOHN MUCKLER TOOK over as Oilers head coach in 1989–90 and had immediate success, as Edmonton won the Stanley Cup. The team added several pieces during the year and Muckler handled the shuffle brilliantly.

In 1990–91, Edmonton once again finished well, behind Los Angeles and Calgary during the regular season and third in the Smythe Division with a 37–37–6 record and a goal differential of 0 (272–272 goals for and against).

Muckler drove his Oilers deep into the postseason, winning series against the Calgary Flames in seven games (with the final two contests going to overtime) and Wayne Gretzky and his Los Angeles Kings in six games. But the Minnesota North Stars made quick work of Edmonton in five games. It was clear at that time the Oilers wouldn't be the class of the Smythe Division for much longer.

Rookies on the 1990–91 team:

- D Francois Leroux: 1 game, 0–2–2
- RW Igor Vyazmikin: 4 games, 1–0–1
- LW David Haas: 5 games, 1–0–1
- RW Max Middendorf: 3 games, 1–0–1
- LW Brad Aitken: 3 games, 1–0–1
- LW Dan Currie: 5 games, 0–0–0
- C Shaun Van Allen: 2 games, 0–0–0
- RW Tomas Srsen: 2 games, 0–0–0

The eight men who suited up for Edmonton as rookies in 1990–91 saw very little playing time. It's a further reflection that the Oilers' draft-and-development system was no longer producing.

It's also true Muckler had little time to nurture legit prospects like Leroux and Van Allen, as the Oilers were still in the window to win.

NO. 12 OVERALL: C TYLER WRIGHT
Swift Current Broncos (WHL)

Wright was the third Bronco (Peter Soberlak, Tim Tisdale) drafted by Edmonton and the 31st WHL player selected from the WHL.

Wright had a strong draft season, scoring 41–51–92 in 66 games (1.39 points per game). Among first-round selections, Wright's points per game was the highest in team history to that time, exceeding Paul Coffey's mark of 1.36.

He played a gritty style and had a fairly complete skill set. Draft reports suggested a two-way centre with enough offence to play on a top line as a complementary type.

Wright finished up his junior career and spent his first season with the Cape Breton Oilers (65 games, 14–27–41) of the AHL. He took on all comers and showed some range but was a little shy as an offensive player.

He split time between the AHL and NHL for his entry deal, playing a total of 41 games with the Oilers over four seasons.

Sather sent him to the Pittsburgh Penguins, where Wright found a way to survive as a utility player with a range of skills. He would finish with 613 NHL games.

Wright emerged as a scout of note after his career, climbing the ladder and working as scouting director with the Columbus Blue Jackets, the Detroit Red Wings, and, beginning in 2019, the Edmonton Oilers.

NO. 20 OVERALL: LW MARTIN RUCINSKY
Litvinov HC (Czech)

The 12th Czechoslovakian player selection by Edmonton was a home run. Along with Jaroslav Pouzar and Josef Beranek, the Czech contribution by Rucinsky and others to the Edmonton franchise is often overlooked, possibly because he spent so little time with the Oilers.

Rucinsky was an older player (20) when he was drafted, coming off a strong season (49 games, 23–18–41) with Litvinov.

He arrived in the Edmonton organization in fall 1991 and played two games in Edmonton and 35 in Cape Breton before he was suddenly traded to the Quebec Nordiques for goalie Ron Tugnutt and defenceman Brad Zavisha.

Rucinsky would play 961 games, scoring 241 goals and 612 points in a fine career.

Scouting report and legacy: Rucinsky was a fantastic winger to observe, with great speed and high skill. Many of his most electric moments came in international competition, where the big ice allowed more room to wheel. Rucinsky had a fine shot and scored 20-plus goals four times during his career.

Rucinsky was the first of what became a too-common occurrence: Oilers scouts identifying a quality player and management trading him out of town before the club received the benefits of astute drafting.

NO. 34 OVERALL: G ANDREW VERNER
Peterborough Petes (OHL)

Verner is typical of most Oilers goalie draft picks since Grant Fuhr was taken in 1981. He had a solid draft year and stumbled a little during the rest of his junior career, but not enough to discourage Edmonton from signing him.

Once in pro hockey, Verner played well in his first year, outperforming starter Wayne Cowley. In year two with the AHL Cape Breton Oilers, Cowley was the better goalie, but Verner wasn't far behind.

By his third year in the minors, Joacquin Gage and Steve Passmore passed both Verner and Cowley, and Verner found himself playing for the Canadian national team. Credit to him,

Verner played pro in Europe through 2010 in what was a productive career spent entirely outside the NHL.

NO. 56 OVERALL: RW GEORGE BREEN
Cushing Academy (USHS, Massachusetts)

Breen was the ninth high school player out of Massachusetts to
be drafted by Edmonton and the second from Cushing Academy
(Greg Louder).

Breen was 6'2" and 200 pounds and went to Providence,
improving each year of his NCAA career. He turned pro with the
Cape Breton Oilers, scoring 11 goals in 50 games for the 1995–96
team, a shy total for a player who was already at an advanced age
(22) for a prospect. He did not pursue his hockey career past 1997.

NO. 78 OVERALL: LW MARIO NOBILI
Longueuil College-Francais (QMJHL)

At 6'2" and 185 pounds and 20 on the day Edmonton drafted
him, Nobili could have turned pro in 1991 but stayed in junior
for an extra season. He played one season for the Tulsa Oilers
(CHL) before building a career in Europe that lasted the rest of
the decade. He played some Quebec Senior league hockey after
returning to Canada.

NO. 93 OVERALL: LW RYAN HAGGERTY
Westminster High School (USHS, Connecticut)

Haggarty was drafted for his scoring ability and showed well at
times during a four-year career at Boston College. In 137 games
at B.C., Haggarty scored 58 goals.

He turned pro with the Cape Breton Oilers but lasted only half a season before heading for the ECHL, where he would remain through 1997–98. He did not pursue a hockey career beyond that point.

NO. 144 OVERALL: RW DAVID OLIVER
Michigan (NCAA)

At this point in franchise history, Edmonton had drafted from Michigan State, Michigan Tech, and Western Michigan, but Oliver was the first player the NHL team drafted from the Michigan Wolverines.

Oliver played Tier 2 with the Vernon Lakers, scoring 92 goals in 116 games and establishing himself as an impressive scorer at that level.

He scored 13 in 27 games as a freshman and got himself drafted by Edmonton. He exploded in his final three seasons, scoring 94 goals in 125 games.

When he turned pro, Oliver had immediate success with both the Cape Breton Oilers of the AHL (32 games 11–18–29) and the Edmonton Oilers (44 games, 16–14–30) in 1994–95, aged 23. He made the Oilers out of camp, but the NHL and NHLPA were in the middle of negotiations on a collective bargaining agreement that would drag into the regular season.

In 1995–96, Oliver scored 20 goals, one of four Oilers to do it as the team began to climb back to respectability.

In 1996–97, he started off slow, scoring just one goal in 17 games. Oliver was claimed on waivers by the New York Rangers, as the Oilers were once again flush with strong options on the wing.

For his career, Oliver would total 49 goals in 233 games and was still scoring 20-plus as late as 2005–06 with Iowa of the AHL.

During the later portions of this book, I'll list players who earned more NHL time than they received. Oliver is on that list.

NO. 166 OVERALL: C GARY KITCHING
Thunder Bay Flyers (USHL)

The USHL of the early 1990s was a good junior league but didn't produce players at the current level of excellence. Players chosen from the league who made the NHL during Kitching's time include Sean Pronger and Greg Johnson.

Kitching did not play in the NHL, but he did score a pile of goals while he was in the USHL. After that, he spent four seasons at Ferris State University (CCHA) before playing a season of pro hockey in the Colonial Hockey League.

NO. 210 OVERALL: F VEGAR BARLIE
Oslo (Norway)

Barlie played well for Norway at the 1990 World Junior Championships but never played in North America. He had a good career in Norway, winning several championships.

NO. 232 OVERALL: G EVGENY BELOSHEIKEN
CSKA Moscow (RSL)

Belosheiken was 25 when the Oilers drafted him and did come over for one season in the AHL (1991–92). He played on the Russian team at the Canada Cup (1987) and was on the 1988 Olympic gold medal–winning team. Belosheiken also won gold at the 1986 World Hockey Championships.

NO. 254 OVERALL: RW JUHA RIIHIJARVI
Oulu Karpat (Liiga)

Riihijarvi was 22 when Edmonton drafted him and already an established scorer in Finland's best league.

Riihijarvi came over and played for the 1993–94 Cape Breton Oilers, scoring 10–15–25 in 57 games. That would be considered less-than-replacement-level NHL production, especially for a player who was 23 at the time.

He returned to Finland and scored at will, then played in Sweden (Malmo, SEL) for years as a productive scorer. Riihijarvi also spent time playing in Switzerland, Austria, and Italy before retiring in 2010.

1991 Draft Summary
How did the Oilers scouts do in this draft? Very well. The first two picks, both in the first round, were spent on players who had substantial offence in good leagues. (Number in parentheses is points per game.)

- Tyler Wright (WHL) age 17: 66 games, 41–51–92 (1.39)
- Martin Rucinsky (Czech) age 19: 49 games, 23–18–41 (0.85)
- Andrew Verner (OHL) age 17: 46 games, 3.52 .897
- George Breen (USHS) age 17: numbers are unavailable
- Mario Nobili (QMJHL) age 19: 70 games, 33–52–85 (1.21)
- Ryan Haggarty (USHS) age 17: numbers are unavailable
- David Oliver (NCAA) age 19: 27 games, 13–11–24 (0.89)
- Gary Kitching (USHL) age 19: 46 games, 29–64–93 (2.02)
- Vegar Barlie (Norway) age 18: numbers are unavailable

- Evgeny Belosheiken (RSL) age 24: numbers are unavailable
- Juha Rihijarvi (Finland Jr.) age 20: 42 games, 29–41–70 (1.67)

NHL Career Games Played

Fraser and his scouts followed a historically bad draft (1990) with a success via the 1991 selections. Three men would play in the NHL, and all had some degree of success:

1. Martin Ruckinsky: 961
2. Tyler Wright: 613
3. David Oliver: 233

If an NHL team could deliver that kind of return on every draft, said team would contend for the Stanley Cup every year and win a few along the way.

Most of the games played by these three men happened elsewhere in the NHL, but the job of the scouts is to procure talent. The general manager will use it as required for the parent team.

Here's how the 1991 draft class ranked in terms of total NHL games played:

1. 1979 (4,143 games)
2. 1980 (3,841 games)
3. 1981 (2,215 games)
4. 1983 (1,810 games)
5. **1991 (1,807 games)**
6. 1987 (1,602 games)
7. 1985 (1,206 games)
8. 1989 (1,137 games)
9. 1988 (1,135 games)

10. 1984 (607 games)
11. 1982 (394 games)
12. 1986 (50 games)
13. 1990 (0 games)

Through 1991, this draft was the fifth best all-time by Edmonton—and that's some excellent company.

The Oilers were still a playoff team and remained capable of winning a round or two, but they badly needed a string of quality drafts. Could Fraser and his team manage it?

Trades That Involved Draft Picks

On August 9, 1988, the Oilers traded Wayne Gretzky, Mike Krushelnyski, and Marty McSorley to the Los Angeles Kings for Jimmy Carson, Martin Gelinas, and first-round picks in 1989, 1991 (No. 20, Martin Rucinsky), and 1993.

On February 7, 1989, the Oilers traded Keith Acton and a 1991 sixth-round pick (Dmitri Yushkevich) to Philadelphia for Dave Brown.

On November 2, 1989, the Oilers traded Jimmy Carson, Kevin McClelland, and a fifth-round pick in the 1991 draft (Brad Layzell) to the Detroit Red Wings for Adam Graves, Joe Murphy, Petr Klima, and Jeff Sharples.

On November 10, 1990, the Oilers traded a ninth-round pick (Brent Brekke) to Quebec Nordiques for Max Middendorf.

On June 12, 1991, the Oilers traded John Leblanc and a 10th-round selection (Teemu Numminen) to the Winnipeg Jets for the fifth-round selection used on Ryan Haggarty.

THE 1992 DRAFT

For the 1991–92 season, Ted Green replaced John Muckler as coach. Muckler's two seasons in the job resulted in a Stanley Cup win in 1990 and a third-round exit the following year.

After the franchise spent almost 10 years with Sather as coach and two under Muckler, Green was given his chance and started well. Edmonton finished the season with a 36–34–10 record and 82 points.

No Oilers player finished in the top 10 scorers, but Joe Murphy and Bernie Nicholls found the scoring range in the playoffs and Bill Ranford was solid in goal as Edmonton once again moved past the Los Angeles Kings in the opening round.

Edmonton defeated the Vancouver Canucks in the second round in six games, with Murphy and Ranford once again leading the team.

The Oilers ran into a strong Chicago Blackhawks club in the third round and fell in four straight games.

Oilers rookies this season included:

- Josef Beranek: 58 games, 12–16–28
- Louie DeBrusk: 25 games, 2–1–3
- Dan Currie: 7 games, 1–0–1
- Steve Rice: 3 games, 0–0–0
- Francois Leroux: 4 games, 0–0–0
- Martin Rucinsky: 2 games, 0–0–0

Several productive careers either began or continued their way to regular duty with the Oilers in 1991–92. Rucinsky would have a regular spot for the next 16 seasons in the NHL.

NO. 13 OVERALL: LW JOE HULBIG
St. Sebastian's High School (USHS, Massachusetts)

Ranked No. 10 on the final Central Scouting list of North American skaters in 1992, Hulbig had size (6'3", 215 pounds) and a power forward's reputation. As it turned out, his first two seasons at Providence College saw him miss games and produce lower-than-expected offence. In his final two seasons of college, Hulbig was scoring just more than a point per game and played a physical style.

When he turned pro as a member of the Oilers organization, Hulbig scored at a disappointing rate (73, 18–28–46 with the 1996–97 Hamilton Bulldogs) and was well behind players in his age range on the team.

By July 1999, after completing his entry contract, Hulbig signed as a free agent with the Boston Bruins.

NO. 37 OVERALL: LW MARTIN REICHEL
Freiburg EHC (Germany DEL 2)

Reichel was an impressive scorer in the German second league (Bundeslegia) on his draft day and would move up to the top German league (DEL) when he turned 20. He played 14 successful seasons in the DEL and was part of the German Olympic team in 2002. He did not sign with Edmonton.

NO. 61 OVERALL: D SIMON ROY
Chicoutimi Cataractes (QMJHL)

Ranked No. 37 among North American skaters for the 1992 draft, Roy had good size and could help offensively. He made the all-rookie QMJHL team in 1992 and blossomed offensively in his final two seasons in junior. Roy did not sign with Edmonton and did not play pro hockey.

NO. 65 OVERALL: LW KIRK MALTBY
Owen Sound Platers (OHL)

Maltby was drafted as a 19-year-old (turned 19 in December 1991) after a dominant 50-goal season in the OHL. As an older prospect, the offence (50 goals) had to be viewed in context; a younger player scoring 50 would have been chosen far earlier in the draft.

Maltby turned pro right away and scored enough to make it interesting with the Cape Breton Oilers of the AHL (73 games, 22–23–45). Although he didn't project as a scoring winger at the NHL level, Maltby displayed the tools to emerge as a quality two-way winger. Checking, penalty killing, and suppressing offence while chipping in 10–15 goals a year proved to be Maltby's ticket to an NHL career.

He scored 11 goals as an NHL rookie in 1993–94, which fell to eight goals the following year. Maltby spent a little time in the AHL during his fourth pro season. That same season, in March 1996, Edmonton traded Maltby to the Detroit Red Wings for defenceman Dan McGillis.

He found a home in Detroit, playing 13 seasons with the Red Wings in that two-way checking role.

Maltby is the answer to an amazing trivia question about Oilers draft picks. Can you name the player Edmonton chose in the draft who won four Stanley Cups, none of them with the Oilers? Maltby won four in Detroit and finished his career with 1,072 games, 128 goals, and 132 assists. He also played in 169 playoff games, an enormous total for a role player. None of those playoff games came as a member of the Oilers.

NO. 96 OVERALL: LW RALPH INTRANUOVO
Soo Greyhounds (OHL)

Intranuovo was a small (5'8") skill forward whose signature move was gaining the offensive zone, curling back, and then setting up a play. It was reminiscent of Denis Savard of the Chicago Blackhawks during his great career.

Intranuovo was a brilliant AHL player, posting tremendous numbers during his entry deal. (Number in parentheses is points per game.)

- 1993–94 (age 20): 66 games, 21–31–52 (0.788)
- 1994–95 (age 21): 70 games, 46–47–93 (1.329)
- 1995–96 (age 22): 52 games, 34–39–73 (1.404)

He played in the NHL during those years, but only 14 games (1–2–3). He looked to have caught a break in September 1996 when the Toronto Maple Leafs claimed him on waivers, but the Leafs tried to sneak him back through waivers a month later and Edmonton grabbed him.

Intranuovo would play three more seasons in the high minors (AHL and IHL) in North America and then head for Germany, Austria, and Italy, where he would fill European nets through 2013.

There's very little doubt he could have had a more substantial NHL career if he had played in the current NHL.

NO. 109 OVERALL: G JOAQUIN GAGE
Portland Winterhawks (WHL)

A workhorse (63 games in his draft year) who had good size (6'0", 218 pounds) for the era, Gage was the first Oilers draft pick to play in an NHL game (among goalies) since Mike Greenlay, who was selected six years earlier.

Gage finished his junior career well and divided his rookie pro season between the AHL Cape Breton Oilers (54 games, 4.13 goals-against average, and a .877 save percentage) and the Edmonton Oilers (two games).

The following year he played 16 games in Edmonton, with a 3.77 goals-against average and an .871 save percentage.

Gage had a lot of competition during his first run with the Oilers. The organization was high on Steve Passmore, and Fred Brathwaite was getting NHL time and looked like he might back up Bill Ranford (and then Curtis Joseph) for some time.

Gage got lost in the flood and found himself bouncing around minor league cities (in the ECHL and AHL) for a couple of years. He signed again with Edmonton in 2000 and played five games that season, posting his strongest NHL numbers (3.46 goals-against average, .880 save percentage).

After that, Gage signed in Europe, where he played in the British Super League, in Sweden, in Germany, and in Italy before calling it a career.

NO. 157 OVERALL: LW STEVE GIBSON
Windsor Spitfires (OHL)

Gibson was born in October 1992, so he was almost 20 on his draft day. His scoring totals in the OHL spiked so much year-over-year (15 to 49), it was no surprise an NHL team would take a chance on him.

Gibson remained in the OHL at 20, scoring 48 goals as an overage player. He turned pro at 21 and found himself pushed down to the ECHL's Wheeling Thunderbirds (one league below the AHL), where he scored a point per game.

Gibson peaked in the AHL, where he played just 19 games, but he did have a long career in various North American leagues. He retired after the 2003–04 season.

NO. 181 OVERALL: LW KYUIN SHIM
Sherwood Park Crusaders (AJHL)

Born in South Korea, Shim played his junior hockey in Sherwood Park, just outside Edmonton. He had good size (6'1", 205 pounds) and began his first post-draft season with Northern Michigan University. At the end of that season, Shim jumped to the WHL and played a couple of games for the Tri-City Americans. He would split the following season with the Americans and Medicine Hat Tigers, scoring 16–16–32 in 56 games.

After that, Shim enrolled at (and played for) Concordia University, but by 1995–96 he was playing in the CHL for the Tulsa Oilers. He was back at Concorida later in the decade. He did not play pro hockey after the season in Tulsa.

NO. 190 OVERALL: C COLIN SCHMIDT
Regina Midgets

Schmidt was 18 when he was drafted and went right to Colorado College, where he produced impressive offence. In his final two seasons of college hockey, he posted 115 points in 85 games, an impressive total.

He turned pro in 1996–97, playing 15 games with the Hamilton Bulldogs (2–2–4), and spent the rest of the year in the ECHL. That was the conclusion of his hockey career, but he entered the business world and eventually came back to Canada. Those college scoring seasons showed real promise.

NO. 205 OVERALL: RW MARKO TUOMAINEN
Clarkson University (NCAA)

Tuomainen was 20 and in the United States on his draft day after playing (but not much) back home in Finland (Liiga) as a teenager.

A 6'3", 203-pound winger who could take care of himself, Tuomainen emerged as a quality college winger over his four seasons at Clarkson. In 135 NCAA games, he scored 82 goals and 190 points.

Tuomainen turned pro at 22 and was immediately successful in the AHL (58 games, 25–35–60) with the Cape Breton Oilers. Edmonton moved its affiliate to Hamilton (Bulldogs) beginning in 1996–97, and Tuomainen scored 31 goals.

After that, having played in just four games with Edmonton, Tuomainen went back to Finland and played two seasons in the Liiga for Helsinki.

In the summer of 1999, Tuomainen signed with the Los Angeles Kings. He would play one full season with the Kings and parts of two others with the club. In all, he would play in 79 NHL games.

NO. 253 OVERALL: LW BRYAN RASMUSSEN
St. Louis Park High School (USHS, Minnesota)

Rasmussen was drafted out of high school with good size (6'2", 180 pounds), and he continued to have success in the USHL (Rochester Mustangs) in his first post-draft season. In his second year at that level, the offence fell away, and Rasmussen attended University of St. Thomas (MIAC) to complete his playing career.

1992 Draft Summary

The 1992 draft consisted of one quality pick and a few cups of coffee, but overall, it can be judged a success. What did the numbers have to say? (Number in parentheses is points per game.)

- Joe Hulbig (USHS) age 17: 17 games, 19–24–43 (2.53)
- Martin Reichel (Germany Div. 1) age 17: 27 games, 15–16–31 (1.15)
- Simon Roy (QMJHL) age 17: 63 games, 3–24–27 (0.43)
- Kirk Maltby (OHL) age 18: 64 games, 50–41–91 (1.42)
- Ralph Intranuovo (OHL) age 17: 65 games, 50–63–113 (1.74)
- Joaquin Gage (WHL) age 17: 63 games, 4.44 goals-against average, .871 save percentage
- Steve Gibson (OHL) age 18: 63 games, 49–40–89 (1.41)
- Kyuin Shim (AJHL) age 17: 55 games, 38–38–76 (1.38)
- Marko Tuomainen (NCAA) age 19: 29 games, 11–13–24 (0.83)
- Bryan Rasmussen (USHS) age 17: numbers are unavailable

The math suggests the Oilers' scouts got it right for much of the 1992 draft. Hulbig, Reichel, Maltby, and Intranuovo were all solid-to-excellent picks, and later selections were also productive. For the second draft in a row, math endorsed the Edmonton list.

Scouting director Fraser procured a useful player (Maltby) and Sather dealt him for defenceman Dan McGillis (and then Janne Niinimaa). Good deals all around.

NHL Career Games Played

Five players made the NHL from the Oilers' 1992 draft.

1. Kirk Maltby: 1,072
2. Marko Tuomainen: 79
3. Joe Hulbig: 55
4. Joaquin Gage: 23
5. Ralph Intranuovo: 22

The 1992 draft was the seventh-most-successful draft in Oilers history, although the best player chosen wasn't a scoring champion.

The lesson of Maltby is this: he was a very successful checking forward for a long time in the NHL. He also scored 50 goals in junior. NHL checkers played feature roles as amateurs; it's a universal truth.

Here's how the 1992 draft class ranked in terms of total NHL games played:

1. 1979 (4,143 games)
2. 1980 (3,841 games)
3. 1981 (2,215 games)
4. 1983 (1,810 games)
5. 1991 (1,807 games)
6. 1987 (1,602 games)
7. **1992 (1,251 games)**
8. 1985 (1,206 games)
9. 1989 (1,137 games)
10. 1988 (1,135 games)
11. 1984 (607 games)
12. 1982 (394 games)
13. 1986 (50 games)
14. 1990 (0 games)

Trades That Involved Draft Picks

On June 12, 1991, the Oilers traded John Leblanc and a 1992 10th-round pick (Teemu Numminen) to the Winnipeg Jets for a 1991 fifth-round selection (Ryan Haggarty).

On September 11, 1991, the Oilers traded a sixth-round pick (Jiri Dopita) to the Boston Bruins for Norm Foster.

On October 2, 1991, the Oilers traded defenceman Steve Smith to the Chicago Blackhawks for defenceman Dave Manson and a third-round pick (Maltby) in the 1992 draft.

On June 20, 1992, the Oilers dealt pick No. 85 overall (Chris Ferraro) to the New York Rangers for No. 96 (Ralph Intranuovo) and No. 190 overall (Colin Schmidt).

THE 1993 DRAFT

If you were an Oilers fan in the fall of 1992, a unique experience was about to play out for you over the NHL season. The Oilers became bottom-feeders for the first time.

Edmonton's leading scorer that year (Petr Klima) finished with 48 points, and the team had only two players who scored 20 or more goals.

The team lost 50 NHL games in a season for the first time, going 26–50–8 overall. Edmonton had a goal differential of minus-95, courtesy of 242 goals for and 337 against.

It was a miserable season, with favourites like Esa Tikkanen being dealt away for futures. The Oilers rookies in 1992–93 consisted of two-way players and hopeful scorers:

- Shjon Podein: 40 games, 13–6–19
- Vladimir Vujtek: 30 games, 1–10–11
- Steven Rice: 28 games, 2–5–7
- Tyler Wright: 7 games, 1–1–2
- Dan Currie: 5 games, 0–0–0

Steven Rice was the big name, one of the major pieces coming over from the New York Rangers in the Mark Messier trade (October 1991).

NO. 7 OVERALL: C JASON ARNOTT
Oshawa Generals (OHL)

The poor showing in the regular season allowed Edmonton to pick inside the top 10 overall for the first time since 1981.

Arnott had an October 1974 birthday, meaning he was older than most of the draft-eligible players in 1993. His final junior season (56 games, 41–57–98, 1.75 points per game) reflected a dynamic offensive prospect and his size (6'5", 220 pounds) and rugged style made him a perfect combination of skill and grit.

Scouting report and legacy: Arnott arrived out of the draft as a full-grown man and had an immediate impact (33 goals in 78 games, 1993–94). Edmonton needed a big centre with skill and Arnott was a perfect fit for a team that was trying to gather impact youth.

His four-plus seasons in Edmonton were mostly a success, but the first half of the 1997–98 season saw him struggle badly. After an especially poor performance, he told the gathered media, "I just wasn't into it," and that unleashed the fan base during home games and made the situation untenable.

General manager Glen Sather, whose template for the Oilers featured talent, speed, and men with size who could play a rugged game, was hesitant to deal his big centre but finally pulled the trigger when New Jersey winger Billy Guerin was made available.

Arnott would play in 1,244 NHL games, scoring 417 goals, 521 assists, and 938 points. He won a Stanley Cup with the New Jersey Devils in 2000.

No. 7 overall pick in 1993 Jason Arnott was the most talented forward drafted by Edmonton since Jari Kurri (fourth round, 1980). However, a trade forced by the fan base meant the Oilers never saw Arnott's full potential at centre. *(Steve Babineau/NHLI via Getty Images)*

Arnott was the most talented forward drafted by Edmonton since Jari Kurri (fourth round, 1980). The big regret for all involved was a trade forced by an unforgiving fan base. Despite getting real value in the deal for Arnott, Sather's template required strength up the middle, and with Arnott gone, Edmonton continued the chase for an impact centre.

NO. 16 OVERALL: D NICK STADJUHAR
London Knights (OHL)

At 6'3", 206 pounds, and having posted 61 points in 49 games, Stadjuhar had a fairly complete skill set on his draft day.

Once he reached the AHL, Stadjhuar showed well in 54 games, posting 12 goals and 26 points with the Cape Breton Oilers. At that point, his career trajectory suggested an NHL career of some promise.

While Stadjuhar was playing in the AHL, an off-ice incident left him with a concussion and he did not return to his previous level of quality. He did play in the minors through 2000–01, but his two NHL games with Edmonton in 1995–96 were the extent of his big-league career.

He was the final of three first-round selections acquired in the trade that sent Wayne Gretzky to the Los Angeles Kings in 1988.

NO. 33 OVERALL: RW DAVID VYBORNY
HC Sparta Praha (Czech)

Vyborny was 18 when he was drafted and had completed his first season (52 games, 20–24–44) in the Czech league. After he was drafted, Vyborny played one more year for HC Sparta Praha before coming over to North America and playing for Edmonton's AHL farm club in 1994–95.

That was the season shortened by the NHL-NHLPA contract dispute, with the league playing just 48 games. Vyborny flourished with the Cape Breton Oilers (76 games, 23–38–61) but did not get a call to the NHL, so he went back to the Czech league the following year.

He would remain there until signing as a free agent with the expansion Columbus Blue Jackets in June 2000. He would play seven seasons with the Blue Jackets, scoring 113–204–317 in 543 games.

Vyborny had NHL talent in 1994–95, and at that time Edmonton's skill lines were unsettled on right wing. Despite an inviting situation, Vyborny couldn't break through.

This was a case of the scouts getting it right, but the NHL coaching staff valuing other, perhaps less skilled, players above Vyborny.

NO. 59 OVERALL: LW KEVIN PADEN
Detroit Jr. Red Wings (OHL)

Paden's major appeal for the Oilers was his size (6'4", 222 pounds), despite delivering pedestrian offence (54 games, 14–9–23) in his draft year.

Fraser and the Oilers were in constant search of Coke machines on skates from the mid-80s until he retired in 2000, and then beyond with new scouting directors.

Paden peaked with four AHL games and played mostly in the ECHL until 2001.

NO. 60 OVERALL: LW ALEXANDER KERCH
Dynamo Riga (Latvia)

A prolific scorer as a teenager, Kerch was a left winger who shot right. He was 5'10" and 187 pounds—a little small for the NHL, but his skill was worthy of a draft pick. He came right over to North American in time for the 1993–94 season, scoring well with the Cape Breton Oilers (57 games, 24–38–62) and playing in five games with the Edmonton Oilers. The following year he played a little for the Providence Bruins (AHL) but was soon back in Russia and played hockey around Europe through 2006.

NO. 111 OVERALL: LW MIROSLAV SATAN
Trencin Dukla (Czech)

In the 40-plus-year history of the Oilers at the draft table, perhaps no single selection is more of a lightning rod for fans than the Satan pick.

Satan scored 11 goals in 38 Czech league games during his draft year. The fact he was a regular in the league at 17 was impressive, but there were other, more impressive scorers (Ziggy Palffy scored 38 goals) for Trencin that season.

He exploded in year two, scoring 42 goals in 39 games to lead the entire league at 18. At that point, it was clear Edmonton had delivered a strong pick from the fifth round of the 1993 draft.

Scouting report and legacy: Satan arrived in North America in his draft-plus-two season and tore apart the AHL. In Oilers draft history, no forward tore the cover off the ball like Satan as a member of the Cape Breton Oilers in 1994–95.

To show how dominant Satan was in the AHL, here are the most impressive Oilers rookie pro forwards who played in the AHL during the 10-year period leading up to Satan's arrival:

PLAYER	YEAR	STATS	PTS/ GAME
MIRO SATAN	1994–95	25 games, 24–16–40	1.60
DAN CURRIE	1988–89	77 games, 29–36–65	0.84
ESA TIKKANEN	1985–86	15 games, 4–8–12	0.81
DAVID VYBORNY	1994–95	76 games, 23–38–61	0.80
RALPH INTRANUOVO	1993–94	66 games, 21–31–52	0.79

Inexplicably, Edmonton would not make room for the super scorer until 1995–96, and even then, he was used sparingly.

Sather traded Satan to Buffalo in March 1997. He would score more than 300 goals after leaving Edmonton, winning a Stanley Cup with the Pittsburgh Penguins in 2009.

The trade was probably the poorest in Sather's career as Oilers general manager, considering the Gretzky transaction was a sale (massive dollars exchanged hands in the Gretzky deal).

It's also a major reason why one of Edmonton's best draft summers under Barry Fraser is rarely thought of as a success.

The Satan disconnect (scouts found him, but management and coaches didn't see what he was despite clear evidence) created a chasm in the team's pipeline. What happens if a scouting staff hits a massive draft home run and the evaluators at the other end (GM, coach) don't recognize the talent and derail the asset?

Satan was the first. It would happen again.

NO. 163 OVERALL: D ALEX ZHURIK
Dynamo Minsk (RSL)

Zhurik was a big (6'4", 214 pounds) and physical defender who came over to North America and played in the OHL for his final junior seasons.

He turned pro with the AHL Cape Breton Oilers and played capably for three seasons in the minors. Zhurik spent 1998–99 back in Russia, then returned to the Oilers organization for another season in the AHL.

He was clearly NHL calibre but never played in the league. Zhurik returned to Russia and finished his career in 2004–05.

NO. 189 OVERALL: D MARTIN BAKULA
University of Alaska-Anchorage (NCAA)

Another Czech player (23 when drafted), this time by way of Alaska-Anchorage, Bakula played in Czechoslovakia through 1990 and began his college career in the fall of 1991.

After two seasons showing two-way ability in the NCAA, Edmonton drafted and signed Bakula. He stepped right into the AHL (Cape Breton Oilers) and played well, although his defensive acumen took some time to show itself at the AHL level. In his second season in Cape Breton, Bakula tightened up on the back end but did not receive an NHL call.

He would return to the Czech Republic in the fall of 1995 having never played in the NHL.

NO. 215 OVERALL: D BRAD NORTON
Cushing Academy (USHS, Massachusetts)

A giant (6'6", 251 pounds) defenceman who posted 36 points in 31 games for the Academy his draft year, Norton settled in as an effective two-way talent in college (UMass-Amherst).

As often happens with high school defencemen, some of Norton's offence stayed back and Norton was a big shutdown type with some puck-moving ability as a pro.

He didn't play for Edmonton in the NHL (he made the team but was suspended for a preseason incident) but landed with the Florida Panthers in 2001–02 and played parts of several seasons in the NHL.

NO. 241 OVERALL: LW OLEG MALTSEV
Chelyabinsk Traktor (RSL)

A big winger (6'3", 213) who was 30 when Edmonton drafted him, Maltsev had been a regular in Russia's highest league for several years, scoring 21 times in his draft year. Although Maltsev did leave Russia to play in other countries, he did not sign with the Oilers and did not play in North America.

NO. 267 OVERALL: D ILYA BYAKIN
Landschut (DEL)

Like Maltsev, Byakin was 30 and had been playing in the top Russian league for years by the time he was free to sign in North America. Edmonton plucked him from the German league and Byakin came over right away,

He was an impact player in the AHL (12 games, 2–9–11) and an impressive offensive defender in the NHL (44 games, 8–20–28)

in his first North American season. He signed with the San Jose Sharks the following season but played just 13 games there before returning to Russia. He would play in Sweden and the IHL as well after leaving the NHL.

1993 Draft Summary

This draft is rarely mentioned as being anything but a disappointment, but from the scouts' point of view it was a massive home run. The numbers from draft-year performances suggested Edmonton had struck gold more than once. (Number in parentheses is points per game.)

- Jason Arnott (OHL) age 17: 56 games, 41–57–98 (1.75)
- Nick Stadjuhar (OHL) age 17: 49 games, 15–46–61 (1.24)
- David Vyborny (Czech) age 17: 52 games, 20–24–44 (0.85)
- Kevin Paden (OHL) age 17: 54 games, 14–9–23 (0.43)
- Alexander Kerch (Latvia) age 25: 42 games, 23–14–37 (0.88)
- Miro Satan (Czech) age 17: 38 games, 11–6–17 (0.45)
- Alex Zhurik (Russia Jr.) age 17: 1 game, 0–0–0
- Martin Bakula (NCAA) age 22: 35 games, 9–15–24 (0.69)
- Brad Norton (USHS) age 17: numbers are unavailable
- Oleg Maltsev (RSL) age 29: 39 games, 21–15–36 (0.92)
- Ilya Byakin (DEL) age 29: 44 games, 12–19–31 (0.70)

Just three years after the worst draft in history (1990), the scouts uncovered exceptional quality and depth. As was the case in 1992, the scouts' decisions were supported by math. Even Satan impressed, scoring 11 goals in a men's league at 17.

NHL Career Games Played

1. Jason Arnott: 1,244
2. Miro Satan: 1,050
3. David Vyborny: 543
4. Brad Norton: 124
5. Ilya Byakin: 57
6. Alexander Kerch: 5
7. Nick Stadjuhar: 2

It took more than a decade for Fraser and his staff to exceed any of the first three (1979–81) magic drafts, but 1993 finally did it. There would be no Stanley Cups, and trades changed the course of this draft, with Stanley Cups being won in New Jersey and Pittsburgh instead of Edmonton. It doesn't alter the brilliance of draft weekend.

In terms of total NHL games played, 1993 was an all-timer:

1. 1979 (4,143 games)
2. 1980 (3,841 games)
3. **1993 (3,025 games)**
4. 1981 (2,215 games)
5. 1983 (1,810 games)
6. 1991 (1,807 games)
7. 1987 (1,602 games)
8. 1992 (1,251 games)
9. 1985 (1,206 games)
10. 1989 (1,137 games)
11. 1988 (1,135 games)
12. 1984 (607 games)
13. 1982 (394 games)

14. 1986 (50 games)
15. 1990 (0 games)

Trades That Involved Draft Picks

On August 9, 1988, the Oilers traded Wayne Gretzky, Mike Krushelnyski, and Marty McSorley to the Los Angeles Kings for Jimmy Carson, Martin Gelinas, and a 1989 first-round pick (Jason Miller), a 1991 first-round pick (Martin Rucinsky), and the No. 16 pick in the 1993 draft (Nick Stadjuhar).

On August 27, 1992, the Oilers traded Vincent Damphousse and the No. 85 overall pick in the 1993 draft (Adam Wiese) to the Montreal Canadiens for Shayne Corson, Brent Gilchrist, and Vladimir Vujtek.

On December 11, 1992, the Oilers traded Kevin Lowe to the New York Rangers for Roman Oksiuta and the No. 60 overall pick in the 1993 draft (Alexander Kerch).

On June 20, 1993, the Oilers traded Martin Gelinas and No. 137 overall (Nicholas Checco) to the Quebec Nordiques for Scott Pearson.

6

NADIR'S RAIDERS 1.0: OILERS REACH A NEW LOW, BUT THE DRAFT PICKS IMPROVE

THE 1994 DRAFT

THE 1993-94 SEASON started poorly again, but Glen Sather fired coach Ted Green after a disastrous 3–18–3 start and took over coaching the team. The Oilers improved to 22–27–11 the rest of the way and showed promise under youngsters such as Doug Weight and Jason Arnott.

The team's overall goal differential improved to minus-44 (261–305) from the previous year's minus-95 (242–337).

Top rookies for 1993–94:

- Jason Arnott: 78 games, 33–35–68
- Dean McAmmond: 45 games, 6–21–27
- Kirk Maltby: 68 games, 11–8–19
- Brent Grieve: 24 games, 13–5–18
- Adam Bennett: 48 games, 3–6–9
- Peter White: 26 games, 3–5–8
- Roman Oksiuta: 10 games, 1–2–3
- Boris Mironov: 14 games, 0–2–2
- Todd Marchant: 3 games, 0–1–1
- Tyler Wright: 5 games, 0–0–0
- Marc Laforge: 5 games, 0–0–0
- Darcy Martini: 2 games, 0–0–0
- Brad Zavisha: 2 games, 0–0–0
- Josef Cierny: 1 game, 0–0–0
- Fred Brathwaite: 19 games, 3.54 .889

The 15 rookies employed during the 1993–94 campaign represent a record number for the Oilers in team history. Brathwaite signed as an undrafted free agent, the best free-agent goalie procured as a first-year pro during the Fraser era.

Sather used the 1994 offseason as an opportunity to return to signing undrafted free agents. Defenceman Greg De Vries and left winger Dennis Bonvie would go on to play in the NHL and support the 1994 draft group.

NO. 4 OVERALL: C JASON BONSIGNORE
Niagara Falls Thunder (OHL)

Analytics as a draft tool wouldn't arrive for more than a decade, so it's only with hindsight we can look back on the Bonsignore selection and see if math could have helped Barry Fraser and his staff.

Using the eye test—the "saw him good" model—Bonsignore was something close to perfect. A giant, right-handed centre, he was highly skilled and had the look of a future superstar. For an Edmonton team that had just drafted Jason Arnott, another big centre, in 1993, the appeal of two big men in the middle was too much to resist. Should Edmonton have chosen Bonsignore at No. 4 overall in 1994? Scouts say yes.

What did the math say? Here are the offensive numbers for each forward chosen between No. 4 and No. 10 in the 1994 draft. (Number in parentheses is points per game.)

- Jeff O'Neill: 66 games, 45–81–126 (1.91)
- Jeff Friesen: 66 games, 51–67–118 (1.79)
- Ethan Moreau: 59 games, 44–54–98 (1.66)
- Jason Bonsignore: 58 games, 22–64–86 (1.48)
- Ryan Smyth: 72 games, 50–55–105 (1.46)
- Jason Wiemer: 72 games, 45–51–96 (1.33)
- Brett Lindros: 15 games, 4–6–10 (.667)

Math suggests Edmonton would have been wiser to select Jeff O'Neill, who did in fact enjoy a solid NHL career. Math liked Bonsignore, though, slightly more than Ryan Smyth, whom Edmonton would take later in the round.

Bonsignore had a less impressive season in the year after his draft, scoring 27–35–62 in 59 games (just over a point per game). He also played one NHL game and scored his first goal in the league.

In 1995–96, his second year after the draft, Bonsignore played three separate levels of hockey but impressed in only one:

- OHL: 18 games, 10–16–26 (1.44)
- AHL: 12 games, 1–4–5 (0.42)
- NHL: 20 games, 0–2–2 (0.10)

Bonsignore arrived in pro hockey in the fall of 1996 and was promptly optioned to the AHL Hamilton Bulldogs. Here are his numbers at age 20 compared to the best performers in the previous decade in their AHL debuts in the Oilers organization:

PLAYER	YEAR	STATS	PTS/ GAME
MIRO SATAN	1994–95	25 games, 24–16–40	1.60
DAN CURRIE	1988–89	77 games, 29–36–65	0.84
DAVID VYBORNY	1994–95	76 games, 23–38–61	0.80
RALPH INTRANUOVO	1993–94	66 games, 21–31–52	0.79
JASON BONSIGNORE	1996–97	78 games, 21–33–54	0.69

By the time he arrived in pro hockey, Bonsignore's offence no longer appeared to be "in the range" for a top pick, and in fact he was at the bottom of a list of mixed-bag Oilers prospects who had thrived as AHL rookies.

Sather traded Bonsignore in the winter of 1997, and he is generally regarded as being the biggest draft bust on Fraser's watch. A No. 4 overall pick doesn't have to be a superstar, but he has to contribute. In fact, that's what Sather told the scouts before the 1994 draft.

In evaluating the Bonsignore selection, I'm less inclined to give a harsh grade to Fraser because Bonsignore was in fact a highly successful offensive player in junior. He wasn't an overager, he had all the tools, and he clearly interviewed well.

Teams would get smarter about drilling down on prospects a decade or more after the Bonsignore pick, but given the tools available in 1994, I think Fraser and his staff can be accused only of choosing the wrong player. That's many miles from being delinquent on doing due diligence.

Bonsignore would play in just 79 NHL games. It remains a very difficult conversation among Oilers fans.

PROSPECT SPOTLIGHT
NO. 6 OVERALL: LW RYAN SMYTH, MOOSE JAW WARRIORS (WHL)

In describing Ryan Smyth as "100 percent desire," there's a danger of underestimating his genuine talents. Smyth was, in fact, as implied by his junior team's nickname, a warrior.

Scouting report and legacy: As a kid, Smyth worked at the Banff Springs Hotel in his hometown. As it happened, Team Canada 1987 stayed there and trained in the town leading up to the 1987 Canada Cup series. One day during the camp, a car driven by Oilers winger (and member of Team Canada) Glenn Anderson struck Smyth and sent him to hospital. Smyth would be okay, but the story is part of the team's history and ties fans together in the legend of the Oildrop.

Smyth and Anderson would play together briefly as Oilers in 1995–96, one generation passing the torch to the next.

Ryan Smyth's two greatest talents, without a doubt, were his anticipation and his willingness to sacrifice to make a play. He was also a sublime passer and knew where to go in order to score goals. That skill should never be overlooked. Smyth's "garbage" goals were legendary, but they all counted the same as the beautiful goals.

Smyth played most of his career on a skill line, partly because he was so good at retrieving pucks along the wall. He was relentless in his determination to win battles and used what size he had (6'2", 192 pounds) effectively.

Smyth became known during his career as "Captain Canada" because of his frequent appearances at the World Championships and other international events. He represented Canada on the gold-medal Olympic team in 2002, World Championship teams in 2003 and 2004, the gold-medal World Cup team in 2004, plus the 1995 World Junior team and the 2012 Spengler Cup team.

He is one of the most successful draft picks in the history of the Oilers, playing in 1,270 NHL games.

NO. 32 OVERALL: LW MIKE WATT
Stratford Cullitons (MOJHL)

Watt was a big winger with some skill who came out of Tier 2 in Ontario on his way to Michigan State. By his sophomore year in college, he was scoring more than a point per game and he flourished in his junior year (24–17–41 in 39 games), and Edmonton signed him to a pro contract.

In 1997–98, the Oilers were overrun with rugged wingers and some fast ones too, so Watt had to steal playing time from

Drafted No. 6 overall in 1994, left winger Ryan Smyth is one of the most successful draft picks in Oilers history, playing in 1,270 NHL games. He served as an alternate captain for every team he played with in the NHL. *(AP Photo/Paul Chiasson, CP)*

the likes of Ryan Smyth, Dean McAmmond, Valeri Zelepukin, and Rem Murray.

He played most of his rookie pro season with the AHL's Hamilton Bulldogs, scoring 24–25–49 in 63 games. When he did get the call to the Oilers in his first year, he found offence eluded him (14 games, 1–2–3).

That summer, GM Sather shipped him off to the New York Islanders in exchange for goaltender Eric Fichaud. (The Oilers were in search of goaltending help.)

Watt played two seasons with the Islanders and then had stops with the Nashville Predators and Carolina Hurricanes. Shoulder problems shortened his NHL career to 157 games.

NO. 53 OVERALL: D COREY NEILSON
North Bay Centennials (OHL)

Neilson was a gigantic, right-handed defenceman with some offensive potential (62 games, 3–35–38 with North Bay in his draft year).

He ran in place offensively for his two seasons between the draft and turning 20, and Edmonton did not sign him, so he returned for a final year of junior.

He peaked with nine AHL games, spent several years in the ECHL, and then found a hockey home in England with the Nottingham Panthers of the EIHL. When he retired from the team, he spent a couple of years coaching in Nottingham.

NO. 60 OVERALL: D BRAD SYMES
Portland Winterhawks (WHL)

A tough-as-nails WHL defenceman, Symes took a regular shift in the league at 16 and had two full seasons before his draft day (on which he was 18).

Symes didn't bring a lot of offence to pro hockey, and he didn't stand out defensively. He peaked with five AHL games and spent two-plus seasons in the ECHL before completing his playing career.

NO. 79 OVERALL: RW ADAM COPELAND
Burlington Cougars (OPJHL)

Copeland was a typical Fraser draft pick, a big forward with good skill and some size (6'1", 215 pounds). He filled the net in Tier 2 but had two quiet years in college (Miami of Ohio) before blossoming (40 points in 40 games) as a junior. His senior year saw the same kind of production, and Edmonton signed him. He split his first pro season between the ECHL and AHL and didn't deliver enough offence to move up. Edmonton did not retain him beyond his entry deal (three years), and he had a short career in various lower North American leagues.

NO. 95 OVERALL: RW JUSSI TARVAINEN
KalPa (Liiga)

Tarvainen was a big skill winger taken from a region Edmonton had much success in over the years. He didn't play much in his draft year but had a strong World Junior Championships in 1995 and by 1996 was producing impressive offence in Liiga. He jumped to the SEL in 2003 and spent a year in Switzerland before heading back to Finland. He did not sign with the Oilers.

NO. 110 OVERALL: LW JON GASKINS
Dubuque Fighting Saints (USHL)

A massive winger (6'4", 220 pounds) with shy offence (30 games, 6–13–19 in his draft year), Gaskins went to Michigan State and established clearly he wasn't going to score enough to turn pro. He did play in eight ECHL games.

NO. 136 OVERALL: C TERRY MARCHANT
Niagara Scenics (NAHL)

Marchant is the younger brother of Todd Marchant, who enjoyed a strong NHL career that included several seasons in Edmonton. At the time he was drafted, his brother Todd had been a member of the Oilers organization for about three months.

Terry was bigger (6'1", 205) pounds than his older brother and not as fast. Terry had enjoyed a big season with the Scenics (42 games, 27–40–67), but it wasn't clear how well NAHL offence would translate to higher leagues.

He didn't score well in his first two seasons at Lake Superior State University, but finished strong, including a senior year (36 games, 17–22–39) above a point per game.

Edmonton signed Marchant, and he turned pro with the Hamilton Bulldogs. In 47 games, he scored 12 times and had 20 points. He moved on to the IHL for two seasons and then hit the ECHL for four seasons, followed by several years in the lower minors.

NO. 160 OVERALL: D CURTIS SHEPTAK
Olds Grizzlys (AJHL)

Sheptak was a big (6'3", 196 pounds) offensive defenceman (27–34–61 in 50 games) in Tier 2 in Alberta.

He showed his rugged style and some offence during four seasons in Northern Michigan. He did not sign in Edmonton but played in both the AHL and IHL as a first-year pro, and with the Saint John Flames in 1999–00. He played a couple of years in Finland (Liiga) and a year in Germany before playing in lower leagues in Europe and North America.

NO. 162 OVERALL: RW DMITRI SHULGA
Tivali Minsk (Russia)

At 6'2", 207 pounds, Shulga had true power-forward size. A left shot who played the opposite wing, common among Russian forwards, he scored well at the World Junior Championships and lower leagues but didn't play a full season in Russia's highest league until 2000. He did not sign in Edmonton.

NO. 179 OVERALL: G CHRIS WICKENHEISER
Red Deer Rebels (WHL)

A big (6'2", 209 pounds) goaltender, Wickenheiser had a .854 save percentage in his draft and a 5.04 goals-against average. He improved the following season and by 1996–97 (his fourth season in the league), Wickenheiser delivered a .913 save percentage. He turned pro with the Hamilton Bulldogs but played just four AHL games in the league, with the rest spent in the ECHL and lower leagues. He wrapped up his playing career in 2000–01.

NO. 185 OVERALL: D ROB GUINN
Newmarket Royals (OHL)

Average in size and neither a puck mover nor a shutdown type, Guinn did bring a physical element to the game and played with a great deal of heart.

After completing his junior career, Guinn attended St. Mary's University (Halifax) and then played for several years in the UHL and other lower leagues in the United States. He passed away after his final season in 2007–08.

NO. 188 OVERALL: D JASON REID
St. Andrew's College (Ontario High School)

Reid attended the University of Vermont for four seasons after he was drafted and spent three pro seasons in the ECHL. He did not stand out as a junior beyond size (6'2", 205 pounds), which would have been the appeal for Fraser and Oilers scouts.

NO. 214 OVERALL: G JEREMY JABLONSKI
Victoria Cougars (WHL)

Jablonski split time between the Cougars and Fort McMurray Oil Barons (AJHL) in his draft year, then played seven games for the Melfort Mustangs (SJHL) the following year, and that was the end of his playing career.

NO. 266 D LADISLAV BENYSEK
Olomouc (Czech)

Benysek had good size (6'1", 194 pounds) and began his North American career at 19 with the Cape Breton Oilers. He struggled defensively (and was not alone), so he spent the following years back in the Czech Republic. Benysek tried his luck again in 1997–98 (age 22) and had advanced enough to be considered a legit NHL prospect.

In September 1999 the Anaheim Ducks claimed him on waivers, and the following year Benysek became a regular with the fledgling Minnesota Wild. He would play 161 NHL games, just two with Edmonton.

1994 Draft Summary

When a team gets two of the first six picks in a draft, there are great expectations. Did the math tip off the organization about the future? (Number in parentheses is points per game.)

- Jason Bonsignore (OHL) age 17: 58 games, 22–64–96 (1.66)
- Ryan Smyth (WHL) age 17: 72 games, 50–55–105 (1.46)
- Mike Watt (MOJHL) age 17: 48 games, 34–34–58 (1.21)
- Corey Neilson (OHL) age 17: 62 games, 3–35–38 (0.61)
- Brad Symes (WHL) age 17: 71 games, 7–15–22 (0.31)
- Adam Copeland (OPJHL) age 17: 39 games, 28–44–72 (1.85)
- Jussi Tarvianen (Liiga) age 17: 42 games, 3–4–7 (0.17)
- Jon Gaskins (USHL) age 17: 30 games, 6–13–19 (0.63)
- Terry Marchant (NAJHL) age 17: 42 games, 27–40–67 (1.60)
- Curtis Sheptak (AJHL) age 18: 50 games, 27–34–61 (1.22)
- Dmitry Shulga (RSL) age 17: 2 games, 0–0–0
- Chris Wickenheiser (WHL) age 17: 29 games, 5.04 goals-against average, .854 save percentage
- Rob Guinn (OHL) age 17: 63 games, 2–8–10 (0.16)
- Jason Reid (Ontario HS) age 17: numbers are unavailable

- Jeremy Jablonski (WHL) age 18: 17 games, 6.29 goals-against average, .856 save percentage
- Ladislav Benysek (Czech) age 18: numbers are unavailable

The team was fishing in the right areas at the draft. Most of the early selections were productive offensive players in draft seasons. Although there is still disappointment attached to this draft these years later, the team did add a huge piece of the future to the prospect list.

NHL Career Games Played

1. Ryan Smyth: 1,270
2. Ladislav Benysek: 161
3. Mike Watt: 157
4. Jason Bonsignore: 79

Edmonton would deal Bonsignore for significant return in the years to come, and Smyth had an enormous impact with the Oilers over many years.

Here's how the 1994 draft class ranked in terms of total NHL games played:

1. 1979 (4,143 games)
2. 1980 (3,841 games)
3. 1993 (3,025 games)
4. 1981 (2,215 games)
5. 1983 (1,810 games)
6. 1991 (1,807 games)
7. **1994 (1,667 games)**
8. 1987 (1,602 games)
9. 1992 (1,251 games)

10. 1985 (1,206 games)
11. 1989 (1,137 games)
12. 1988 (1,135 games)
13. 1984 (607 games)
14. 1982 (394 games)
15. 1986 (50 games)
16. 1990 (0 games)

Fraser's scouting staff had recovered from the disaster of 1990, but as summers rolled along the Bonsignore selection became a point of contention for fans.

It's only now, when we apply modern draft metrics to Edmonton's decision, that we see it was not a pick out of the blue, but rather a selection that was a slight reach and turned out poorly for all involved.

Trades That Involved Draft Picks

On June 16, 1993, the Oilers traded forward Petr Klima to the Tampa Bay Lightning for No. 60 overall in the 1994 draft (Brad Symes).

On September 1, 1993, the Oilers traded F Craig Simpson to the Buffalo Sabres for forward Jozef Cierny and the No. 95 overall pick in the 1994 draft (Jussi Tarvainen).

On September 10, 1993, the Oilers traded a 10th-round pick (Tomas Pisa) to the San Jose Sharks for forward Link Gaetz.

On September 15, 1993, the Oilers traded defenceman Brian Glynn to the Ottawa Senators for No. 185 overall (Rob Guinn) in the 1994 draft.

On December 6, 1993, the Oilers traded a 1994 fourth-round pick (Tavis Hansen) to the Winnipeg Jets for defenceman Fredrik Olausson and pick No. 160 in the 1994 draft (Curtis Sheptak).

On December 6, 1993, the Oilers traded Geoff Smith and a 1994 fourth-round pick (Dave Nemirovsky) to the Florida Panthers for No. 53 overall in the 1994 draft (Corey Neilson) and No. 146 in the 1994 draft (Chris Kibermanis).

On March 15, 1994, the Oilers traded Dave Manson and a 1994 sixth-round pick (Chris Kibermanis) to the Winnipeg Jets for D Boris Mironov and the No. 4 overall selection (Jason Bonsignore) and No. 79 overall selection (Adam Copeland).

THE 1995 DRAFT

The 1995 draft was held in Edmonton for the first and only time. The Oilers held the No. 6 overall selection and the 10,000 fans in attendance at Northlands Arena were pumped for a successful draft by the hometown Oilers. Chants of "Doan, Doan, Doan!" could be heard as the Oilers advanced to the stage to make the selection. Edmonton did not choose Shane Doan, and that fact became a very famous draft moment.

Despite drafting early in 1993 and 1994, Edmonton remained well inside the top 10 for the 1995 draft due to another season marked by struggle.

In 1994–95, the season started late due to the owners locking out the players. The team's record (in 48 games) was 17–27–4 under two coaches (George Burnett, Ron Low), with the high draft pick being one of the few things that went right during the entire year.

Here are the rookies for the Oilers in 1994–95:

- David Oliver: 44 games, 16–14–30
- Todd Marchant: 45 games, 13–14–27
- Roman Oksiuta: 26 games, 11–2–13
- Jason Bonsignore: 1 game, 1–0–1

- Ralph Intranuovo: 1 game, 0–1–1
- Dennis Bonvie: 2 games, 0–0–0
- Ryan Smyth: 3 games, 0–0–0
- Marko Tuomainen: 4 games, 0–0–0

In September 1995, the Oilers signed Rem Murray as an undrafted free agent. He proved to be an astute addition, as he had enough offence to play up and down the lineup and the utility to play all three forward positions and both special teams.

NO. 6 OVERALL: C STEVE KELLY
Prince Albert Raiders (WHL)

The Oilers did not choose Doan, despite media legend John Short being led to believe the organization's view on the gap between Doan and Edmonton's pick (Steve Kelly) as being razor thin.

Kelly's major asset was tremendous foot speed and scouting reports had him putting all kinds of pressure on opponents because of it. However, Kelly's offence in junior did not merit such a high selection. In the 1995 draft, selections No. 5 through 9 all came from the WHL, and the differences in offensive output were striking. (Number in parentheses is points per game.)

- No. 5 overall Daymond Langkow: 72 games, 67–73–140 (1.94)
- No. 6 overall Steve Kelly: 68 games, 31–41–72 (1.06)
- No. 7 overall Shane Doan: 71 games, 37–57–94 (1.32)
- No. 8 overall Terry Ryan: 70 games, 50–60–110 (1.57)
- No. 9 overall Kyle McLaren: 47 games, 13–19–32 (0.68)

One of Kelly's coaches in Prince Albert, Rod Dallman, told the *Tampa Bay Times*, "He's a very exciting hockey player who fits the mold of a Mike Modano–type player. He has the ability to set the pace of the game by using his speed."

Kelly scored 101 points in his draft-plus-one season, but his first AHL campaign was shy (48 games, 9–29–38) for a high draft pick on his way to a quality NHL career.

Sather traded him in December 1997 (along with fellow draft disappointment Jason Bonsignore) for defenceman Roman Hamrlik and Paul Comrie.

Kelly's speed kept him in the league through 2008, but he was a part-time player for most of his career. He played in just 149 games.

NO. 31 OVERALL: RW GEORGES LARAQUE
St. Jean Lynx (QMJHL)

Laraque was a massive winger (6'4", 245 pounds) whose junior numbers (62 games, 19–22–41) projected him as a fourth-line enforcer, which is what he became—one of the best of his era.

Laraque was a great enforcer, so feared as a fighter that he was rarely engaged during the peak of his career. He was the most intimidating fighter on the team in a decade and could spend most of a shift moving the puck along the wall in the offensive zone, miles from danger.

He was part of what still ranks as Edmonton's best fourth line, along with Boyd Devereaux and Jim Dowd in 1999–00.

He scored 13 goals and 29 points in his best NHL season and played in 695 games during his career.

NO. 57 OVERALL: D LUKAS ZIB
Ceske Budejovice HC (Czech)

Another defender with NHL size (6'1", 214 pounds), Zib played in the Czech Republic for several years. His defensive play improved, and he moved to different leagues across Europe (Liiga, Russia, Germany) before returning to the Czech league, where he played until 2015. He was an effective two-way defenceman at that level but did not play in North America.

NO. 83 OVERALL: G MIKE MINARD
Chilliwack Chiefs (BCJHL)

Minard delivered a solid season (.898 save percentage) with the Chiefs and got himself drafted in 1995. He played in the OHL in his draft-plus-one season and played a lot for the Detroit Whalers (42 games, 3.32 goals-against average, .895 save percentage).

In the AHL, Minard posted good–to–very good numbers through the late 1990s and made his NHL debut in 1990–00. He played 60 minutes, gave up three goals, and won the game, posting a save percentage of .917.

It was his first and last NHL game. He would enjoy two more solid AHL seasons before landing in the ECHL and lower leagues to complete his career in 2008.

His one NHL game was quality. It's extremely rare for a player to play that well in his debut and not receive another opportunity.

NO. 109 OVERALL: D JAN SNOPEK
Oshawa Generals (OHL)

Snopek was a Czech offensive defenceman who came to North America to play against the best available talent and to raise his profile. It worked well, as he was chosen by Edmonton in his second year of eligibility (aged 19 on his draft day).

Snopek was a quality passer and puck mover (64 games, 14–30–44 in his draft year) and built on his success in his draft-plus-one season. Edmonton didn't sign him, so he played two AHL games (Saint John Flames), spent a year in the SHL, and then settled into a long career in the Czech league. He finished up with two seasons in Liiga and two more in Italy, retiring in 2014.

NO. 161 OVERALL: C MARTIN CERVEN
Trencin Dukla (Slovak)

Cerven was drafted from Trencin Dukla, but was another in a fairly long line of Czech players drafted during the Fraser era. Cerven was the 17th Czech chosen, with the successes up to this point including Jaroslav Pouzar, Martin Rucinsky, Miro Satan, David Vyborny, and Josef Beranek.

Cerven came immediately to North America and played in the WHL. He scored reasonably well (72 games, 27–25–52 in his final season with the Seattle Thunderbirds of the WHL), but the Oilers didn't sign him, instead trading Cerven to the Philadelphia Flyers for a conditional pick in 1997.

NO. 187 OVERALL: D STEPHEN DOUGLAS
Niagara Falls Thunder (OHL)

A 6'6", 235-pound defensive defenceman, Douglas began his draft year in the OPJHL but quickly moved up to the OHL, where he played a depth role (32 games, 0–2–2, 15 PIM).

Edmonton chose him based on size and intimidation factor, and that part of his game kicked in when Douglas moved to the

QMJHL in time for the 1995–96 campaign. In 1996–97, he had 383 PIM for two teams. Edmonton did not sign him and he played just 10 ECHL games before spending a full season in the WPHL.

NO. 213 OVERALL: D JIRI ANTONIN
Pardubice HC (Czech)

Yet another Czech rounded out the 1995 draft, and a big defence-man (6'5", 209 pounds) too. Antonin had played in Czech junior hockey before being drafted by Edmonton and remained at one level or another of Czech hockey for the next 20 years. He did not sign in Edmonton but did play one year in Poland.

1995 Draft Summary

The fans had it right; Shane Doan was the correct pick in 1995. Did math tell the Oilers that Kelly was a poor pick? (Number in parentheses is points per game.)

- Steve Kelly (WHL) age 17: 68 games, 31–41–72 (1.06)
- Georges Laraque (QMJHL) age 17: 62 games, 19–22–41 (0.66)
- Lukas Zib (Czech) age 17: 22 games, 3–0–3 (0.14)
- Mike Minard (BCHL) age 17: 40 games, 3.50 goals-against average, .898 save percentage
- Jan Snopek (OHL) age 18: 64 games, 14–30–44 (0.69)
- Martin Cerven (Slovak) age 17: numbers are unavailable
- Stephen Douglas (OHL) age 17: 32 games, 0–2–2 (0.06)
- Jiri Antonin (Czech Jr.) age 19: 33 games, 5–15–20 (0.61)

Kelly was a poor pick because he was chosen No. 6 overall with more talented players on the board. Edmonton was focused on speed and that cost the team. Combined with the no-hit 1990 draft and the Bonsignore miss, Oilers fans yelling "DOAN!" at Northlands during the draft meant Kelly became a lightning-rod pick in an instant. It was not a success.

NHL Career Games Played

Here are the players drafted by Edmonton in 1995 who made it to the NHL:

1. Georges Laraque: 695
2. Steve Kelly: 149
3. Mike Minard: 1

Here's how the 1995 draft class ranked in terms of total NHL games played:

1. 1979 (4,143 games)
2. 1980 (3,841 games)
3. 1993 (3,025 games)
4. 1981 (2,215 games)
5. 1983 (1,810 games)
6. 1991 (1,807 games)
7. 1994 (1,667 games)
8. 1987 (1,602 games)
9. 1992 (1,251 games)
10. 1985 (1,206 games)
11. 1989 (1,137 games)
12. 1988 (1,135 games)
13. **1995 (845 games)**
14. 1984 (607 games)
15. 1982 (394 games)
16. 1986 (50 games)
17. 1990 (0 games)

I have 1,000 games as a pass/fail line in the sand; this is the fifth time in 17 seasons Fraser and his scouts get an F. The 1980s failures came after incredible success in adjacent draft seasons, but from 1990 on, the Oilers needed great draft performances that did not come. The Kelly selection, both at the time and looking back, was a failure in the drafting process. Edmonton no longer made offence a priority, even at the top of the draft.

Trades That Involved Draft Picks

On March 13, 1995, the Oilers traded Brad Zavisha and a sixth-round selection in 1995 (Jamie Sokolsky) to the Philadelphia Flyers for Ryan McGill.

THE 1996 DRAFT

The 1995–96 Oilers spent a fourth consecutive season outside the playoffs, but there were signs of better days ahead. Despite delivering an unimpressive 30–44–8 record and a goal differential of minus-64 (240–304), Doug Weight scored 104 points and became the first Oilers player to hit the century mark since Mark Messier in 1989–90.

The club had several splendid rookies:

- Miro Satan: 62 games, 18–17–35
- Ryan Smyth: 48 games, 2–9–11
- Brett Hauer: 29 games, 4–2–6
- David Roberts: 6 games, 2–4–6
- Ralph Intranuovo: 13 games, 1–2–3
- Greg De Vries: 13 games, 1–1–2
- Jason Bonsignore: 20 games, 0–2–2
- Tyler Wright: 23 games, 1–0–1
- Dennis Bonvie: 8 games, 0–0–0

- Bryan Muir: 5 games, 0–0–0
- Nick Stadjuhar: 2 games 0–0–0
- Joaquin Gage: 16 games, 3.77 goals-against average, .871 save percentage

NO. 6 OVERALL: C BOYD DEVEREAUX
Kitchener Rangers (OHL)

Edmonton drafted a checking forward sixth overall in 1996, repeating the mistake of 1995, when Steve Kelly was chosen in front of more talented offensive players.

Here are the junior offensive numbers for the five most recent first-round selections for the Oilers (including Devereaux). (Number in parentheses is points per game.)

- Jason Arnott 1992–93: 56 games, 41–57–98 (1.75)
- Jason Bonsignore 1993–94: 58 games, 22–64–86 (1.48)
- Ryan Smyth 1993–94: 72 games, 50–55–105 (1.46)
- Steve Kelly 1994–95: 68 games, 31–41–72 (1.06)
- Boyd Devereaux 1995–96: 66 games, 20–38–58 (.88)

As much as the Bonsignore selection disappointed, he delivered enough offence to project as an NHL skill player.

Kelly in 1995 was a poor selection from the standpoint of Fraser and the scouts not being able to identify a fast but limited offensive forward.

Devereaux was something else again, as the scouting staff (or management) clearly wanted to use the pick on a quality checking centre. That's poor usage of a No. 6 overall selection, then and now. Consider Daniel Briere, who was drafted at No. 24 overall and had a draft-year points-per-game total of 2.43. He would play in 973 NHL games, averaging 59 points per 82 games.

Devereaux, a fine checking centre, would play in 627 games and average 23 points per 82 games.

It's unfair to place the blame on Fraser and his scouts if Sather and upper management were focused on a checking centre, but there was a major disconnect in the Oilers organization during the 1990s. Simply put, Briere was more valuable because his scoring ability was far more difficult to procure than a checking centre like Devereaux.

The Oilers failed to get full value for their early picks in the 1990s because the club did not consider the rarest skills on the board to be the most valuable.

That's a major problem, and it contributed to Edmonton's lack of success after 1990 far more than misspent free-agent dollars. Combined with noxious trades like the Miro Satan deal, the Oilers were at a distinct disadvantage.

NO. 19 OVERALL: D MATTHIEU DESCOTEAUX
Shawinigan Cataractes (QMJHL)

Descoteaux was a big (6'4", 208 pounds) and physical shutdown defenceman who blossomed offensively in his final junior season (70 games, 12–37–49). Scoring spikes by junior players aged 19 are common, but those gaudy numbers rarely translate to pro hockey.

Descoteaux showed well defensively as an AHL rookie in 1997–98, holding his own on a defensive crew that included future NHL players Bryan Muir, Ladislav Benysek, Scott Ferguson, and Sean Brown. His offensive output as a rookie (67 games, 2–8–10) reflected the expected output from his entire junior résumé.

Edmonton dealt him to Montreal midway through the final (third) season of his entry-level deal, and he would play his only five NHL games for the Canadiens in 2000–01.

NO. 32 OVERALL: D CHRIS HAJT
Guelph Storm (OHL)

At 6'3", 206 pounds, Chris Hajt was almost a perfect physical copy of his father, Bill Hajt. The father was a quality shutdown defender with some offence who played for the Saskatoon Blades of the WHL, spent two seasons in the minors, and then played 854 effective games for the Buffalo Sabres.

The younger Hajt also spent two seasons in the AHL after turning pro, but his offensive game was nonexistent and his defensive prowess, while solid, did not move the needle enough to make up for his puck-moving shortfalls.

He spent 10 seasons in pro hockey, eight of them with at least some AHL appearances.

NO. 59 OVERALL: D TOM POTI
Cushing Academy (USHS, Massachusetts)

Poti was one of the most naturally talented defencemen the Fraser scouting staff drafted over 21 seasons. He had size (6'3", 197 pounds), speed, and the ability to make a beautiful pass and a tremendous shot. He could skate the puck to safety and had a massive wingspan that was useful at both ends of the ice.

Poti had some issues, led by defensive lapses that often ended up in disaster and (at times) a lack of creativity in the offensive zone once he had established possession inside the opponent's end.

Injuries were also an issue for Poti, who had groin, back, and pelvis injuries, among others, over a long career. Perhaps most unusual were his myriad food allergies, which made road trips difficult but never affected his ability to play the game.

Poti played much of his career inside the top-four defence and was useful on special teams. He had his share of critics while in Edmonton, but Poti's natural talent was on display while he was an Oiler. He played more of a defensive role later in his career and that became his strength.

Poti played 824 NHL games between 1998 and 2013.

NO. 114 OVERALL: RW BRIAN URICK
Notre Dame (NCAA)

Urick was a regular and an effective player (36 games, 12–14–26) for the Fighting Irish. In his final three seasons with Notre Dame, he delivered impressive offence and led the team in points as a sophomore.

He turned pro in 1999–00 but did not score enough to stay in the AHL. His scoring in the ECHL (21 goals in 45 games) earned him an AHL berth for 2000–01, but the numbers (50 games, 11–8–19) were again shy and he did not continue his pro hockey career.

NO. 141 OVERALL: RW BRYAN RANDALL
Medicine Hat Tigers (WHL)

Randall was the fifth member of the Tigers drafted in 1996 and had a late birthday (August 1978) with plenty of time to develop.

Randall's big appeal was his size (6'4", 210 pounds), and he did have some offensive potential. It didn't convert into scoring success until Randall was traded to the Kelowna Rockets in 1997–98. In 25 games, he scored 8–12–20, including five goals on the power play. He did not sign with the Oilers, but played in lower pro leagues for a few years and for the University of Saskatchewan in 2001.

NO. 168 OVERALL: RW DAVID BERNIER
St. Hyacinthe Lasers (QMJHL)

A skill winger with good size (6'2", 187 pounds) Bernier scored 10–18–28 in 65 games in his draft year and improved slightly in the following season.

His final junior season saw Bernier blossom, with 35 goals and 88 points in 70 games. He did not sign with Edmonton but was drafted by the Anaheim Ducks. He would return to junior for an even more impressive campaign, although injuries shortened his year. Bernier played low minors after turning pro, eventually returning to St. Hyacinthe and the senior team.

NO. 170 OVERALL: RW BRANDON LAFRANCE
Ohio State University (NCAA)

LaFrance had been a fine scorer in Tier 2 CJHL, scoring 84 points in 53 games for the Ottawa Jr. Senators at age 18 in 1994–95.

In his freshman season with Ohio State, he scored well (11–5–16 in 32 games) in a support role. The goals never came, the feature role never arrived, and LaFrance entered pro hockey in the ECHL. He played until 2009, most of his games coming in Quebec's LNAH league.

NO. 195 OVERALL: RW FERNANDO PISANI
St. Albert Saints (AJHL)

Pisani was a local legend in St. Albert, with his scoring exploits (103 points in 58 games) enough to get him drafted.

He entered Providence College in the fall of 1996, contributing quietly early before emerging as a useful two-way winger halfway through college. That template—incremental progress early followed by a blossoming offence—would be a consistent part of Pisani's hockey career.

After completing college, Pisani turned pro in 2000 with the Hamilton Bulldogs. His scoring numbers were just average (12–13–25 as an AHL rookie in 52 games), but Pisani would deliver 60 points in 79 games for Hamilton the following year.

By 2002–03 he was pushing for an NHL job, eventually replacing Daniel Cleary on the No. 3 line as a productive two-way right winger. In his second NHL season, Pisani scored 16 goals while also serving in a mentor role to young arrivals from the farm. It was a role he would play well through the rest of his career.

In 2005–06, Pisani scored a career-high 18 goals in the regular season and almost equalled it in the playoffs. During a magical run by Edmonton that spring, Pisani spearheaded the offence with brilliant and timely goals.

During the Stanley Cup Final that spring, Pisani scored one of the most famous goals in franchise history. It was Game 5. The Oilers needed a win to avoid elimination, and Edmonton defenceman Steve Staios was in the penalty box.

The Hurricanes were exiting their own zone sleepily, with little momentum, and a poorly timed pass entered the middle of the ice while Pisani, onside, raced toward it. No Carolina player recognized the danger in time, and Pisani beat the final defender to the puck and raced in on Cam Ward. Brilliant shot shelf, and music! The Oilers are still in the Final.

After the memorable season, Pisani continued in his role as contributing winger and mentor but was also suffering from ulcerative colitis. The impact of that illness derailed his career and changed Pisani's life.

His final complete campaign was 2006–07. The illness shortened his career by several seasons.

NO. 221 OVERALL: G JOHN HULTBERG
Kingston Frontenacs (OHL)

Hultberg had a reasonable save percentage in his draft year (.891) and played in the world's best junior league. He maintained that level of goaltending, but did not progress and peaked out in the lower minors.

1996 Draft Summary

After the disappointment of the 1995 draft, the fifth-worst Oilers draft to that time, Barry Fraser and the scouting staff needed a recovery draft. It was a little ironic in that the team grabbed its checking centre at No. 6 overall and a top skill defender in the third round plus a fine two-way right winger in the eighth round, but it was a success by any measure. Here's what the math says. (Number in parentheses is points per game.)

- Boyd Devereaux (OHL) age 17: 66 games, 20–38–58 (0.88)
- Matthieu Descoteaux (QMJHL) age 17: 69 games, 2–13–15 (0.22)
- Chris Hajt (OHL) age 17: 63 games, 8–27–35 (0.56)
- Tom Poti (USHS) age 18: 29 games, 14–59–73 (2.52)

- Brian Urick (NCAA) age 18: 36 games, 12–14–26 (0.72)
- Bryan Randall (WHL) age 17: 64 games, 4–5–9 (0.14)
- David Bernier (QMJHL) age 17: 65 games, 10–18–28 (0.43)
- Brandon Lafrance (NCAA) age 18: 32 games, 11–5–16 (0.50)
- Fernando Pisani (AJHL) age 18: 58 games, 40–63–103 (1.78)
- John Hultberg (OHL) age 18: 40 games, 3.69 goals-against average, .891 save percentage

At No. 6 overall, Devereaux is one of many early picks of defencemen in the 1980s that show the organization's failure to recognize that using early picks on substantial offensive players is key to winning. On the other hand, Poti's high school stats were fantastic.

NHL Career Games Played

1. Tom Poti: 824
2. Boyd Devereaux: 627
3. Fernandi Pisani: 462
4. Chris Hajt: 6
5. Matthieu Descoteaux: 5

The 1996 draft was rare for Edmonton because three men played more than 400 games. The Oilers have enjoyed stunning successes in some draft summers, but it is rare for the organization to have put a cluster together in one draft.

Here's how the 1996 draft class ranked in terms of total NHL games played:

1. 1979 (4,143 games)
2. 1980 (3,841 games)
3. 1993 (3,025 games)
4. 1981 (2,215 games)
5. **1996 (1,924 games)**
6. 1983 (1,810 games)
7. 1991 (1,807 games)
8. 1994 (1,667 games)
9. 1987 (1,602 games)
10. 1992 (1,251 games)
11. 1985 (1,206 games)
12. 1989 (1,137 games)
13. 1988 (1,135 games)
14. 1995 (845 games)
15. 1984 (607 games)
16. 1982 (394 games)
17. 1986 (50 games)
18. 1990 (0 games)

Trades That Involved Draft Picks

On July 28, 1995, the Oilers received a 1996 first-round pick (Marty Reasoner) and a 1997 first-round pick (Matt Zultek) from the St. Louis Blues as compensation for signing forward Shayne Corson.

On August 4, 1995, the Oilers dealt a 1996 first-round pick (Marty Reasoner) and a 1997 first-round pick (Matt Zultek) to the St. Louis Blues for goalie Curtis Joseph and the rights to college winger Mike Grier.

On December 4, 1995, the Oilers traded centre Peter White and a 1996 fourth-round pick (Jason Sessa) to the Toronto Maple Leafs for winger Kent Manderville.

On January 11, 1996, the Oilers traded goalie Billy Ranford to the Boston Bruins for winger Marius Czerkawski, the rights to defenceman Sean Brown, and the No. 19 overall pick in the 1996 draft (Matthieu Descoteaux).

On June 22, 1996, the Oilers traded centre Tyler Wright to the Pittsburgh Penguins for selection No. 170 overall in the 1996 draft (Brandon LaFrance).

7

OILERS ARE BACK!

THE 1997 DRAFT

THE 1996-97 OILERS, under coach Ron Low, made the playoffs—for the first time in five seasons. Some parts of the last Stanley Cup team remained, represented by veteran defenceman Kevin Lowe, winger Kelly Buchberger, and the midseason acquisition of scorer Petr Klima.

The key players on the team were Doug Weight and Curtis Joseph, acquisitions by Glen Sather from other organizations, as well as draft picks Jason Arnott and Ryan Smyth. The rookies in 1996–97 were as follows:

- Mike Grier: 79 games, 15–17–32
- Rem Murray: 82 games, 11–20–31
- Mats Lindgren: 69 games, 11–14–25
- Dan McGillis: 73 games, 6–16–22
- Greg De Vries: 37 games, 0–4–4
- Steve Kelly: 8 games, 1–0–1

- Ralph Intranuovo: 5 games, 1–0–1
- Drew Bannister: 1 game, 0–1–1
- Joe Hulbig: 6 games, 0–0–0
- Sean Brown: 5 games, 0–0–0
- Barrie Moore: 4 games, 0–0–0
- Craig Millar: 1 game, 0–0–0

This period for the Oilers was unusual in that the pipeline was producing rookies, but they weren't draft picks. Rem Murray and Greg De Vries were signed as undrafted free agents and Grier, Lindgren, and McGillis were trade acquisitions by Sather. Barry Fraser's men were not able to establish themselves as NHL players during these years, represented above by Steve Kelly and Joe Hulbig.

NO. 14 OVERALL: LW MICHAEL RIESEN
Biel HC (Swiss-B)

Riesen was the highest-drafted Swiss player when Edmonton chose him in the first round, the first to be chosen in that round. It is notable that he did not play in Switzerland's highest league in his draft year.

A right-shooting winger who played the left side, he stayed in Switzerland in his first post-draft season, scoring well for hometown Davos (16 goals in 32 games).

He came to North America in 1998–99, going just 6–17–23 in 60 games for the Hamilton Bulldogs. Although he was clearly skilled, Riesen took some time to deal with the physical nature of the league.

In year two with Hamilton, Riesen played on a line with Brian Swanson (centre) and Daniel Cleary, with all three men flourishing. Riesen was the goal-scorer on the line, posting 29–31–60 in 73 games.

He broke camp on "the Bulldog Line" with the Oilers in the fall of 2000, new coach Craig MacTavish bringing the trio to the NHL as a unit. In 12 games, he faltered and looked hesitant, matching his initial games with Hamilton in the AHL. He and Swanson were sent back to the AHL, with only Cleary winning full-time work in 2000–01.

On July 1, 2001, Riesen was part of a major deal that saw Edmonton send him and Doug Weight (its best player) to the St. Louis Blues for a package of players. Riesen returned to Switzerland, where his skill was on display through 2014.

NO. 41 OVERALL: G PATRICK DOVIGI
Erie Otters (OHL)

Dovigi had good size (6'1", 203 pounds) and pushed for a starting job in the OHL at age 17, where his save percentage was .878. He took a step back the following year, posting just .862 with the Otters and eventually losing the starting job to Steve Valiquette. He struggled in the starting role in Erie during his final year, eventually being traded to St. Mike's in Toronto, where he played better (.878). The Oilers did not sign him.

NO. 68 OVERALL: D SERGEI YERKOVICH
Las Vegas Thunder (IHL)

Yerkovich was 23 when Edmonton picked him, a veteran of the top Russian league and newly famous as an enforcer with the Thunder in Las Vegas (167 PIM). He had size (6'3", 209 pounds) and some two-way skill. He stayed in Vegas for a second year and was less successful defensively, then moved up to Hamilton in 1998–99, where he spent two seasons in Edmonton's system. In his second year, he played well enough to be considered one of the best defenders in Hamilton, but big Bert Robertsson got the call instead. Yerkovich would return to Russia and play four more years in Europe.

NO. 94 OVERALL: D JONAS ELOFSSON
Farjestads BK (SEL)

Elofsson was a two-way defender of average size and did not progress during the seasons after his draft. Elofsson would enjoy a 10-year career in Sweden, with a brief detour to Finland, but did not play in North America.

NO. 121 OVERALL: LW JASON CHIMERA
Medicine Hat Tigers (WHL)

In his draft season with Medicine Hat, Chimera scored 16–23–39 in 71 games. Six forwards on that team outscored him, but none of them could skate like Chimera. He would score more than 30 goals in each of his two final junior seasons and turn pro with the Hamilton Bulldogs in 1999–00.

Chimera started his pro career the same way things went in Medicine Hat, scoring 15 goals and 28 points in 78 games with the Hamilton Bulldogs. Solid, but nothing earth-shattering. As happened in junior, Chimera would use that experience (and his speed) to score 54 and then 77 points in the seasons that followed.

Each fall, Oilers general manager Kevin Lowe would talk to the media about Chimera and then coach Craig MacTavish would send him back. The coach loved his speed but wanted responsible players, and Chimera had some lessons to learn.

Chimera's speed and scoring ability made him a legit NHL prospect, but he was not able to establish himself on an NHL skill line for any length of time.

In 2002–03, Chimera stayed with Edmonton, scoring 14 goals in 66 games. He struggled in 2003–04 and spent the lockout season (2004–05) playing in Italy. During the lockout, he was traded twice, first to the Phoenix Coyotes and then to the Columbus Blue Jackets.

Once in Columbus, Chimera found his way as a fast winger who could score 15–20 goals a season, forecheck like a demon, and help on the penalty kill. He lacked consistency, which hurt him and meant he was off to a new team every few years. He would play in 1,107 NHL games, ranking No. 9 among all Oilers draft picks between 1979 and 2020. He had a fine career.

NO. 141 OVERALL: C PETER SARNO
Windsor Spitfires (OHL)

Sarno had excellent offensive instincts and was an outstanding passer. Though he was just average in size (5'11", 185 pounds) and speed, he was a quality junior beginning in his draft season (20–63–83 in 66 games) and scored 121 and 130 points in the final two years in Windsor.

Turning pro with the Hamilton Bulldogs in 1999–00, Sarno posted 10–36–46 in 67 games. During this period, one of the early innovators in hockey analytics was Tim Barnes (now of the Washington Capitals). He noted that an AHL rookie, age 20, who delivered a point per game in the league was very likely to play on a skill line in the NHL. Sarno delivered .686 points per game at 20 and would play just seven games in the NHL.

Sarno delivered strong AHL seasons through 2006 (Edmonton traded him in 2004 in exchange for goalie Tyler Moss) and played another five seasons in Europe. He delivered offence in every league he played in save the NHL, where he scored one goal in seven games.

NO. 176 OVERALL: D KEVIN BOLIBRUCK
Peterborough Petes (OHL)

Bolibruck was 20 by the time Edmonton drafted him. The Ottawa Senators had picked him in 1995, but he didn't sign and re-entered the draft. He had average size for a defenceman (6'1", 200 pounds) and his speed did not stand out in junior or in the minors. His big defensive asset was positioning and wingspan, but it got him only as far as the AHL, where he spent two years in the Oilers system and three more in Rochester, Houston, and Bridgeport Sound. After that, Bolibruck played several years in Europe.

NO. 187 OVERALL: C CHAD HINZ
Moose Jaw Warriors (WHL)

Hinz was an undersized centre who posted strong numbers in junior (draft year: 72 games, 37–47–84) but was a little shy of delivering enough offence to make the NHL. He emerged as a solid two-way centre in the AHL and would later play in Europe for several seasons.

Hinz didn't play in the NHL, but he did get a call when Jarret Stoll came down with tonsillitis. He dressed for a game against Phoenix and took the pregame skate but did not play in the game.

NO. 205 OVERALL: D CHRIS KERR
Sudbury Wolves (OHL)

Kerr was a shutdown defender with some size (6'3", 210 pounds) but played very little after his draft day, finally becoming a regular in the OPJHL in 1998–99. He did not sign with Edmonton.

NO. 231 OVERALL: G ALEXANDER FOMITCHEV
St. Albert Saints (AJHL)

Fomitchev, from Moscow, played on a strong Saints team in 1996–97, posting a save percentage of .910. He moved up to the WHL and played well (.898, .901, and .912) in three seasons as a starter.

Fomitchev played mostly in the low minors as a pro and then in Russia for several seasons before retiring in 2013.

1997 Draft Summary

Although the 1997 draft gets a passing grade, the picks at the top of Edmonton's draft did not enjoy success. Here are their numbers. (Number in parentheses is points per game.)

- Michel Riesen (NLA-B) age 17: 38 games, 16–16–32 (0.84)
- Patrick Dovigi (OHL) age 17: 36 games, 3.88 goals-against average, .878 save percentage
- Sergei Yerkovich (IHL) age 22: 76 games, 6–19–25 (0.33)
- Jonas Elofsson (SuperElite J20) age 17: 20 games, 4–10–14 (0.70)
- Jason Chimera (WHL) age 17: 71 games, 16–23–39 (0.55)
- Peter Sarno (OHL) age 17: 66 games, 20–63–83 (1.26)
- Kevin Bolibruck (OHL) age 19: 46 games, 4–26–30 (0.65)

- Chad Hinz (OHL) age 17: 72 games, 37–47–84 (1.17)
- Chris Kerr (OHL) age 17: 45 games, 3–10–13 (0.29)
- Alexander Fomitchev (AJHL) age 17: 41 games, 2.88 goals-against average, .910 save percentage

Riesen's offence came in the second Swiss league. Looking back, that may have indicated his offence wouldn't be enough. On the other hand, Chimera's offence in the WHL wasn't impressive and he would emerge as an NHL player and stay in the league a long time.

NHL Career Games Played
1. Jason Chimera: 1,107
2. Michel Riesen: 12
3. Peter Sarno: 7

Chimera would play forever, mostly due to his exceptional speed. He did not occupy a spot among the skill lines for most of those seasons. By 1997, it had been a few years since the Ryan Smyth draft, and Edmonton remained without a substantial skill prospect at any of the forward positions.

Here's how the 1997 draft class ranked in terms of total NHL games played:
1. 1979 (4,143 games)
2. 1980 (3,841 games)
3. 1993 (3,025 games)
4. 1981 (2,215 games)
5. 1996 (1,924 games)
6. 1983 (1,810 games)
7. 1991 (1,807 games)

8.   1994 (1,667 games)
9.   1987 (1,602 games)
10. 1992 (1,251 games)
11. 1985 (1,206 games)
12. 1989 (1,137 games)
13. 1988 (1,135 games)
14. 1997 (1,126 games)
15. 1995 (845 games)
16. 1984 (607 games)
17. 1982 (394 games)
18. 1986 (50 games)
19. 1990 (0 games)

Trades That Involved Draft Picks

On July 28, 1995, the Oilers received a 1996 first-round pick (Marty Reasoner) and a 1997 first-round pick (Matt Zultek) from the St. Louis Blues as compensation for signing forward Shayne Corson.

On August 4, 1995, the Oilers dealt a 1996 first-round pick (Marty Reasoner) and a 1997 first-round pick (Matt Zultek) to the St. Louis Blues for goalie Curtis Joseph and the rights to college winger Mike Grier.

On August 24, 1995, the Oilers traded a 1997 sixth-round selection (Larry Shapley) to the Vancouver Canucks for Brett Hauer.

On March 18, 1997, the Oilers traded Jeff Norton to the Tampa Bay Lightning for Drew Bannister and the No. 141 overall selection in the 1997 draft (Peter Sarno).

On June 18, 1997, the Oilers traded the rights to Martin Cerven to the Philadelphia Flyers for the No. 187 overall selection (Chad Hinz).

THE 1998 DRAFT

The 1997–98 Oilers once again made the playoffs and again won a round of the playoffs (a classic series against the Colorado Avalanche). Edmonton finished third in the Pacific Division.

Edmonton was led by Doug Weight, Dean McAmmond, Curtis Joseph in goal, and defenceman Bo Mironov, all acquired via trade. The top-performing draft pick was Ryan Smyth, who was solidifying his role as a first-line winger with a rugged edge.

Sather traded one of his prize draft picks, Jason Arnott, and picked up another rough skill winger (Bill Guerin).

The top Oilers rookies in 1997–98 were:

- Scott Fraser: 29 games, 12–11–23
- Boyd Devereaux: 38 games, 1–4–5
- Craig Millar: 11 games, 4–0–4
- Joe Hulbig: 17 games, 2–2–4
- Mike Watt: 14 games, 1–2–3
- Steve Kelly: 19 games, 0–2–2
- Sean Brown: 18 games, 0–1–1
- Georges Laraque: 11 games, 0–0–0
- Terran Sandwith: 8 games, 0–0–0
- Bryan Muir: 7 games, 0–0–0
- Dennis Bonvie: 4 games, 0–0–0
- Ladislav Benysek: 2 games, 0–0–0
- Scott Ferguson: 1 game, 0–0–0

NO. 13 OVERALL: RW MICHAEL HENRICH
Barrie Colts (OHL)

Henrich was No. 5 on the North American list (Central Scouting) on draft night but fell to Edmonton at No. 13 overall. Red Line Report ranked him No. 4 overall.

Henrich was a good goal-scoring winger (41 in 66 games) in his draft year, and brought good size (6'2", 209 pounds). He was described as a power winger with good speed, and the 41 goals (an increase from nine the previous year) seemed to indicate there was a future player of note on the way.

Henrich continued to score in his final two seasons of junior (38 goals both times) but flatlined once he arrived in the AHL with the Hamilton Bulldogs in 2000–01. As an AHL rookie, he scored just five goals in 73 games, and just 14 in his second season in the minors.

The Oilers cut him loose and Henrich found his way to Europe before leaving hockey after the 2013–14 season.

NO. 67 OVERALL: D ALEX HENRY
London Knights (OHL)

Henry was a big (6'5", 220 pounds) enforcer who played defence and was ranked No. 31 overall in the final North American rankings for Central Scouting. His issues were regarding quickness and skating, but he made the NHL (177 games) and had a career because he was a feared fighter. Fraser spent a lot of picks on players just like Henry, and this would have to be considered a successful pick based on Henry making the NHL.

NO. 99 OVERALL: C SHAWN HORCOFF
Michigan State University (NCAA)

Horcoff is one of Edmonton's best "value picks" from outside the first round over 40-plus years of drafting.

Scouting report and legacy: Horcoff was a versatile two-way centre who rose through the roster quickly and found himself playing in the middle between Ryan Smyth and Ales Hemsky in June 2006. Horcoff was a creative playmaker who could score, but his utility didn't stop there. Good in the face-off circle and on both special teams, he was an integral part of Edmonton's dream playoff run in 2006. Horcoff was a leader and eventually Oilers captain, and one of the best value picks in Fraser's 20-year run as scouting director in Edmonton. In Oilers draft history there are just six men who were drafted outside the first round and then went on to play five-plus seasons on a skill line in the NHL (Mark Messier, Glenn Anderson, Jari Kurri, Esa Tikkanen, Miroslav Satan, Shawn Horcoff). That's a helluva list.

NO. 113 OVERALL: G KRISTIAN ANTILA
Ilves Jr. (Finland)

Antila was the classic size for a modern goalie (6'3", 202 pounds) and played well for Finland in various junior tournaments leading up to his draft day.

When Antila arrived in pro hockey, he found a home in Finland's top league (Liiga) and that was his highest level of play beyond a two-game stint with the Hamilton Bulldogs (AHL).

NO. 128 OVERALL: D PAUL ELLIOTT
Lethbridge Hurricanes (WHL)

Elliott posted 11–27–38 in 72 games for two WHL teams in his draft season. Big enough for NHL defence (6'1", 210) and skilled enough to project into a two-way role, Elliott had two more good seasons at that level and then added another at age 20 when Edmonton didn't sign him.

NO. 144 OVERALL: LW OLEG SMIRNOV
Elektrostal Kristall (WPHL)

Smirnov was drafted out of the Russian third-tier league, which was unusual in 1998. He made the top league (RSL) in 1998–99 and began scoring goals and playing more in 2001–02. He hung around playing a secondary role in the RSL until 2005–06, then played in Belarus and more secondary Russian leagues. He did not sign with Edmonton or play in North America.

NO. 159 OVERALL: D TREVOR ETTINGER
Cape Breton Screaming Eagles (QMJHL)

Ettinger was a big (6'5", 225 pounds) enforcer type who played both defence and forward during his brief career. He posted 300-plus penalty minutes twice during a physical junior career, spending an extra year in the QMJHL when the Oilers did not sign him. He eventually signed with the Columbia Blue Jackets organization. He was a member of the Jackets minor league team (Syracuse Crunch) at the time of his death by suicide, per ESPN.

NO. 186 OVERALL: G MIKE MORRISON
Exeter High School (USHS, New Hampshire)

Morrison had a lot of good indicators on draft day, including size (6'3", 202 pounds) and a solid year in high school (2.35 goals-against average).

He went straight to Maine (NCAA) after the draft and posted impressive save percentages, except for one season (.917, .894, .924, .921), before he was signed by the Oilers.

In his first year (Columbus Cottonmouths, ECHL) Morrison struggled (.892), but he played very well for the Toronto Roadrunners

(AHL), posting a .913 save percentage in 2003–04. He improved the following year (.939) and made his NHL debut in 2005–06.

In 21 games, he posted an .884 save percentage and became famous for expert work in the postgame shootout to settle ties. The Oilers lost him on waivers to the Ottawa Senators in March 2006. He played in the minors through the end of the decade.

NO. 213 OVERALL: D CHRISTIAN LEFEBVRE
Baie-Comeau Drakker (QMJHL)

Another big (6'5", 216 pounds) defender, Lefebvre had been drafted two years earlier by the Calgary Flames. He played well for the Granby Prédateurs at the 1996 Memorial Cup, and that has been enough to get drafted over the years. It's rarely enough to get drafted twice, but he did not play much during the two drafts (1996 and 1998) and didn't play at all after the draft. Fraser's ongoing desire to bring in big defencemen wasn't unique to the Oilers, but Lefebvre's story has quite a bit of mystery to it.

NO. 241 OVERALL: RW MAXIM SPIRIDONOV
London Knights (OHL)

Spiridonov was one of the best Russian-born scorers ever to play in the OHL, posting 85 goals and 151 points in 121 games.

He was not a success in the minor leagues, scoring inconsistently in the IHL and the AHL in his early twenties. In 2001, he signed with Ufa of the RSL (Russia) and began a long and productive career in that league, scoring well (led the league in scoring in 2002–03) in the RSL and then KHL when the league's name changed. Combined, he scored 125 goals in 475 games in the league and played for a long time, finishing in 2013–14. He didn't play in the NHL, but at the peak of his career he would have had a shot at regular play.

1998 Draft Summary

As happened in 1997, one player chosen in 1998 (Horcoff) made the draft successful, but the first-round selection was a disappointment. The math loved his scoring, but he was shy of a point per game. (Number in parentheses is points per game.)

- Michael Henrich (OHL) age 17: 66 games, 41–22–63 (0.95)
- Alex Henry (OHL) age 17: 62 games, 5–9–14 (0.23)
- Shawn Horcoff (NCAA) age 18: 34 games, 14–13–27 (0.79)
- Kristian Antila (Finland Jr.) age 17: 8 games, 3.31 goals-against average, .897 save percentage
- Paul Elliott (WHL) age 17: 72 games, 11–27–38 (0.53)
- Oleg Smirnov (Rus Div 3) age 17: 23 games, 5–9–14 (0.61)
- Trevor Ettinger (QMJHL) age 17: 50 games, 1–2–3 (0.06)
- Mike Morrison (USHS) age 18: 27 games, 2.35
- Christian Lefebvre (QMJHL) age 19: 8 games, 0–0–0
- Maxim Spiridonov (OHL) age 19: 66 games, 54–44–98 (1.48)

Horcoff was the big success here, and there were math reasons to like him (he scored well and was young for the NCAA) but no one on the list posted extreme numbers aside from Spiridonov (who would have passed through the draft twice).

NHL Career Games Played

1. Shawn Horcoff: 1,008
2. Alex Henry: 177
3. Mike Morrison: 29

Ironically, Horcoff would emerge as the first forward chosen who spent substantial time inside the Oilers skill lines for five or more years, connecting him to Messier, Anderson, Kurri, and Tikkanen at least marginally (skill players chosen outside the first round).

By the time Horcoff arrived in the NHL, Fraser would be gone.

Here's how the 1998 draft class ranked in terms of total NHL games played:

1. 1979 (4,143 games)
2. 1980 (3,841 games)
3. 1993 (3,025 games)
4. 1981 (2,215 games)
5. 1996 (1,924 games)
6. 1983 (1,810 games)
7. 1991 (1,807 games)
8. 1994 (1,667 games)
9. 1987 (1,602 games)
10. 1992 (1,251 games)
11. **1998 (1,214 games)**
12. 1985 (1,206 games)
13. 1989 (1,137 games)
14. 1988 (1,135 games)
15. 1997 (1,126 games)
16. 1995 (845 games)
17. 1984 (607 games)

18. 1982 (394 games)
19. 1986 (50 games)
20. 1990 (0 games)

Trades That Involved Draft Picks

On July 16, 1997, the Oilers traded Vladimir Vujtek and a 1998 third-round selection (Dimitry Afanasenkov) to the Tampa Bay Lightning for Brantt Myhres and the No. 67 overall pick in the 1998 draft (Alex Henry).

On August 12, 1997, the Oilers traded Jiri Slegr to the Pittsburgh Penguins for a 1998 third-round pick (Brian Gionta).

On March 24, 1998, the Oilers traded Dan McGillis and a 1998 second-round pick (Jason Beckett) to the Philadelphia Flyers for Janne Niinimaa.

On June 27, 1998, the Oilers traded a 1998 third-round pick (previously acquired from Pittsburgh-Brian Gionta) to the New Jersey Devils for the rights to Fredrik Lindquist, the No. 113 overall pick in the 1998 draft (Kristian Antila), and the No. 144 overall pick in the 1998 draft (Oleg Smirnov). Note: Lindqvist would play for the Oilers under the name Fredrik Bremberg.

THE 1999 DRAFT

The Oilers finished second in the new Northwest Division for 1998–99, the team's 33–37–12 record trailing the Colorado Avalanche but clear of the Calgary Flames and Vancouver Canucks.

Edmonton was no match for the Dallas Stars in the playoffs, losing in four straight. Dallas would go on to win the first Stanley Cup in franchise history. There were some good rookies, including two draft picks who enjoyed solid NHL careers:

- Tom Poti: 73 games, 5–16–21

- Sean Brown: 51 games, 0–7–7
- Georges Laraque: 39 games, 3–2–5
- Craig Millar: 24 games, 0–2–2
- Fredrik Lindquist (Bremberg): 8 games, 0–2–2
- Dan Lacouture: 3 games, 0–0–0

Poti had exceptional puck-carrying ability and was a good passer, but coverage issues and a nonphysical style made him something less than a crowd favourite in Edmonton. Laraque, an enforcer, would emerge as one of the most popular Oilers ever with his physical game and ability to hold on to the puck for extended periods.

NO. 13 OVERALL: LW JANI RITA
Jokerit (Liiga)

Rita was ranked No. 5 on the European list from Central Scouting and had good size (6'1", 206 pounds) for a winger. He played with some edge and owned a plus shot.

The worry about Rita on draft day surrounded how much offence he would bring. In his draft year, he played 41 games for Jokerit in Finland's best league but had limited minutes and scored just three goals. In his draft-plus-one season, he increased his goal total to six, but remained a part-time player. Rita stayed an additional season in Finland, scoring 5–10–15 in 50 games. One of his career highlights came at the 2001 World Junior Championships, where Rita scored eight goals in seven games.

He arrived in North America with some questions about his ability to score in pro hockey despite that good shot. In his first AHL season, he scored 25 goals in 76 games, but was unable to increase his scoring prowess and got very little NHL time during his entry deal.

The Oilers dealt Rita to the Pittsburgh Penguins in January 2006. He got a 30-game audition with the Penguins but once again, his offence was found wanting.

He would return to Finland and enjoy a solid career with Jokerit, retiring in 2016.

NO. 36 OVERALL: LD ALEXEI SEMENOV
Sudbury Wolves (OHL)

At 6'6", 210 pounds, Semenov is one of the tallest players ever drafted by Edmonton. A defensive defender with great wingspan but lacking speed, he became one of the better draft picks of this player type chosen during the Fraser era of 1979–2000.

He was ranked No. 75 by Central Scouting on the North American list, so this could be categorized as a "reach" selection. A reach selection involves a team choosing a player out of order. In this case, using all four of Central Scouting's lists (NA goalie, NA skater, Euro goalie, Euro skater), Semenov should have been chosen around No. 100–110 based on ranking.

After his draft, Semenov had two strong seasons in the OHL, including an impressive spike in offence. As he was big and strong, but not a puck mover or exceptional passer, there was little expectation he would be a strong offensive player in the NHL.

In the AHL, he settled in as a big shutdown blue with speed issues, but his wingspan and ability to defend made him a good prospect.

In 2002–03, he made the NHL and played 46 games, and in 2003–04 he improved defensively in 46 games. At that point in his career, it was possible to project Semenov as a No. 5–6 defender who could help at even strength and on the penalty kill for years. He would play 211 NHL games and was still playing defence in the KHL in 2020–21, aged 39.

NO. 41 OVERALL: LW TONY SALMELAINEN
HIFK Helsinki (Liiga)

Salmelainen was Euro No. 13 on Central Scouting's list, so was chosen right in the window of expectation.

A small and skilled winger with better finishing skills than Rita, he played well during his entry deal but at 5'9", 185 pounds, didn't bring elite skill and could not find a regular job in the NHL.

The Oilers gave him a cup of coffee in 2003–04 and after that he couldn't break into the lineup. At the trade deadline in 2006, Edmonton sent him to the Chicago Blackhawks in a deal for Jaroslav Spacek.

He (like Rita with Pittsburgh) would get a full audition in Chicago and land shy of NHL duty. After that, Salmelainen played in Russia and Switzerland before heading back to Finland for a final season in 2013–14.

NO. 81 OVERALL: G ADAM HAUSER
Minnesota (NCAA)

Hauser was drafted by Edmonton at age 19 after his freshman year at Minnesota. He was a starter in his first season (40 games, .876) and got better from there (.909, .902, and .913) through his college career.

He did not sign with Edmonton but played for the Providence Bruins and Manchester (New Hampshire) Monarchs of the AHL, and even got one NHL game in with the Los Angeles Kings. In

Manchester for three seasons (2003–06), Hauser posted outstanding save percentages (.926, .933, and .919) and earned more than just one NHL game, but it never came. He finished in Germany, with his time in Manchester of the AHL and in college representing consistent excellence.

NO. 91 OVERALL: LC MIKE COMRIE
Michigan (NCAA)

The Oilers would have had a lot of local knowledge on Comrie, who lit up the AJHL in Sherwood Park and St. Albert (two bedroom communities near Edmonton) for two seasons before he landed at Michigan.

Comrie was ranked No. 34 on the North American (NA) list from Central Scouting, meaning he should have landed somewhere between No. 45 and 55 overall.

He fell due to size (5'10", 185 pounds) and possessing a pure offensive style. In his time in Michigan, he scored a point per game as a draft-eligible freshman and posted 59 points in 40 games in year two.

Comrie, who had a lot of self-confidence, deemed himself ready for the pros and jumped to the WHL (where he scored at will, 39–40–79 in 37 games) with the intent to gain free agency at the end of the year.

After a long negotiation with new general manager Kevin Lowe (who had taken over from Glen Sather in the spring of 2000), Comrie arrived in the NHL in the final days of 2000 (he played his first NHL game on December 30).

Comrie quickly settled in as a pure skill centre, scoring 22 points in 41 games in his rookie NHL season. In 2001–02, he blossomed with 33 goals and 60 points in 82 games. In year three with Edmonton, he had some injury issues but still managed 20 goals and 51 points in 69 games.

Playing in his hometown was difficult for Comrie, and Lowe had a budget that he planned to follow. Contract negotiations became difficult and the Oilers eventually traded him (there was a deal to Anaheim that fell through followed by a trade to Philadelphia).

Comrie's career was shortened by injury, and he was a one-dimensional player, but few third-round picks by Edmonton have been more productive. He would finish his career with 589 NHL games and 365 points.

NO. 139 OVERALL: RD JONATHAN FAUTEUX
Val d'Or Foreurs (QMJHL)

Fauteux was ranked No. 50 on the NA list for Central Scouting, so had fallen significantly when Edmonton chose him. A right-shot defenceman who had a career year in the season of his draft (59 games, 15–33–48), he was unable to build on it and in fact faded in the season after his draft. He did turn pro with the Hamilton Bulldogs but had little success and was done with pro hockey in 2002.

NO. 171 OVERALL: F CHRIS LEGG
London Nationals (WJBHL)

Legg was ranked No. 182 by Central Scouting (NA), meaning he was unlikely to be drafted based on ranking. Legg flourished in Junior B, but barely moved the needle offensively at Brown University. He played ECHL hockey but was out of the pro game after one season.

NO. 199 OVERALL: LD CHRISTIAN CHARTIER
Saskatoon Blades (WHL)

No. 84 on the Central NA list, Chartier had to wait a long time to get drafted. He had a poor draft season but recovered with two solid seasons in the WHL to complete his junior career after being dealt to the Prince George Cougars.

He did not sign with Edmonton but had a solid run in the AHL with the St. John's Maple Leafs and later in Germany.

NO. 256 OVERALL: LW THOMAS GROSCHL
Leksands (SEL)

A big scoring winger, Groschl scored well in Swedish junior (15–14–29 in 33 games) in the year after he was drafted and came to North America in 2000–01, but did not deliver strong offence in the ECHL (5–11–16 in 59 games), effectively ending his status as an NHL prospect.

1999 Draft Summary
The Oilers drafted a mixed bag of talent in 1999, but there was value in the middle. (Number in parentheses is points per game.)

- Jani Rita (Liiga) age 17: 41 games, 3–2–5 (0.12)
- Alexei Semenov (OHL) age 17: 28 games, 0–3–3 (0.11)
- Tony Salmelainen (Sarja U-20) age 17: 21 games, 13–10–23 (1.1)
- Mike Comrie (NCAA) age 17: 42 games, 19–25–44 (1.05)
- Jonathan Fauteux (QMJHL) age 17: 59 games, 15–33–48 (0.81)
- Chris Legg (WOHL) age 18: 50 games, 36–32–68 (1.36)

- Christian Chartier (WHL) age 17: 62 games, 2–14–16 (0.26)
- Tamas Groschl (Hungary) age 18: 22 games, 9–10–19 (0.86)

Rita played in the same league as Salmelainen in his draft year, posting similar numbers (20 games, 9–13–22), but also spent 41 games playing very little in the top league. Edmonton drafted an intriguing player, but he was poorly developed in Finland.

Comrie was going to be the star of this group—he was 17 and posting more than a point per game in college. Fauteux was an intriguing player based on his draft-day stats.

NHL Career Games Played

Barry Fraser's second-to-last draft as Oilers scouting director saw the first five selections make the NHL, but only one player would enjoy a career of 500-plus games:

1. Mike Comrie: 589
2. Alexei Semenov: 211
3. Tony Salmelainen: 70
4. Jani Rita: 66
5. Adam Hauser: 1

All five men had moments after draft day that implied possible NHL success, and all made it to the world's best league. For multiple reasons, it was not to be.

Here's how the 1999 draft class ranked in terms of total NHL games played:

1. 1979 (4,143 games)
2. 1980 (3,841 games)

3. 1993 (3,025 games)
4. 1981 (2,215 games)
5. 1996 (1,924 games)
6. 1983 (1,810 games)
7. 1991 (1,807 games)
8. 1994 (1,667 games)
9. 1987 (1,602 games)
10. 1992 (1,251 games)
11. 1998 (1,214 games)
12. 1985 (1,206 games)
13. 1989 (1,137 games)
14. 1988 (1,135 games)
15. 1997 (1,126 games)
16. 1999 (937 games)
17. 1995 (845 games)
18. 1984 (607 games)
19. 1982 (394 games)
20. 1986 (50 games)
21. 1990 (0 games)

I established a line in the sand for success in Fraser-era drafts—1,000 games. He missed that mark in 1999.

Trades That Involved Draft Picks

On March 20, 1999, the Oilers traded Bo Mironov, Dean McAmmond, Jonas Elofsson, and a 1999 second-round pick (Dmitri Levinsky) to the Chicago Blackhawks for Ethan Moreau, Dan Cleary, Chad Kilger, Christian Laflamme, and the No. 46 overall selection in the 1999 draft (Alexei Semenov).

On March 20, 1999, the Oilers traded Mats Lindgren and a 1999 eighth-round pick (Radek Martinek) to the New York Islanders for Tommy Salo.

On March 23, 1999, the Oilers traded a 1999 fourth-round pick (Jonathan Zion) and a 2000 second-round pick (Kris Vernarsky) to the Toronto Maple Leafs for Jason Smith.

On June 26, 1999, the NHL awarded Edmonton selection No. 41 (Tony Salmelainen) as a compensatory selection for losing free agent Curtis Joseph in free agency.

On June 26, 1999, the Oilers traded Craig Millar to the Nashville Predators for the No. 91 overall pick (Mike Comrie).

Junior Points per Game

In the final 20 years of this book, we'll spend more time on the math of the draft. I wanted to point out how important offence in junior was as a predictor of success even in the years 1979–99.

Here is a list of every first-round pick by Edmonon who played as a forward and played in one of the CHL leagues (WHL, OHL, or QMJHL). Notice how the junior points per game correlates to future success most of the time.

PLAYER	YEAR	LGE	AGE	PTS/ GAME	NLGP	NHL PTS/ GAME
JASON ARNOTT	1993	OHL	17	1.75	1,244	0.754
JASON BONSIGNORE	1994	OHL	17	1.65	79	0.203
RYAN SMYTH	1994	WHL	17	1.46	1,270	0.663
TYLER WRIGHT	1991	WHL	17	1.29	613	0.243

PLAYER	YEAR	LGE	AGE	PTS/ GAME	NLGP	NHL PTS/ GAME
PETER SOBERIAK	1987	WHL	17	1.10	0	0.000
STEVE KELLY	1995	WHL	17	1.06	149	0.141
SCOTT METCALFE	1985	OHL	17	1.03	19	0.158
KIM ISSEL	1986	WHL	17	1.00	4	0.000
MICHAEL HENRICH	1998	OHL	17	0.95	0	0.000
BOYD DEVEREAUX	1996	OHL	17	0.88	627	0.286
SCOTT ALLISON	1990	WHL	17	0.58	0	0.000

In viewing these numbers, there may be an urge to point out that the great successes (Arnott and Smyth) were top-10 picks. I would draw your attention to Steve Kelly and Boyd Devereaux, also chosen well inside the top 10 overall. It also reiterates that there was no math reason to call out Fraser on Jason Bonsignore's draft day.

Devereaux did play in the NHL for several years, but as a depth forward. Those player types are easily available every year— it's the Arnotts and Smyths NHL teams should be looking for in each draft. As you can see, from the mid-80s through 1993, Edmonton was drafting in the wrong area of the draft pool. Tyler Wright is the exception.

Although there's far more that goes into the making of an NHL defenceman, having some offensive upside is a valuable tool for the next level. Edmonton's pursuit of enforcer types and shutdown defenders in the first round often sent them too far down the draft lists. Here are the numbers from 1979 to 1999 for defencemen:

PLAYER	YEAR	LGE	AGE	PTS/ GAME	NLGP	NHL PTS/ GAME
PAUL COFFEY	1980	OHA	18	1.36	1,409	1.087
KEVIN LOWE	1979	QMJHL	19	1.26	1,254	0.344
SELMAR ODELEIN	1984	WHL	17	0.72	18	0.111
JEFF BEUKEBOOM	1983	OHL	17	0.36	804	0.198
JIM PLAYFAIR	1982	WHL	17	0.24	21	0.286
MATTHIEU DESCOTEAUX	1996	QMJHL	17	0.22	5	0.400
FRANCOIS LEROUX	1988	QMJHL	17	0.19	249	0.092
JASON SOULES	1989	OHL	17	0.19	0	0.000

Coffey and Lowe were big successes. Both were older but offered a range of skills. Odelein was injured but had a nice résumé; Beukeboom had success. Playfair's career was also derailed by injury. Fraser needed to be drafting players, even defencemen, who brought a little more offence than did Leroux and Soules.

THE 2000 DRAFT

The 1999–2000 season saw several changes in the organization. Ron Low, who had successfully coached the Oilers to three straight playoff appearances, could not reach a contract agreement with general manager Glen Sather.

Kevin Lowe, the team's first-ever draft pick, stepped in to coach the team and brought the 1999–2000 Oilers in with a second-place finish in the Northwest Division, although the team would lose again in the first round of the playoffs.

In the offseason, there was more change, as Sather left on June 9, 2000. He was general manager for five Stanley Cup wins, head coach in four of them. He created the template for the fast and exciting teams, contributed to the development of several of the best players to play the game, and left a legacy of excellence his predecessors have been unable to continue.

Rookies on the 1999–2000 team:

- Paul Comrie: 15 games, 1–2–3
- Dan Lacouture: 5 games, 0–0–0
- Mike Minard: 1 game, 3.00 goals-against average, .917 save percentage

Only Minard was an Oilers draft pick. Among the top 10 scorers on the team, only Ryan Smyth and Tom Poti were draft picks.

NO. 17 OVERALL: LW ALEXEI MIKHNOV
Yaroslavl Torpedo (Russia 3)

Mikhnov was a big winger who could play both sides and had significant scoring potential. At 6'5", 218 pounds, and slow afoot, there were some concerns about his NHL potential on draft day. Aside from the speed issue, he was not an eager participant in the defensive side of the game.

It took forever for Edmonton to get him to North America (2006–07) and once he was there, his eyesight was discovered to be an issue. He spent one year in North America, played two games, and then returned to Russia, where he enjoyed a strong career in the top Russian league through 2018–19. This was not a strong pick, and he was a reach selection (at No. 19 on the European Central Scouting list, he would have been expected to go in the middle-to-late second round).

Mikhnov would be Barry Fraser's last first-round selection, as he finished with a string of six forwards (Steve Kelly, Boyd Devereaux, Michel Riesen, Michael Henrich, Jani Rita, Alexei Mikhnov) who did not enjoy NHL careers on a skill line. In fact, only Devereaux would spend significant time in the league.

NO. 35 OVERALL: LW BRAD WINCHESTER
Wisconsin (NCAA)

Another huge winger, Winchester continued the Fraser-era pursuit of big and skilled players.

Winchester ranked No. 36 on the North American Central Scouting list, meaning he was a slight reach selection.

Edmonton looked at Winchester as a possible power forward, but he didn't score enough in the USHL or college to suggest he would cover that bet. Despite size, he had trouble in a checking role because he didn't use his size effectively.

In Winchester's rookie pro season (2003–04), he scored 13 goals and 19 points in 65 games with the Toronto Roadrunners

(AHL). He increased those totals in 2004–05, going 22–18–40 in 76 games.

In 2005–06, he got a cup of coffee and scored a big goal in the Stanley Cup playoffs in spring 2006. He scored the third goal in a 4–2 win in Game 2 of the series against the Detroit Red Wings.

The next season he was a full-time Oilers player, scoring 4–5–9 in 59 games. Head coach Craig MacTavish famously said, "He needs a second opinion," and general manager Kevin Lowe set him free after the 2006–07 campaign.

Winchester landed with the Dallas Stars, then the St. Louis Blues, and finally the Anaheim Ducks. He played in 390 NHL games, never impacting the game enough offensively to find a home in the world's best league.

NO. 83 OVERALL: LD ALEXANDER LJOBIMOV
Samara CSK (Russia)

Ranked No. 28 in Central Scouting's European listings for 2000, he was a slight bargain choice by the time the Oilers chose him. Ljobimov was 20 on draft day, came over for one season (played with the wonderfully named Odessa Jackalopes of the ECHL), and returned to Russia, where he played until 2007.

Edmonton liked him because of his performance at the World Junior Championships. It didn't work out and is an example of why short tournaments are not a good barometer of overall ability and should be regarded with suspicion.

NO. 113 OVERALL: LC LOU DICKENSON
Mississauga Ice Dogs (OHL)

There was a lot to like on draft day about Dickenson, who had an August 2002 birthday, making him one of the youngest players in the draft. He was fast and skilled and had some size.

He also fell a lot from his final Central Scouting rank (No. 32), meaning teams passed on him multiple times when he should have been in draft range. Sometimes picks that fall work out well, but Dickenson did not spike as a player in the two years after his draft. Edmonton did not sign him, but he had a long career outside the NHL, retiring in 2017. He was one of the players who starred in the television show *Making the Cut*, focusing on players with talent who needed exposure to land pro contracts.

NO. 152 OVERALL: LD PAUL FLACHE
Brampton Bitallion (OHL)

A gigantic (6'6", 220 pounds) defenceman who played the enforcer role for Brampton in his draft year, Flache would not sign with Edmonton by 2002, although they liked his work ethic and size. Flache re-entered and was chosen by the Atlanta Thrashers. He would not play in the NHL.

NO. 184 OVERALL: RW SHAUN NORRIE
Calgary Hitmen (WHL)

Norrie was a big, rugged winger who was shy offensively on his draft day. His output in his draft year (12–13–25 in 67 games) improved in his draft-plus-one season (24–24–48 in 72), but his size (6'3", 193 pounds) and penalty minutes (106 in 2000–01) were the drawing card. Norrie did not sign with Edmonton and landed at the University of Lethbridge after his junior career ended. He had an edge to his game but couldn't move the game offensively.

NO. 211 OVERALL: C JOE CULLEN
Colorado College (NCAA)

Cullen was an awkward skater but had offensive skill, so the Oilers took a chance at a point in the draft when everyone is a long shot. Cullen had a strong senior year (20–15–35 in 42 games) with Colorado College and turned pro with some promise.

His first AHL season (14–16–30 in 69 games for the Toronto Roadrunners in 2003–04) was his best in pro, but he could not sustain success. He stayed in the AHL until the middle of the decade and then played several seasons in Italy.

NO. 215 OVERALL: C MATTHEW LOMBARDI
Victoriaville Tigres (QMJHL)

There are just a few examples of late-round picks not signing with the Oilers and then emerging as quality NHL players. Lombardi is one of them.

Lombardi's numbers in his draft year weren't special (65 games, 18–26–44), but he blossomed in the two years that followed. That's not unusual, as players near age 20 become more dominant in junior. However, Lombardi had a massive final season (130 points in 66 games) and didn't resemble a seventh-round selection by the time player, agent, and team began to negotiate a contract. Lombardi had a fantastic Memorial Cup, ending the tournament as the leading scorer. Edmonton didn't sign him, and the Calgary Flames took advantage.

NO. 247 OVERALL: LD JASON PLATT
Omaha Lancers (USHL)

The Oilers liked Platt for his passing ability and work ethic, but he had no standout physical skills. He didn't post much offence at Providence College and played just a depth role in the AHL after Edmonton signed him. He played until 2008 in various North American leagues.

NO. 274 OVERALL: RW EVGENY MURATOV
Neftekhimik (RSL)

Muratov was a small skill winger who had talent with the puck but lacked NHL speed. He would enjoy a 10-year career in the top Russian league.

2000 Draft Summary
The final Barry Fraser draft was not a success. Kevin Prendergast would take over for the 2001 season. (Number in parentheses is points per game.)

- Alexei Mikhnov (Rus3) age 17: 40 games, 22–13–35 (0.88)
- Brad Winchester (NCAA) age 18: 33 games, 9–9–18 (0.55)
- Alexander Ljubimov (RSL) age 19: 18 games, 0–1–1 (0.06)
- Lou Dickenson (OHL) age 17: 66 games, 21–25–46 (0.70)
- Paul Flache (OHL) age 17: 54 games, 1–0–1 (0.02)
- Shaun Norrie (WHL) age 17: 67 games, 12–13–25 (0.37)

- Joe Cullen (NCAA) age 18: 29 games, 4–6–10 (0.34)
- Matthew Lombardi (QMJHL) age 17: 65 games, 18–26–44 (0.68)
- Jason Platt (USHL) age 18: 49 games, 1–6–7 (0.14)
- Evgeny Muratov (RSL) age 18: 37 games, 11–9–20 (0.54)

None of the selections in Fraser's final draft stood out offensively in his draft season. Mikhnov scored well, but in a league far down the Russian depth chart. Dickenson and Lombardi were solid CHL scorers but were not standouts in their draft years.

NHL Career Games Played

The final names who would make the NHL from a Fraser draft:
1. Matt Lombardi: 536
2. Brad Winchester: 390
3. Alexei Mikhnov: 2

Only Winchester would contribute to the Oilers in any meaningful way. Lombardi, on the other hand, must be held as an extreme value pick, and the scouts deserve credit no matter what happened with the contract negotiations.

Here's how the 2000 draft class ranked in terms of total NHL games played:
1. 1979 (4,143 games)
2. 1980 (3,841 games)
3. 1993 (3,025 games)
4. 1981 (2,215 games)
5. 1996 (1,924 games)
6. 1983 (1,810 games)
7. 1991 (1,807 games)

8. 1994 (1,667 games)
9. 1987 (1,602 games)
10. 1992 (1,251 games)
11. 1998 (1,214 games)
12. 1985 (1,206 games)
13. 1989 (1,137 games)
14. 1988 (1,135 games)
15. 1997 (1,126 games)
16. 1999 (937 games)
17. **2000 (928 games)**
18. 1995 (845 games)
19. 1984 (607 games)
20. 1982 (394 games)
21. 1986 (50 games)
22. 1990 (0 games)

I established the 1,000-game line in the sand for Fraser, and he missed in his two final seasons.

Seven of 22 drafts, or 32 percent, are considered failures by the 1,000-game metric. Four of 22, or 18 percent, brought 2,000-plus games to the NHL and should be viewed as elite drafts. Fraser's curse was that three of the first four drafts were elite and he spent a decade chasing another (1993) and could not find it.

Trades That Involved Draft Picks

On March 11, 1999, the Oilers traded Mikhail Shtalenkov to the Phoenix Coyotes for a fifth-round pick (Matt Koalska).

On March 23, 1999, the Oilers traded a 1999 fourth-round pick (Jonathan Zion) and a 2000 second-round pick (Kris Vernarsky) to the Toronto Maple Leafs for Jason Smith.

On June 12, 2000, the Oilers traded a fifth-round pick (previously a Coyotes selection, which became Matt Koalska) to the Nashville Predators for Patrick Cote. This was Kevin Lowe's first trade, and it was made so Edmonton would have enough qualifying players available for the coming expansion draft.

On June 24, 2000, the Oilers traded Roman Hamrlik to the New York Islanders for Eric Brewer, Josh Green, and the No. 35 overall pick in the 2000 draft (Brad Winchester).

On June 25, 2000, the NHL awarded Edmonton a compensatory selection for losing free agent Marty McSorley (No. 211 overall, Joe Cullen).

On June 25, 2000, the NHL awarded Edmonton a compensatory selection for losing free agent Bob Essensa (No. 274 overall, Evgeny Muratov).

On June 25, 2000, the Oilers traded a 2000 ninth-round pick (Andreas Lindstrom) to the Boston Bruins for a 2001 ninth-round pick.

EVALUATION
BARRY FRASER, SCOUTING
DIRECTOR 1979-2000

In his fascinating book *The Road to Hockeytown*, Jimmy Devellano discusses the goal of a scouting director and his staff: "We're trying to determine if the player can get to the next level, that's the real job. Most people can sit and watch a game and tell you who the best player on the ice is, but the good scout will be able to judge whether or not a player can go a step or two higher. We in the hockey business call it projecting."

SUCCESS IN THE FIRST 30 SELECTIONS OF EACH DRAFT

Fraser chose 27 players in the top 30 of the draft. The first three (Kevin Lowe, Paul Coffey, Grant Fuhr) are now in the Hockey Hall of Fame. Jeff Beukeboom, Martin Rucinsky, Jason Arnott, and Ryan Smyth were other first-round picks who delivered productive careers. In spite of many years of poor production, specifically 1984–1990, the overall draft record in the first round is impressive. Nine men (34.6 percent) played 500-plus NHL games.

SUCCESS IN THE FIRST 100 SELECTIONS OF EACH DRAFT

While Fraser was chief scout, Edmonton chose 67 players between Nos. 31 and 100 in the draft. Mark Messier, Glenn Anderson, and Jari Kurri all made the HHOF and represent breathtaking draft value. The club also drafted several men who would be productive for multiple seasons between selections 31 and 100, including Walt Poddubny, Esa Tikkanen, Geoff Smith, Josef Beranek, Kirk Maltby, Georges Laraque, David Vyborny, Tom Poti, Shawn Horcoff, and Mike Comrie. A total of 12 men (16.9 percent) played 500-plus NHL games.

SUCCESS AFTER THE FIRST 100 SELECTIONS OF EACH DRAFT

There were 143 players chosen at pick No. 100 or later on Fraser's watch. Andy Moog, Steve Smith, Todd Ewen, Kelly Buchberger, Shaun Van Allen, Shjon Podein, Miro Satan, Fernando Pisani, Jason Chimera, and Matthew Lombardi all had productive careers. Nine players (6.5 percent) played 500-plus NHL games.

SUCCESS IN WHAT DEVELLANO CALLS "PROJECTING"

Messier is the king of projection. He scored one goal in the WHA in the year Edmonton drafted him. Andy Moog, Esa Tikkanen, Shawn Horcoff, and many others would qualify. It's difficult to compare Fraser to others because he was in the position a long time, but it's clear that many draft picks blossomed into quality players in the years following the draft.

SUCCESS IN ADDRESSING TEAM NEEDS

The early drafts would have taken any team on a Stanley Cup run. There's nothing but praise due to Fraser and his staff in the first five years. However, the pursuit of complementary players during the period when the Oilers should have been readying themselves for turnover (brought on by success and then increased salary) was poor. That's on general manager Glen Sather but also on the scouting staff. The 1982 draft was a harbinger for the decade to follow, and beginning in 1985 the forwards chosen in the first round were shy offensively almost without exception through 1993.

BEST FIRST-ROUND PICK

Paul Coffey was an integral part of the Oilers' best teams and an impact player in an Oilers uniform. Grant Fuhr would also be a worthy name here, for the same reasons.

LEAST SUCCESSFUL FIRST-ROUND PICK

Jason Bonsignore was the No. 4 overall pick in the 1994 draft and played in 79 NHL games for his career. It's important to note that Bonsignore's numbers on draft day suggested a successful NHL player.

BEST PICK AFTER THE FIRST ROUND

Mark Messier. The Oilers enjoyed some great picks later on in the year, such as Glenn Anderson, Miro Satan, and Esa Tikkanen, but Messier is the king.

WHAT STYLE DID FRASER EMPLOY?

There's plenty of evidence to suggest Fraser was less than democratic in compiling the final draft list. A famous example is Tomas Kaberle, an obscure yet talented prospect Oilers scouts Chris McCarthy and Kent Nilsson identified early in his draft year. As Guy Flaming reported in Hockey's Future, McCarthy had Kaberle in his first round and couldn't get Fraser to list him. The Toronto Maple Leafs drafted Kaberle and enjoyed great success with the player.

WHAT PLAYER TYPE DID FRASER LOOK FOR AT THE DRAFT?

In the August 10, 1979, edition of the *Edmonton Journal*, Fraser told columnist Terry Jones about the team's priorities:

"Most scouts believe the thing is skating. I don't believe that. The big thing to me is the pumper inside his chest. Desire. If you watch a kid enough in junior, you know if he comes to play every day. That's the kind of player we're looking for before we look at anything else."

Fraser did draft the fiercest player of his generation (Messier), a fearless speed demon (Anderson), and a tough-as-nails defenceman (Lowe) the same weekend he talked about "the pumper" with Jones. They were also very talented with the puck.

There's plenty of evidence the Oilers' priorities changed. As I've woven through this book, there were years when Fraser and his scouts were looking for the next Dave Hunter (checking winger) over speed, skill, and other elements important to success. That's "the pumper" scouting in action.

In 1995, 16 years after the quote about the "pumper in the chest," Edmonton chose speed-demon winger Steve Kelly over heart-and-soul winger Shane Doan at the draft (making its only appearance in Edmonton).

Legendary media icon John Short asked Fraser at the time about the gap between Kelly and Doan, and Fraser indicated it was razor-thin. That decision—that selection—flies in the face of the 1979 quote.

Fraser was a scouting director for such a long time, and the priorities of the organization changed over those 20-plus seasons.

WAS FRASER THE BEST SCOUTING DIRECTOR IN NHL HISTORY?

It's impossible to know for certain, but Fraser would be in the conversation for the best of all time. Other candidates during the universal draft (1969-plus) era include Del Wilson

(Montreal Canadiens), Jim Devallano (New York Islanders), Scott Bradley (Boston Bruins), and Ken Holland (Detroit Red Wings). Beyond that, there are brilliant scouts such as Gerry Ehman (Islanders), Gerry Melynk (Philadelphia Flyers), Håkan Andersson (Detroit Red Wings), and others who rarely get recognition but were fantastic team builders at the grassroots level.

Fraser's work from 1979 to 1981 brought six Hall of Fame players to the Oilers. Here are the names by games played and by decade while Fraser served as the Oilers' chief scout (700-plus games):

1979–88

1. Mark Messier: 1,756
2. Paul Coffey: 1,409
3. Kevin Lowe: 1,254
4. Jari Kurri: 1,251
5. Kelly Buchberger: 1,182
6. Glenn Anderson: 1,129
7. Esa Tikkanen: 877
8. Grant Fuhr: 868
9. Steve Smith: 804
10. Jeff Beukeboom: 804
11. Shaun Van Allen: 794
12. Andy Moog: 713

1989–98

13. Ryan Smyth: 1,270
14. Jason Arnott: 1,244
15. Jason Chimera: 1,107
16. Kirk Maltby: 1,072
17. Miroslav Satan: 1,050
18. Shawn Horcoff: 1,008
19. Martin Rucinsky: 961
20. Tom Poti: 824

THE BARRY FRASER ALL-STAR TEAM

Over 22 drafts, Fraser and his scouting staff procured a lot of talent for the Oilers. Including all draft picks, here is the Barry Fraser All-Star Team:

- Goalie: Grant Fuhr
- Defenceman: Paul Coffey
- Defenceman: Kevin Lowe
- Centre: Mark Messier
- Left Wing: Glenn Anderson
- Right Wing: Jari Kurri

The lesson of Barry Fraser's success is also woven into his later failure. NHL teams should pursue skill with every selection. Checkers and role players are more plentiful and can be found as mature assets via trade and free agency. In fact, many junior scorers develop into pro checkers, but junior checkers can't score enough to remain in the game.

In the 1979, 1980, and 1981 drafts, Fraser and his scouts took pure skill players such as Mark Messier (dominant in his league in a small sample), Glenn Anderson, and Jari Kurri. Defenceman Paul Coffey had supreme puck skills.

In the first rounds of the 1982 (Jim Playfair) and 1983 (Jeff Beukeboom) drafts, the organization drafted defensive defencemen.

Instead of using Coffey as the example of success, Fraser began drafting defence-first options. This may have been due to the extreme number of generational forward talents on the big club (Wayne Gretzky plus Kurri, Messier, and Anderson), but the nature of sports is those names won't be together forever—certainly not with free agency and the exploding salaries of the 1980s.

I've identified the first round in 1985 as the point when the Oilers as an organization turned their back on the success forged by the Fraser staff from 1979 to 1981.

The reason I focused on 1985 was first-round selection Scott Metcalfe, chosen No. 20 overall. After that draft, Fraser said they chose him because "he's something like Dave Hunter was coming out of junior."

The Fraser brilliance was Messier, Anderson, Kurri, and Coffey, and the organization chose to pursue players who most resembled Hunter in the first round.

The rest of the NHL caught up and passed Edmonton before the 1990 draft shutout.

The last truly skilled pick of the golden era of Fraser drafting was Esa Tikkanen (No. 80 in 1983) and the last truly skilled first-rounder (before Jason Arnott in 1993) was Paul Coffey in 1980.

The Barry Fraser era had enormous highs followed by a long coda of disappointment.

His career is difficult to sum up in a paragraph, but the goal of a scout is to provide great talent to his team. The pieces provided by Fraser sent the Oilers to five Stanley Cup victories. He delivered fantastic talent; that's the job, and his résumé is among the best in the history of the game.

8

A BRAND-NEW DAY: KEVIN PRENDERGAST REPLACES A LEGEND

THE 2001 DRAFT

KEVIN PRENDERGAST TOOK over as scouting director after Barry Fraser's 22-year run in the role. That's a lot of history to see walk out the door, but fans believed it could serve as a breath of fresh air, a renewal for the scouts.

Prendergast told Guy Flaming of Hockey's Future, "Our staff works as a team and whomever the player is that we take we're taking him as a team and there might be three or four scouts who don't like the player but the other nine guys on staff do like him."

Kevin Lowe hired Craig MacTavish as his coach, and MacT guided his first Oilers club to 39 wins and 93 points and a first-round exit. The Oilers were competitive in these years, but big-market teams were grabbing the best talent (Curtis Joseph, Doug Weight, Bill Guerin) and the Oilers weren't drafting enough of their own solutions.

Ryan Smyth, Tom Poti, and Georges Laraque were the most productive homegrown talents. The system did provide some productive newcomers. Rookies on the 2000–01 team:

- Mike Comrie: 41 games, 8–14–22
- Shawn Horcoff: 49 games, 9–7–16
- Domenic Pittis: 47 games, 4–5–9
- Dan Lacouture: 37 games, 2–4–6
- Brian Swanson: 16 games, 1–1–2
- Michel Riesen: 12 games, 0–1–1
- Jason Chimera: 1 game, 0–0–0
- Chris Hajt: 1 game, 0–0–0

In April 2001, Edmonton won a fairly large bidding war for free agent Ty Conklin. He would have a star-crossed career with Edmonton but played 215 games in the NHL.

In July 2001, Edmonton signed QMJHL undrafted free agent Marc-Andre Bergeron. He was an impressive offensive defence-man with defensive chaos in his game, but like Conklin, he would go on to a substantial NHL career.

PROSPECT SPOTLIGHT
NO. 13 OVERALL: RW ALES HEMSKY, HULL OLYMPIQUES (QMJHL)

Legend has it every time Prendergast went to see Hemsky he had a poor game, but a draft year that included 100 points in 68 games suggested Edmonton was dealing in high-octane offence.

He played one more (brilliant) year in the QMJHL before turning pro and going directly to the NHL at age 19.

Scouting report and legacy: Hemsky arrived in the NHL with ridiculous skill and a tendency to put himself into difficult situations and to pay the price physically. He was most often the best player on his line and was fantastic in the spring and summer of 2006. Fans would call the sports stations and confess Hemsky was the biggest reason to attend Oilers games during the era, especially after 2006.

Hemsky was fast and elusive; he could stickhandle through every opponent and then do it again on the way back to centre—and he did it a few times. His vision and passing were electric, and he could post numbers at even strength and on the power play. Per 82 games with the Oilers, he averaged 18–42–60.

His peak seasons were age 22–25, and after that Hemsky had a series of injuries that took their toll. He remained productive but wasn't available every game.

When Jordan Eberle arrived, Hemsky remained the more productive right winger in year one, but Eberle had an enormous second year and at that point the die seemed cast. It was clear a youth movement was coming and eventually he was dealt.

Hemsky was a key player for Edmonton in the run to the 2006 Stanley Cup and one of the most entertaining players to ever play for the team—a home run for the scouts.

The lesson of Fraser's 1985–2000 period—draft skill in the first round—was adhered to by Prendergast in his first draft.

NO. 43 OVERALL: LD DOUG LYNCH
Red Deer Rebels (WHL)

Lynch was a big defenceman, similar to those in the Fraser era, but he could move the puck, had a plus shot, and used his wingspan (6'3", 214 pounds) effectively on defence.

Lynch had a strong pro debut with the AHL Toronto Roadrunners (74 games, 11–25–36), and he was named to the AHL All-rookie team for 2003–04. He also played in two NHL games.

Lynch hurt his wrist the following year and was dealt to the St. Louis Blues in the blockbuster Chris Pronger trade coming out of the lockout in 2005. The surgery to fix his wrist left him a completely different player, and his career path would not take him to the NHL.

NO. 52 OVERALL: LC EDDIE CARON
Phillips-Exeter Academy (USHS, New Hampshire)

Caron was a high-scoring high school player (30–20–50 in 17 games) when the Oilers chose him in the second round of the 2001 draft. He had size (6'2", 214 pounds) and was ranked No. 29 on the North American list of Central Scouting (he was falling a little in the draft when he was chosen).

At the University of New Hampshire, he had a quiet freshman year (6–7–13). He transferred to Yale to play with friend Chris Higgins, but Higgins turned pro and Caron posted another down season at UNH. A quick pro career spent in Greenville left player and organization disappointed.

Right winger Ales Hemsky, drafted No. 13 overall in 2001, was a key player for Edmonton in the run to the 2006 Stanley Cup and a home run for the scouting staff. *(AP Photo/David Zalubowski)*

NO. 84 OVERALL: LD KENNY SMITH
Harvard (NCAA)

Oilers scouts had been tracking Smith back to his USHL days and chose him earlier than Central Scouting's list (No. 74 NA) implied he should go. He was a two-way defender and a little older (turned 20 in December 2001), but he would not push for an NHL job during his pro career.

NO. 133 OVERALL: G JUSSI MARKKANEN
Tappara Tampere (Liiga)

Although he was 26 on draft day, Markkanen would go on to become one of the more successful goalies drafted by Edmonton. A small tweak in drafting style saw the Prendergast scouts select older Europeans instead of big defencemen and enforcers from the CHL. Markkanen played well for the Oilers (and briefly, the Rangers) and was valiant in the 2006 playoffs when Dwayne Roloson was injured. He would play in 128 NHL games.

NO. 154 OVERALL: RW JAKE BRENK
Breck High School (USHS, Minnesota)

Brenk had NHL size (6'2", 196 pounds) and plus speed, but his offence was the worry. He spent four years at Minnesota State-Mankato and was unable to deliver enough offence to warrant serious consideration as a pro prospect. His best college season was his senior year (6–13–19 in 33 games). Brenk spent some time in the low minors but was never a serious threat to make the NHL—until he decided to become a referee.

NO. 185 OVERALL: RD MICHAEL SVENSK
Vastra Frolunda (Sweden Jr.)

A physical defenceman who had good size (6'3", 214 pounds), he reached his career peak with 17 games in the SEL (top Swedish league) in 2002–03. He didn't come to North America, as the Oilers had several better options.

NO. 215 OVERALL: LW DAN BAUM
Prince George Cougars (WHL)

A physical winger who was effective in the role of "pest," Baum wasn't a big player (6'1", 194 pounds), but he never backed down. His career was derailed by injuries (headaches, illness), peaking with 85 AHL games.

NO. 248 OVERALL: LD KARL HAAKANA
Jokerit Helsinki (Liiga)

One of the tweaks from the Sather/Fraser draft era to the Lowe/Prendergast group, at least in year one, was the procurement of veteran European players like Markkanen and Haakana. He was 28 at the time of the draft and played in the NHL for the Oilers in 2002–03. He was a bridge to younger players in the system, playing just 13 games with Edmonton.

NO. 272 OVERALL: RD ALES PISA
Pardubice (Czech)

Pisa was younger than Haakana (24 on draft day) and a better skater. He could move the puck effectively and was pretty much a regular (48 games) in Edmonton during 2002–03, before being sent to the New York Rangers at the deadline. Between Pisa and

Haakana, the Oilers did build a bridge to the future, however slight. The picks were different from the Fraser era and had the effect of getting some value for late picks as opposed to buying a lottery ticket. It was a useful, if limited strategy.

NO. 278 OVERALL: LW SHAY STEPHENSON
Red Deer Rebels (WHL)

The final Oilers pick in 2001 played two games in the NHL, although not in Edmonton. He was a big-energy winger with some skill and was noticeable at the 2001 Memorial Cup, so Edmonton took him. He did not sign with the Oilers and re-entered the draft. Carolina picked him but he didn't play for them either. Stephenson would sign as a free agent with the Los Angeles Kings and get in to two games with them in 2006–07.

2001 Draft Summary

Kevin Prendergast had a successful first draft, legend has it mostly because he listened to his scouts. Prendergast flew in to watch Hemsky several times, but he never impressed. Oilers scouts swore by the young Czech and Edmonton benefitted in a big way.

There is no evidence the club was listening to what the math told it in 2001, but the numbers were fascinating. (Number in parentheses is points per game.)

- Ales Hemsky (QMJHL) age 17: 68 games, 36–64–100 (1.47)
- Doug Lynch (WHL) age 17: 72 games, 12–37–49 (0.68)
- Ed Caron (USHS) age 18: 17 games, 30–20–50 (2.94)
- Kenny Smith (NCAA) age 18: 21 games, 0–2–2 (0.10)
- Jussi Markkanen (Liiga) age 25: 52 games, 2.09 goals-against average, .923 save percentage

- Jake Brenk (USHS) age 18: numbers are unavailable
- Mikael Svensk (SuperElite U-20) age 17: 15 games, 1–0–1 (0.07)
- Dan Baum (WHL) age 17: 59 games, 9–14–23 (0.39)
- Kari Haakana (Liiga) age 26: 52 games, 2–8–10 (0.19)
- Ales Pisa (Czech) age 23: 47 games, 10–13–23 (0.49)
- Shay Stephenson (WHL) age 18: 44 games, 1–4–5 (0.11)

The Hemsky pick is a perfect reflection of what happens when scouting and math agree. The brilliant Czech winger was a quality first selection by Prendergast. Lynch was injured in his first AHL year but was also a strong math pick. Later, the Stephenson pick was a worthy "draft and follow" selection, as his very late birth date barely made him eligible for selection, in 2001.

NHL Career Games Played

1. Ales Hemsky: 845
2. Jussi Markkanen: 128
3. Ales Pisa: 53
4. Kari Haakana: 13
5. Doug Lynch: 2
6. Shay Stephenson: 2

Here's how the 2001 draft class compares to the preceding decade in terms of total NHL games played:

1. 1993 (3,025 games)
2. 1996 (1,924 games)
3. 1994 (1,667 games)
4. 1992 (1,251 games)
5. 1998 (1,214 games)

6. 1997 (1,126 games)
7. **2001 (1,043 games)**
8. 1999 (937 games)
9. 2000 (928 games)
10. 1995 (845 games)

The first two drafts of the 2000s were similar, but the key difference was Hemsky. His presence represented a key piece of the next Stanley Cup Final team in Edmonton.

Trades That Involved Draft Picks

On February 4, 2000, the Oilers traded a fourth-round pick in the 2000 draft (Brandon Rogers) to the Washington Capitals for Alexandre Volchkov. This was a Glen Sather deal, one of his last.

On June 25, 2000, the Oilers traded a 2000 ninth-round pick (Andreas Lindstrom) to the Boston Bruins for a 2001 ninth-round pick, No. 272 overall (Ales Pisa).

On November 15, 2000, the Oilers traded Bill Guerin and a first-round pick in 2001 (Shaone Morrisonn) for Anson Carter, the No. 13 overall pick (Ales Hemsky), and the No. 43 overall pick (Doug Lynch). Note: the flip of first-round selections came at the Oilers' option and allowed the team to select Hemsky.

On June 24, 2001, the NHL awarded the Oilers a compensatory selection in exchange for the loss of free agent German Titov. Pick No. 133 was used on Jussi Markkanen.

THE 2002 DRAFT

The Edmonton Oilers missed the playoffs in 2001–02, but coach Craig MacTavish brought his team in at over 90 points and boasting a plus-23 goal differential.

What's more, the team's draft picks were once again having an impact, with Mike Comrie leading the team in scoring and Ryan Smyth playing a big part in the team's success.

It was not a big year for Oilers rookies making their NHL debut:

- Brian Swanson: 8 games, 1–1–2
- Jason Chimera: 3 games, 1–0–1
- Ales Pisa: 2 games, 0–0–0
- Jani Rita: 1 game, 0–0–0
- Ty Conklin: 4 games, 1.63 goals-against average, .939 save percentage

Chimera would have a long career as a middle-six forward, while Conklin would play for a decade in the NHL.

In May 2002, the Oilers signed centre Mike Bishai as an undrafted free agent. He had delivered solid two-way play at Western Michigan University. He would play 14 games with the Oilers in 2003–04.

In the spring of 2002, Edmonton signed forward J.J. Hunter, nephew of the great Canadian skier Jim Hunter. He had some raw talent, and the Oilers invested in him, but he finished shy of the NHL. Hunter and his brothers later reached fame as musical group the Hunter Brothers.

NO. 15 OVERALL: LC JESSE NIINIMAKI
Ilves Tampere (Liiga)

Niinimaki has become a legendary selection through no fault of his own. Heavily scouted by Euro scouts Kent Nilsson and Frank Musil, the Oilers liked his size (6'2", 196 pounds) and gritty style.

Prendergast suggested that Edmonton rated him the top centre in the draft, which sent alarm bells throughout the fan base. Niinimaki was ranked No. 50 on the European Central Scouting list, so a typical landing spot would be No. 125–150 overall.

He would play just 24 games in North America, with injuries derailing any hope of an NHL career.

There was never a chance for the player to cover the bet, and that's on the scouts every time. If a team is going that far off the board, the scouts better be right.

NO. 31 OVERALL: G JEFF DROUIN-DESLAURIERS
Chicoutimi Sagueneens (QMJHL)

Deslauriers had a promising draft year, posting a .900 save percentage in the high-flying QMJHL. At 6'4", 203 pounds, he was the modern prototype for an NHL goalie—big with quickness.

Deslauriers turned pro during a period when Edmonton's ownership (a many-pronged group called the EIG) was cutting corners. So Deslauriers never stayed in one spot during his four AHL seasons, playing for the Edmonton Roadrunners, Hamilton Bulldogs, Wilkes-Barre/Scranton Penguins, and Springfield Falcons. During some of those seasons, he was "loaned" to another organization, as the Oilers didn't have a minor league team.

It's difficult to put an accurate number on how much his career trajectory was negatively affected, but he struggled in the first two years before straightening things out in Wilkes-Barre/Scranton.

As an NHL goalie, Deslauriers showed flashes of brilliance but in 62 NHL games posted a .901 save percentage.

NO. 36 OVERALL: RC JARRET STOLL
Kootenay Ice (WHL)

Stoll was a draft re-entry, having been chosen by the Calgary Flames in 2000 but re-entering the draft in 2000. Stoll brought a gritty style and two-way ability to the centre position and was closer to NHL-ready based on his being two years older than most of the other prospects drafted in 2002.

He delivered impressive offence, which included firing shots from the point on the power play and playmaking ability. He was a rugged player and in his five Edmonton seasons averaged 17–30–47, while peaking at 68 points during the magical 2005–06 season.

The Oilers dealt him in a big trade with the Los Angeles Kings for impact defenceman Lubomir Visnovsky, a trade that led to Stoll winning two Stanley Cups on the West Coast.

NO. 44 OVERALL: RD MATT GREENE
Green Bay Gamblers (USHL)

Greene was 6'3", 229 pounds, and a nasty bit of business who patrolled NHL blue lines for 615 games.

Greene went to North Dakota for three years but left before his senior season, partly because his physical style was a better fit for pro hockey. He played just three seasons with Edmonton. Greene continued the team tradition of having a regular player who could also serve as an enforcer.

Greene was traded to the Los Angeles Kings in the same deal as Stoll and was part of Stanley Cup–winning teams in 2012 and 2014.

NO. 79 OVERALL: LW BROCK RADUNSKE
Michigan State University (NCAA)

Another forward with size (6'4", 200 pounds) Radunske posted pedestrian numbers at Michigan State and played in just 28 games in the AHL after he turned pro. He would head to Europe (Germany) before finding a hockey home in Asia, where he played until 2018. His career highlight came representing South Korea at the Olympic Games in 2018.

NO. 106 OVERALL: LD IVAN KOLTSOV
Cherepovets (Russia Jr.)

Koltsov had good size (6'3", 190 pounds) but didn't bring a lot of offence. Two years after he was drafted, Koltsov was playing in the same league, and instead of moving up the system in Russia he landed in Belarus. He came back to Russia in 2004 and played in Russia's second league but did not flourish. He did not sign with the Oilers.

NO. 111 OVERALL: LC JONAS ALMTORP
MoDo (Sweden Jr.)

Almtorp had a lot of good things on his résumé, including size, speed, and two-way acumen. Almtorp scored well in junior, but the moment he reached SHL (the top Swedish league) the offence ran dry, and he could never recover in the period when Edmonton considered him a prospect. In 2005–06, when he was 21, Almtorp finally showed an offensive pulse in the SHL, and that inspired a trip to North America for the 2007–08 season. Playing for the Springfield Falcons of the AHL, he scored just 2–2–4 in 37 games. He also spent time that season in the ECHL (7–10–17 in 27 games) but it wasn't enough to warrant another year. Beginning in 2008–09 and running through 2014–15, Almtorp was a productive checking centre in the SHL, finally finding his hockey home six years after he was drafted.

NO. 123 OVERALL: RD ROBIN KOVAR
Vancouver Giants (WHL)

One of the most unusual draft moments in Oilers history involves Kovar. Although he was listed as eligible for the draft, the league had previously ruled him ineligible for selection. It caused a stir on the draft floor as other teams reacted to the ploy, but the pick was ruled void. Kovar was not drafted the following season and did not play in the NHL.

NO. 148 OVERALL: G GLENN FISHER
Ft. Saskatchewan Traders (AJHL)

Fisher was just average in size (6'1", 190 pounds) for the position but had impressed in the AJHL before his draft day. He went to the University of Denver and was on two national championship teams during his four years there. His best college season was his senior year, 2006–07, when he posted a .919 save percentage. Edmonton did sign him, but the organization had two superior prospects (Devan Dubnyk, Jeff Deslauriers) at the position. Fisher peaked as a pro with four AHL games and the rest of his time was spent in the ECHL.

NO. 181 OVERALL: LD MIKKO LUOMA
Tappara Tampere (Liiga)

Edmonton drafted another veteran Euro, as had been the case in 2001 with Jussi Markkanen, Kari Haakana, and Ales Pisa. Luoma was 26 on draft day and a year later made his way to North America. Although he played in just three NHL games, Luoma was impressive in the AHL with the Toronto Roadrunners. Instead of staying in the organization, he signed in Sweden, where he spent most of the next decade playing quality hockey in that nation's best league.

NO. 205 OVERALL: LW JEAN-FRANCOIS DUFORT
Cape Breton Screaming Eagles (QMJHL)

Dufort had close to a point per game in his draft year and turned 20 in the months before he was chosen by Edmonton. That usually means a fast track to pro in the draft-plus-one season, but Dufort stayed in the QMJHL for another season. Late in 2002–03, he suffered a severe concussion and his hockey career ended immediately.

NO. 211 OVERALL: LW PATRICK MURPHY
Newmarket Hurricanes (OPJHL)

Murphy stood 6'2", 210 pounds, and played a physical style. In four NCAA seasons with Northern Michigan, he showed a major lack of scoring ability (12 goals in 127 games). Edmonton did not sign him.

NO. 244 OVERALL: LC DWIGHT HELMINEN
Michigan (NCAA)

A shorter player (5'10") built like a truck (190 pounds), Helminen scored well enough at Michigan to get a pro contract. Edmonton didn't plan to sign him and so sent him away in trade to the New York Rangers. After a poor rookie season in the AHL, Helminen found the offensive range at that level and eventually made his way to the NHL with the Carolina Hurricanes and San Jose Sharks. His 27 NHL games were impressive based on where he was chosen in the draft.

NO. 245 OVERALL: LW TOMAS MICKA
Slava Praha (Czech)

Micka was 6'4", 224 pounds, and had already played a game in the top Czech league by draft day. He came over a year later and then played two seasons in the ECHL. He didn't have enough skill to play at a higher level but enjoyed a solid career back in the Czech Republic.

NO. 274 OVERALL: LC FREDRIK JOHANSSON
Frolunda (Sweden Jr.)

Johansson scored well (37 games, 12–20–32) in Swedish junior in his draft season and got a cup of coffee in the SEL the following year. He played a support role for the next two years and then signed with the Oilers for the 2007–08 season. In the AHL (25 games), he showed two-way acumen but was a shy scorer (4–1–5). Johansson spent some time in the ECHL in the same season. After that, he returned to the Swedish second league (Allsvenskan), where he has played for Vasteras IK. He remains in the league 12 years after leaving North America.

2002 Draft Summary

The 2002 draft was the second for the team of general manager Kevin Lowe and scouting director Kevin Prendergast. Unlike 2001, a year that saw Ales Hemsky carry the draft himself, the 2002 draft had two long-term NHL players in Jarret Stoll and Matt Greene. The draft in 2002 more closely resembled a traditional Barry Fraser "after 1981" draft in that skill took a backseat to size and ruggedness. (Number in parentheses is points per game.)

- Jesse Niinimaki (Jr. Liiga) age 18: 27 games, 9–23–32 (1.19)
- Jeff Deslauriers (QMJHL) age 17: 51 games, 3.51 goals-against average, .900 save percentage
- Jarret Stoll (WHL) age 19: 47 games, 32–34–66 (1.40)
- Matt Greene (USHL) age 18: 55 games, 4–20–24 (0.44)
- Brock Radunske (NCAA) age 18: 41 games, 4–9–13 (0.32)
- Ivan Koltsov (Rus 3) age 17: 27 games, 2–2–4 (0.15)
- Jonas Almtorp (Sweden Jr.) age 17: 37 games, 26–18–44 (1.19)
- Glenn Fisher (AJHL) age 18: 47 games, 4.44 goals-against average
- Mikko Luoma (Liiga) age 25: 56 games, 11–18–29 (0.52)
- J-F Dufort (QMJHL) age 19: 68 games, 22–41–63 (0.93)
- Patrick Murphy (OPJHL) age 18: 48 games, 11–21–32 (0.67)
- Dwight Helminen (NCAA) age 18: 39 games, 10–8–18 (0.46)

- Tomas Micka (Czech U-20) age 18: 46 games, 12–16–28 (0.61)
- Fredrik Johansson (SuperElite U-20) age 17: 37 games, 12–20–32 (0.86)

The Niinimaki pick was baffling. He was 18 and playing junior hockey in Finland in his draft year. A massive reach with a first-round pick is the kind of pick a fairly new scouting director might consider a risk. Stoll, even at 19, was the mathematical star of this draft.

NHL Career Games Played
1. Jarret Stoll: 872
2. Matt Greene: 615
3. Jeff Deslauriers: 62
4. Dwight Helminen: 27
5. Mikko Luoma: 3

Here's how the 2002 draft class compares to the preceding decade in terms of total NHL games played:
1. 1993 (3,025 games)
2. 1996 (1,924 games)
3. 1994 (1,667 games)
4. **2002 (1,579 games)**
5. 1998 (1,214 games)
6. 1997 (1,126 games)
7. 2001 (1,043 games)
8. 1999 (937 games)
9. 2000 (928 games)
10. 1995 (845 games)

Prendergast's first two drafts were a success and produced three bona fide NHL players in Hemsky, Stoll, and Greene. In looking at the last 10 seasons of Oilers drafting, the 2002 edition delivered above-average return.

Trades That Involved Draft Picks

On June 29, 2001, the Oilers traded Sergei Zholtok to the Minnesota Wild for the No. 205 overall selection (Jean-Francois Dufort).

On March 19, 2002, the Oilers traded Tom Poti and Rem Murray to the New York Rangers for Mike York and the No. 106 overall selection (Ivan Kolstov).

On June 22, 2002, the Oilers traded the No. 14 overall pick in the 2002 draft (Chris Higgins) to the Montreal Canadiens for selections No. 15 (Jesse Niinimaki) and No. 245 overall (Tomas Micka).

On June 22, 2002, the Oilers traded Jochen Hecht to the Buffalo Sabres for the No. 31 overall (Jeff Deslauriers) and No. 36 overall (Jarret Stoll) selections.

On June 23, the NHL awarded the Oilers a compensatory selection for losing defenceman Igor Ulanov. That pick was No. 123 (Robin Kovar).

THE 2003 DRAFT

The Oilers made the playoffs in 2002–03 but the goal differential (plus-1) fell markedly from plus-23 the previous season. Tommy Salo, the Oilers' starting goalie since 1999, faltered from a .913 save percentage to .899.

Homegrown talent Ryan Smyth led the team in points, and draft picks Shawn Horcoff, Mike Comrie, and rookie Ales Hemsky all finished in the top 10 among the team's scorers. Hemsky led a long and impressive group of rookies in 2002–03:

- Ales Hemsky: 59 games, 6–24–30
- Jason Chimera: 66 games, 14–9–23
- Fernando Pisani: 35 games, 8–5–13
- Alexei Semenov: 46 games, 1–6–7
- Ales Pisa: 48 games, 1–3–4
- Jani Rita: 12 games, 3–1–4
- Marc-Andre Bergeron: 5 games, 1–1–2
- Alex Henry: 3 games, 0–0–0
- Bobby Allen: 1 game, 0–0–0

Hemsky, Pisani, and Bergeron would have an impact on Edmonton's 2006 Stanley Cup run, which fell just short. Chimera would play a long and productive career in the NHL at several stops.

The 2003 draft featured a spectacular pool of talent. Edmonton was focused on skill forwards with size.

NO. 22 OVERALL: RC MARC-ANTOINE POULIOT
Rimouski Oceanic (QMJHL)

The Oilers liked Pouliot's size (6'2", 203 pounds) and the fact he never gave up despite playing on a poor team (he led the Oceanic in points, with the closest player 33 points behind him).

Pouliot was ranked No. 13 by Central Scouting and so went in the range of expectations, but the Oilers left Ryan Kesler, Ryan Getzlaf, Corey Perry, and several others on the board in taking him.

Pouliot had injury issues before the draft. At the Top Prospects game in 2003, Dion Phaneuf leveled him with a vicious (and clean) check. Edmonton drafted him with no way of knowing the parade of injuries that were about to beset Pouliot. In the summer of 2003, he got hurt at the Canadian WJC camp in Calgary (hip) and that had a major impact on his 18-year-old season. It also hurt his performance at the Oilers' rookie camp just two months after being drafted.

In November 2003, he suffered an abdominal injury and missed the Q/Russia prospects game and played only 42 QMJHL games that season, finally having surgery in Montreal in summer 2004 to repair the abdominal tissues.

He played three weeks with a broken wrist during the 2003–04 season.

These injuries had a major impact on Pouliot's draft-plus-one season and likely on his career. How much, we don't know, but we can say that the player did not emerge as a quality regular in a season where outstanding players were readily available when the Oilers made the choice.

Pouliot would play 192 NHL games, with the two men selected after him totaling 1,001 (Ryan Kesler) and 749 (Mike Richards).

NO. 51 OVERALL: RW COLIN MCDONALD
New England Jr. Coyotes (EJHL)

At 6'2" and 219 pounds and with real goal-scoring ability at the junior level (28 goals in 44 games in his draft year), the Oilers were confident McDonald would develop into a plus scorer at the highest levels.

The big winger went to Providence College in his draft-plus-one season, scoring 10 goals in 37 games. It was a quiet season, but freshmen often get limited minutes and Providence's program is well known for a button-down defensive style.

McDonald scored 11, 9, and then 13 goals in his final three seasons of college, so he turned pro with some questions about his goal scoring.

He turned pro in 2007 and it took four seasons in the AHL before he blossomed offensively (42 goals in 2010–11).

By the summer of 2011, he had reached free agency and played just two games in Edmonton. McDonald would sign with the Pittsburgh Penguins and then play for the New York Islanders and Philadelphia Flyers, spending just two full seasons (2012–14) in the NHL.

He played just 148 games, chosen by Edmonton while the rest of the NHL was drafting long-term solutions.

NO. 68 OVERALL: LW JEAN-FRANCOIS JACQUES
Baie-Comeau Drakkar (QMJHL)

Jacques reached legend status with Oilers fans as the "Crazy Train" because of his size (6'3", 231 pounds) and speed (he could fly) combined with an aggressive style.

Jacques scored well in junior and his first season in the AHL (65 games, 24–20–44) had many fans wondering if he could be a real two-way contributor while playing the enforcer role in the NHL.

Then, a funny thing happened to Jacques when he arrived in the NHL—he couldn't score. At all. In his first 53 games, Jacques didn't get credited with a single assist. That's rare for a defenceman, extremely rare for a forward. Jacques scored his first NHL goal on March 3, 2009 (assisted by Ladislav Smid and Zack Stortini), more than three years after making his NHL debut on February 2, 2006.

Jacques spent two seasons as a semi-regular with Edmonton, but back injuries began to affect his ability to play a physical style. He played 166 games in his NHL career.

NO. 72 OVERALL: LC MIKHAIL ZHUKOV
Arbola (Sweden)

Zhukov was another big forward (6'2", 194 pounds on draft day) and a player who had a solid résumé in terms of skill (9–14–23 in 41 games in the Allsvenskan) while playing in Sweden's second league.

The story of Zhukov after his draft involved a small step back in his draft-plus-one season in the Allsvenskan and then back home to Russia, where he played the heart of his career from 2003 to '18. He was never a big scorer in the league but hung around long enough to play 453 games and enjoy some impressive scoring seasons. He never came to North America.

NO. 94 OVERALL: RW ZACK STORTINI
Sudbury Wolves (OHL)

Stortini had the size (6'4", 230 pounds) but wasn't a high-skill junior when Edmonton drafted him (62 games, 13–16–29). They liked his leadership—he was already a captain. He was barely eligible (by four days, born September 11, 1985) for the 2003 draft.

Stortini lacked top-end skill, but Oilers coach Craig MacTavish liked his effort and coachability. Stortini played 29 NHL games in his second pro season and by 2007–08 was an NHL regular. Playing mostly fourth-line minutes, MacTavish came to count on Stortini's low-event shifts (he wasn't scoring, but neither was the opposition). In the three seasons between 2007 and '10, his five-on-five on-ice goals total was 64–61. An NHL coach who has a fourth liner who can hold the opposition at bay values that player. Per 82 games, Stortini averaged just 13 points in the NHL, but he played more games in the league than Pouliot, McDonald, or Jacques because he delivered consistently in an area of the game MacTavish valued.

When MacT left the organization, replacement head coach Pat Quinn played Stortini the same way. One year later, coach Tom Renney effectively ended Stortini's NHL time by severely limiting his minutes. Stortini landed in the AHL by 2011–12 and continued to be a productive player through 2018–19. Few players in this book got more from their ability than Stortini.

NO. 147 OVERALL: RW KALLE OLSSON
Frolunda (Sweden Jr.)

Olsson was an impressive scorer in his draft year (30 games, 22–13–35) but was inconsistent when moving up to the Allsvenskan (second Swedish league), so the Oilers passed on him as a signing. He didn't play in the SHL (top Swedish league) until 2011–12 and was a complementary player through 2018–19. Olsson was a good player but did not develop into an NHL prospect.

NO. 154 OVERALL: RD DAVID ROHLFS
Detroit Compuware (NAHL)

Rohlfs was listed as a defender but would play both defence and forward while at Michigan. He was an impressive scorer in junior but didn't find the range in college until his senior year. A big man (6'3", 215 pounds), the Oilers clearly saw him as a possible power forward, but his pro career peaked in the ECHL and IHL, two leagues below the AHL. Rohlfs fell shy of an NHL career but did play a season in Italy.

NO. 184 OVERALL: RW DRAGAN UMICEVIC
Sodertalje SK (SEL)

Umicevic's unusual name earned him early fame among Oilers fans, who nicknamed him "Trogdor the Burninator" sometime in 2003. He had good size (6'0", 207 pounds) for a skill forward and filled the net (24 games, 19–14–33) in Swedish junior in his draft year, while also playing 22 games (2–3–5) in the SEL.

He showed early there was enough skill for a contract, and the Oilers tried to sign him, but it never happened. Umicevic is still active, having played in Sweden, Finland, Switzerland, Germany, and, most recently, Austria.

NO. 214 OVERALL: RC KYLE BRODZIAK
Moose Jaw Warriors (WHL)

The Oilers rarely draft from Moose Jaw, but when they do, good things often happen. Brodziak was the fourth Warriors player drafted by the team, following Kelly Buchberger, Ryan Smyth, and Chad Hinz.

Brodziak's selection was made possible by the NHL, which awarded Edmonton a compensatory selection for the Robin Kovar mix-up in 2002.

Brodziak was on the radar in 2002 for Edmonton. Quoting Guy Flaming of Hockey's Future, "The vast majority of the credit for the selection falls at the feet of Lorne Davis, the elder states-man of the scouting staff who actually pushed to draft Brodziak a year earlier despite a rather non-descript season in Moose Jaw."

Brodziak played 72 games, scoring 32–30–62 (0.86 points per game) and built on those totals in the following year. When he turned pro, the offence did not follow (32 and 31 points in his first two AHL seasons), but he blossomed (56 points in 62 games) in minors during the third and final year of his entry deal.

At training camp and in preseason during the fall of 2007, Brodziak was quicker and more determined and won regular employment with the big club, even though that meant sending down first-round pick Pouliot.

From there, Brodizak established himself as a valuable utility forward who could play up and down the lineup, centre his own line, and penalty kill for his team.

He even reached the 20-goal plateau for the Minnesota Wild in 2011–12. Edmonton traded Brodziak too early; he spent just two seasons with the team (although there would be a return in 2018–19).

For his career, Brodziak played in 917 games and scored 129 goals along with 167 assists. He was easily the class of the Oilers' draft group for 2003, proving Lorne Davis right all along.

NO. 215 OVERALL: RD MATHIEU ROY
Val d'Or Foreurs (QMJHL)

Roy played 66 games in the NHL and might have had a longer career if he could have stayed healthy. He came out of junior and established himself quickly in the AHL as a reliable two-way defender, but concussions and other maladies had a major impact on him. After leaving the NHL (he also played for the Columbus Blue Jackets and Tampa Bay Lightning), Roy enjoyed a long career in Europe, playing through 2019–20. Better health in his twenties would have given Roy a much better chance to establish himself in the NHL.

NO. 248 OVERALL: LD JOSEF HRABAL
Vsetin (Czech Jr.)

Hrabal was a tall, slender two-way defender on his draft day. He toiled in obscurity in the Czech league and finally came to North America in 2008. He played little and was back in Europe (Sweden) by the end of the 2008–09 season. His career continued in the Czech Republic and he had some fine years, even emerging offensively.

NO. 278 OVERALL: RW TROY BODIE
Kelowna Rockets (WHL)

Bodie was 6'4" on draft day and played a physical game for the Rockets. That wasn't news in 2003, because the team had eight players with over 100 PIM during 2002–03. Bodie played in just 35 games, but the Oilers drafted him because of his size and ability to intimidate.

He became a regular in 2003–04 and improved each season, so the Oilers signed Bodie and sent him to the minors. He split his first season between the ECHL and AHL, scoring well in the ECHL (21–17–38 in 46 games) but not playing much in the AHL (one assist in 20 games).

The following year, 2007–08, he spent the entire year in the AHL, but Edmonton had several enforcers (Tim Sestito, Ben Simon, Jacques) at that level and Zack Stortini in the NHL.

So Bodie signed in Anaheim and played in the NHL during 2008–09, emerging as a regular with the Ducks, then with the

Carolina Hurricanes and finally the Toronto Maple Leafs. He would play 159 NHL games over five seasons, proving the Oilers scouts correct in taking him in the ninth round.

2003 Draft Summary

The 2003 draft brought with it some intriguing numbers. I was fascinated on draft weekend by the close similarities between Pouliot and Brodziak's numbers despite the gap in their selections. (Number in parentheses is points per game.)

- Marc Pouliot (QMJHL) age 17: 65 games, 32–41–73 (1.12)
- Colin McDonald (EJHL) age 17: 44 games, 28–40–68 (1.55)
- J-F Jacques (QMJHL) age 17: 67 games, 12–21–33 (0.49)
- Mikhail Zhukov (Allsvenskan) age 17: 41 games, 9–14–23 (0.56)
- Zack Stortini (OHL) age 17: 62 games, 13–16–29 (0.47)
- Kalle Olsson (SuperElite U-20) age 17: 30 games, 22–13–35 (1.17)
- David Rohlfs (NAHL) age 18: 53 games, 30–14–44 (0.83)
- Dragan Umicevic (Superelite U-20) age 17: 24 games, 19–14–33 (1.38)
- Kyle Brodziak (WHL) age 18: 72 games, 32–30–62 (0.86)
- Mathieu Roy (QMJHL) age 19: 51 games, 11–21–32 (0.63)
- Josef Hrabal (Czech Jr.) age 17: 30 games, 6–7–13 (0.43)
- Troy Bodie (WHL) age 17: 30 games, 4–4–8 (0.27)

Pouliot's offence was low for a first-round pick in the deepest draft in forever, and that was verifiable on draft day. Mike Richards, the next CHL forward chosen, posted a 1.30 point-per-game total. McDonald had a solid résumé, but there were still quality players on the board from established leagues; McDonald would have been better value chosen later. Brodziak was a year older, but a 32-goal season in a good junior league suggested he had talent.

The haul was disappointing, although the parade of injuries to Pouliot can't be blamed on the scouts. The late pick of Brodziak proved to be a godsend, and the 2003 draft was (in terms of NHL games) one of the most successful of the decade.

NHL Career Games Played

1. Kyle Brodziak: 917
2. Zack Stortini: 257
3. Marc Pouliot: 192
4. Jean-Francois Jacques: 166
5. Troy Bodie: 159
6. Colin McDonald: 148
7. Mathieu Roy: 66

Injuries affected the career paths of Pouliot, Jacques, and Roy. We'll never know how much, but that has to be factored into any evaluation. For Prendergast and his scouts, this was a great opportunity that turned into bitter disappointment. Longtime scout Lorne Davis saved them with the Brodziak pick.

Here's how the 2003 draft class compares to the preceding decade in terms of total NHL games played:

1. 1996 (1,924 games)
2. **2003 (1,905 games)**
3. 1994 (1,667 games)
4. 2002 (1,579 games)

5. 1998 (1,214 games)
6. 1997 (1,126 games)
7. 2001 (1,043 games)
8. 1999 (937 games)
9. 2000 (928 games)
10. 1995 (845 games)

NHL games played is an efficient way to measure different draft seasons, but it isn't perfect. The 2003 edition is an example. Edmonton gathered a large number of man games, but none of the players chosen occupied an important roster spot. The 2003 draft is a pass, but also a disappointment.

Trades That Involved Draft Picks

On June 18, 2002, the Oilers traded a third-round pick in the 2003 draft (Ryan Potulny) to the Philadelphia Flyers for C Jiri Dopita.

On June 30, 2002, the Oilers traded their 2003 fourth-round pick (Corey Potter) to the New York Rangers for the rights to goalie Mike Richter.

On October 7, 2002, the Oilers traded right winger Mike Grier to the Washington Capitals for the No. 53 overall pick (Evgeny Tunik) and No. 94 overall pick (Zack Stortini) in the 2003 draft.

On January 17, 2003, the Oilers received the Montreal Canadiens' fifth-round pick (No. 147, Kalle Olsson) in exchange for the right to hire Hamilton Bulldogs coach Claude Julien.

On March 11, 2003, the Oilers traded D Janne Niinimaa and the No. 53 overall pick (Evgeny Tunik) in the 2003 draft for right winger Brad Isbister and left winger Raffi Torres.

On June 21, 2003, the Oilers traded pick No. 17 (Zach Parise) to the New Jersey Devils for pick No. 22 (Marc Pouliot) and No. 68 (Jean-Francois Jacques), all picks in the 2003 draft.

On June 21, 2003, the NHL awarded a compensatory pick to the Oilers for losing free agent Mike Richter. The pick was No. 72 overall, Mikhail Zhukov.

On June 21, 2003, the NHL awarded a compensatory pick to the Oilers for the ineligible Robin Kovar draft selection in 2002. The pick was No. 214 (Kyle Brodziak).

THE 2004 DRAFT

The Oilers missed the playoffs for the second time in four seasons under coach Craig MacTavish in 2003–04. The club had a goal differential of plus-13 (221–208). The frustration of just missing the playoffs would continue to grow later in this decade, sowing the seeds for the famous rebuilds of 2007 and 2010, and the reload of 2015.

Prendergast's picks were beginning to show up as successful NHL players, led by Ales Hemsky (71 games, 12–22–34). The 2003–04 rookies included some recent picks and signings:

- Marc-Andre Bergeron: 54 games, 9–17–26
- Jarret Stoll: 68 games, 10–11–21
- Mike Bishai: 14 games, 0–2–2
- Tony Salmelainen: 13 games, 0–1–1
- Peter Sarno: 6 games, 1–0–1
- Jani Rita: 2 games, 0–0–0
- Doug Lynch: 2 games, 0–0–0

Stoll (draft) and Bergeron (undrafted free agent) arrived quickly in the NHL and would go on to productive careers.

NO. 14 OVERALL: G DEVAN DUBNYK
Kamloops Blazers (WHL)

After 20 years of wasting goalie draft picks, the Oilers finally scored in the first round of the 2004 entry draft. Rumour had it the team was focused on winger Drew Stafford, but Dubnyk was the Oilers' best player available when their turn arrived.

A massive goaltender (6'6", 224 pounds), Dubnyk would get into the butterfly (on his knees so his legs completely cover the bottom of the net) and still have enough size to cover the top of the net.

He was also consistent. In junior, his save percentages were .917 (draft year) followed by .912 and .912 in the two following seasons.

He turned pro in 2006–07, posting a strong .921 save percentage with the Stockton Thunder of the ECHL.

In his three seasons as a starter in the AHL before making it to the NHL, he delivered save percentages of .904, .906, and .915.

As an NHL rookie in 2009–10, he posted an .889 save percentage, a slight surprise. In year two, that elevated to .916 (in 2010–11) and at the end of the decade he had played in 520 NHL games with a .915 save percentage for his career.

Dubnyk spent five years with the Oilers before being dealt.

Oilers general manager Craig MacTavish was never completely convinced of him as an NHL starter, saying, "If you have to ask the question…" then leaving the gathered media to fill in the rest of the sentence.

Coach Dallas Eakins introduced a "swarm" defence that his Oilers defenders had a difficult time executing and Dubnyk was left stone alone on too many plays. In 2013–14, his save percentage fell to .894 (from .921) and Edmonton dealt him to the Nashville

Predators, where he continued to struggle. He regained his confidence with the Arizona Coyotes and then found a second home with the Minnesota Wild.

Dubnyk is the third-most-successful goalie in team draft history, behind Hall of Famer Grant Fuhr and Andy Moog.

NO. 25 OVERALL: LC ROB SCHREMP
London Knights (OHL)

Schremp was a legendary offensive player in junior, known for puck tricks and wizardry that were truly remarkable. In his draft season, he scored 75 points in 63 games, and then exploded in his final two seasons with 90 and 145 points.

He arrived in pro hockey as a phenom, but his attention to detail defensively wasn't strong and he had wide-body skating issues. As an NHL rookie, he didn't score at a point-per-game pace (69 games, 17–36–53) despite being an exceptional puck handler.

In year two in the AHL (2007–08), he posted 76 points in 78 games, despite having knee surgery in May of 2007.

Schremp never did earn the trust of the Edmonton coaching staff and landed with the New York Islanders in 2009–10 (44 games, 7–18–25).

In 2010–11, the Islanders gave Schremp a full shot, but in 45 games his five-on-five on-ice goal differential was 17–35 and his offence (1.59 points per 60 at five on five) wasn't enough to justify the defensive shortcomings. Schremp landed in Atlanta with the Thrashers for a time and then headed for Europe.

His considerable skill wasn't enough to overcome both foot speed and defensive lapses. He would play in 114 NHL games.

NO. 44 OVERALL: RD ROMAN TESLIUK
Kamloops Blazers (WHL)

Tesliuk was a puck-moving defender who could also look after his own end and had a bit of an edge. He increased his offensive totals each season of his junior career, but the Oilers passed on signing him, partly because of recent success in adding names such as Marc-Andre Bergeron to address the issue. Tesliuk played just 24 games pro in the ECHL.

NO. 57 OVERALL: LW GEOFF PAUKOVICH
U.S. National U-18 Team (NAHL)

The Oilers drafted a player they hoped would develop into a power forward in Paukovich. At 6'4", 215 pounds, he scored four goals in 11 games during his draft season and the scouting reports suggested he was growing as a complete player.

At the University of Denver, his rugged style kept him in the lineup and in the penalty box often. He scored well as a freshman (12 goals in 41 games) but couldn't build on that season, scoring just 12 more goals in the following two seasons combined.

The Oilers signed him, but he didn't deliver much offensively in the AHL, eventually settling in at the ECHL level.

NO. 112 OVERALL: LW LIAM REDDOX
Peterborough Petes (OHL)

Reddox came from a junior team in Peterborough that was legendary for two-way forwards. He could hold his own in that area, but also displayed speed and skill, scoring 64 points in 68 games in 2003–04. He exploded for 36 goals and 82 points in the following season, taking a step back offensively in his final season in the OHL.

Reddox turned pro in the ECHL and had a pedestrian season but improved offensively once he arrived in the AHL in 2007–08 (65 games, 16–28–44). He made the NHL in 2008–09 and played exactly 100 games in a depth role, showing two-way acumen and posting 24 points. He would then spend eight productive seasons in the SEL (Vaxjo).

NO. 146 OVERALL: LD BRYAN YOUNG
Peterborough Petes (OHL)

At 6'1", 190 pounds, and bringing shutdown defensive ability, Young could have safely been described as a "tweener" NHL prospect. That's a player who has ability in some or all areas but falls short of being a strong prospect because no one skill stands out.

Young was a good skater who played with an edge and was a reliable player through his junior career. He turned pro in 2006–07, playing in the ECHL and AHL (for two teams—this is the period when the Oilers loaned their players and did not have their own minor league team).

During the 2006–07 season, the parent club in Edmonton had a rash of injuries and rookie pro Young was recalled in an emergency situation. He struggled in the NHL minutes but survived for 15 games, adding two more with the Oilers the following season.

NO. 177 OVERALL: RD MAX GORDICHUK
Kamloops Blazers (WHL)

Gordichuk was the sixth Kamloops player to be drafted by the Oilers over the years, and the third (Dubnyk, Tesliuk) chosen in

2004. Clearly Edmonton liked what was coming out of Kamloops from coach Dean Clark. Gordichuk offered size (6'6", 220 pounds), defended his own end well, and could get the puck out under control. He blossomed offensively in his final two junior seasons but did not sign in Edmonton.

NO. 208 OVERALL: RW STEPHANE GOULET
Quebec Remparts (QMJHL)

Highly touted as a scorer with size (6'3", 208 pounds) as he entered the QMJHL, Goulet disappointed in his first season (6–8–14 in 54 games). After the Oilers took him, Goulet scored 22–25–47 in 69 games in his draft-plus-one season and then scored 51 goals in his final junior season. The Oilers signed him, but Goulet struggled in his entry deal, finally finding the offensive range in the ECHL. He didn't get close to the NHL.

NO. 242 OVERALL: LC TYLER SPURGEON
Kelowna Rockets (WHL)

Spurgeon was an undersized energy centre who was shy offensively (49 games, 8–16–24 in his draft year). He improved in the two junior seasons after he was drafted but was a long shot as an NHL prospect. Edmonton signed him and Spurgeon put in four seasons with the Oilers' minor league teams. After that, he went to Europe (mostly Austria) and as of 2020–21 was playing German Division II hockey.

NO. 274 OVERALL: G BJORN BJURLING

Djurgardens IF Stockholm (SEL)

A goaltender with average size (6'0", 205 pounds) is going to have a tough time making the NHL, but Bjurling's résumé included a stellar .923 save percentage in one of the best leagues in the world. He was 24 when Edmonton drafted him, so there was some urgency for him to come over and compete for work in North America. Bjurling stayed in Sweden and played through 2011.

2004 Draft Summary

Prendergast and his staff had several names of interest (Drew Stafford among them) and Dubnyk in the first round meant a long-term investment. It worked out in time, but the immediate impact of a scoring winger would have helped the organization. (Number in parentheses is points per game.)

- Devan Dubnyk (WHL) age 17: 44 games, 2.51 goals-against average, .917 save percentage
- Rob Schremp (OHL) age 17: 63 games, 30–45–75 (1.19)
- Roman Tesliuk (WHL) age 17: 70 games, 5–19–24 (0.34)
- Geoff Paukovich (NAHL) age 17: 11 games, 4–2–6 (0.55)
- Liam Reddox (OHL) age 17: 68 games, 31–33–64 (0.94)
- Bryan Young (OHL) age 17: 60 games, 0–8–8 (0.13)
- Max Gordichuk (WHL) age 17: 70 games, 0–8–8 (0.11)
- Stephane Goulet (QMJHL) age 17: 54 games, 6–8–14 (0.26)
- Tyler Spurgeon (WHL) age 17: 49 games, 8–16–24 (0.49)
- Bjorn Bjurling (SEL) age 24: 45 games, 2.31 goals-against average, .923 save percentage

Dubnyk was a fine pick. He delivered quality numbers in junior and went on to a long and productive NHL career. Schremp's offence was solid, but he relied heavily on power-play production over his junior career and lacked foot speed. Reddox was an under-the-radar pick who spent some time in the NHL.

NHL Career Games Played

1. Devan Dubnyk: 542
2. Rob Schremp: 114
3. Liam Reddox: 100
4. Bryan Young: 17

The 2004 draft didn't reach the 1,000-game mark, but starting goaltenders bring extra value. However, the low return on a second pick in the first round (Schremp) meant this was the first draft fail by the Prendergast crew (after three passing grades).

Here's how the 2004 draft class compares to the preceding decade in terms of total NHL games played:

1. 1996 (1,924 games)
2. 2003 (1,905 games)
3. 2002 (1,579 games)
4. 1998 (1,214 games)
5. 1997 (1,126 games)
6. 2001 (1,043 games)
7. 1999 (937 games)
8. 2000 (928 games)
9. 1995 (845 games)
10. **2004 (773 games)**

Trades That Involved Draft Picks

On June 30, 2003, the Oilers traded goalie Jussi Markkanen and a 2004 fourth-round pick (Roman Kukumberg) to the New York Rangers for the rights to Brian Leetch.

On December 16, 2003, the Oilers traded centre Mike Comrie to the Philadelphia Flyers for defenceman Jeff Woywitka, the No. 25 overall pick in the 2004 draft (Rob Schremp), and a 2005 third-round pick (Danny Syvret).

On March 3, 2004, the Oilers traded goalie Steve Valiquette, forward Dwight Helminen, and a second-round pick in the 2004 draft (Dane Byers) to the New York Rangers for centre Petr Nedved and goalie Jussi Markkanen.

On June 26, 2004, the Oilers traded left winger Jason Chimera and a 2004 third-round pick (Billy Ryan) to the Phoenix Coyotes for picks No. 57 (Geoff Paukovich) and No. 112 (Liam Reddox).

THE 2005 DRAFT

In 2004–05, there was no NHL season. A lockout by the NHL cost the league an entire year of competition. The Stanley Cup was not awarded for the first time since 1919. Major issues included salary cap and revenue sharing, and the league and players took until July 2005 to find common ground.

The draft lottery was weighted so that weaker teams who had not made recent playoff appearances or enjoyed high draft picks would be favoured. The Oilers, who had not drafted in the top 10 overall in almost a decade, and missed two of three playoffs, saw the lottery deliver them No. 25 overall.

PROSPECT SPOTLIGHT
NO. 25 OVERALL: LC ANDREW COGLIANO, ST. MICHAEL'S BUZZERS (OPJHL)

An undersized speedster who had a nice range of skills even as a junior, Cogiano was virtualy tied with T.J. Oshie on Edmonton's list when the St. Louis Blues chose Oshie just ahead of the Oilers.

Cogliano played two seasons at Michigan (NCAA), delivering impressive offence in his sophomore season (24–26–50 in 38 games). The Oilers signed him and brought him right to the NHL, where Cogliano scored 18–27–45 in 82 games as a rookie. He quickly emerged as one of the leaders of a young group of Oilers forwards who could score goals. Cogliano had some two-way potential, making him unique in the group.

Cogliano played four years in Edmonton before being traded to the Anaheim Ducks. He played in more than 1,000 games and scored 170 goals between his rookie season and 2021, and as of this writing he appears poised to play several more seasons in the league.

Cogliano is fast and durable and delivers strong two-way play. He remains one of the best first-round picks of the Prendergast era.

NO. 36 OVERALL: LD TAYLOR CHORNEY
Shattuck St. Mary's High School (USHS, Michigan)

Chorney was another speedy undersized prospect, this time a defenceman with exciting offensive potential. He played at Shattuck at the same time as No. 1 overall selection Sidney Crosby, and his offensive output in high school (50 games, 4–30–34) suggested a possible future that included an NHL power play.

Chorney played for North Dakota (NCAA) for three seasons after his draft, adding playing time and increasing his point total by year. At the end of his college career (2008) he sprained his knee, and he would have some knee issues during his pro career.

His AHL debut season (2008–09) exposed Chorney defensively, and it took him until year three in the league to become a reliable coverage defenceman. He had a difficult time defensively in his first extended NHL look (42 games in 2009–10), as his on-ice goal differential at five on five (15–33) was easily the worst on the Oilers that season. Edmonton had a veteran group on defence in 2009–10, so Chorney's path to NHL employment was blocked by veterans such as Ryan Whitney, Lubomir Visnovsky, and Ladislav Smid.

Edmonton lost Chorney on waivers to the St. Louis Blues, and he began a journeyman's career through the NHL (Pittsburgh Penguins, Washington Capitals, Columbus Blue Jackets). He played 166 NHL games before heading to Europe and is still an active player.

NO. 81 OVERALL: LD DANNY SYVRET
London Knights (OHL)

Syvret was weeks away from turning 20 when the Oilers drafted him. An undersized puck mover and expert passer, he also had plus speed and was a big part of the Knights' Memorial Cup–winning season in 2005.

Syvret's size (5'11", 203 pounds) was more of an issue in pro hockey, and he struggled in the AHL and during NHL auditions during his entry-level contract 2005–08. Edmonton traded him in summer 2008, and he played a few games over the following seasons with the Philadelphia Flyers and Anaheim Ducks.

NO. 86 OVERALL: LC ROBBY DEE
Breck High School (USHS, Minnesota)

Dee had average size (6'1", 185 pounds), plus speed and a good shot on his draft day, scoring 49 goals in 28 games for his Minnesota high school. The scouting reports suggested he was a good speed forechecker but was not overly physical.

After he was drafted, Dee spent two years with the Omaha Lancers of the USHL, scoring six goals in his first year and 11 in his second. Once he arrived at Maine (NCAA), Dee's offence slowly showed progress until he was just shy of a point per game in his senior year (33 games, 13–22–35). He would play three pro seasons in the ECHL and Germany, plus three games in the AHL.

NO. 97 OVERALL: LC CHRIS VANDEVELDE
Moorhead High School (USHS, Minnesota)

At 6'1", 190 pounds on draft day, VandeVelde had a long stride and decent speed, while scoring well (35–32–67 in 30 games) in high school. He also had several useful secondary skills (faceoffs, intelligent two-way play). The NHL draft guide said he possessed "a good attitude toward his defensive game for a player with his offensive skills."

VandeVelde showed well in the USHL (Lincoln Stars) in 2005–06 (56 games, 16–20–36) and then spent four years with North Dakota (NCAA). He didn't deliver much offensively in his first year, but the final three saw him post respectable totals. He peaked with 41 points in 42 games in his senior year.

He spent most of his three-year entry contract in the AHL, shy on scoring but impressing the Oilers with two-way play and penalty-killing ability.

In 2013–14, he landed with the Philadelphia Flyers and spent three seasons as a No. 4 centre. He finished his NHL time after 278 games.

NO. 120 OVERALL: LW VYACHESLAV TRUKHNO
Prince Edward Island Rocket (QMJHL)

Trukno was a talented offensive winger from Russia who came to Canada to get more draft exposure. His scouting reports said he was "a very good skater with an effortless stride" and was a little bow-legged but solid on his skates with good acceleration. His greatest strength was passing, with backhand passes that were exceptional and difficult to defend. Trukhno also had good two-way acumen.

His draft-year numbers (64 games, 25–34–59) were worthy of a second- or third-round selection, but Edmonton got him in the fourth round. At 6'2", 196 pounds, his availability at No. 120 was a mystery on draft day and even more confusing after two additional junior seasons in which he posted 96 and then 102 points.

Trukno hit the pros in the AHL and, although his scoring was well below a point per game (64 games, 14–21–35), he ranked No. 5 among forwards in 2007–08. There's plenty of room to build after a season like that one, but it would prove to be his best as an Oilers prospect and Trukhno did not make the NHL. He did play several years in Europe, including Austria and Sweden.

NO. 157 OVERALL: LW FREDRIK PETTERSSON
Frolunda (Sweden Jr.)

Pettersson played left wing but shot right, a typical European alignment for wingers. He was undersized (5'10", 185 pounds) but was an explosive skater and an impressive stickhandler. In his draft year he played his junior hockey in Sweden and then moved to the Calgary Hitmen of the WHL, where he spent two seasons, scoring more than 20 goals both times.

NO. 220 OVERALL: LW MATTHEW GLASER
Ft. Saskatchewan Traders (AJHL)

A top scorer (62 games, 25–24–49) for this AJHL team, Glasser fell off offensively the following year and didn't play much or impress during four college seasons with the University of Denver. He played three seasons of pro in the CHL and in the Netherlands.

2005 Draft Summary

The Prendergast scouting department had a good draft, in many ways the best of its time together. The math suggested the club would have success with the players chosen based on draft-year numbers. (Number in parentheses is points per game.)

- Andrew Cogliano (OPJHL) age 17: 49 games, 36–66–102 (2.08)
- Taylor Chorney (USHS) age 17: 50 games, 4–30–34 (0.68)
- Danny Syvret (OHL) age 19: 62 games, 23–46–69 (1.11)
- Robby Dee (USHS) age 17: 28 games, 49–38–87 (3.11)
- Chris VandeVelde (USHS) age 17: 30 games, 35–32–67 (2.23)

- Slava Trukhno (QMJHL) age 17: 64 games, 25–34–59 (0.92)
- Frederik Pettersson (SuperElite U-20) age 17: 24 games, 9–8–17 (0.71)
- Matthew Glasser (AJHL) age 17: 62 games, 25–24–49 (0.79)

Cogliano's scoring numbers were off the charts and earned him first-round value, and most of this draft could be viewed as a positive from a math perspective. VandeVelde was the only one of the depth picks to turn out, but all were solid bets. Four of the eight picks made the NHL, and one of them is still playing as of 2021.

NHL Career Games Played

1. Andrew Cogliano: 1,066
2. Chris VandeVelde: 278
3. Taylor Chorney: 166
4. Danny Syvret: 59

The draft was set up for speed over size, and that was a partial reason for its success. It's also true that skill played a factor. Although Cogliano and VandeVelde spent much of their NHL careers in two-way or checking roles, both were scoring forwards on their draft day. That's the lesson Barry Fraser's final drafts proved time and time again.

Here's how the 2005 draft class compares to the preceding decade in terms of total NHL games played:

1. 1996 (1,924 games)
2. 2003 (1,905 games)

3. 2002 (1,579 games)
4. **2005 (1,569 games)**
5. 1998 (1,214 games)
6. 1997 (1,126 games)
7. 2001 (1,043 games)
8. 1999 (937 games)
9. 2000 (928 games)
10. 2004 (773 games)

Through five drafts, Prendergast had one fail (2004) and three that delivered more than 1,500 NHL games and counting.

Trades That Involved Draft Picks

On December 16, 2003, the Oilers traded centre Mike Comrie to the Philadelphia Flyers for defenceman Jeff Woywitka, the No. 25 overall pick in the 2004 draft (Rob Schremp), and a 2005 third-round pick (Danny Syvret).

On March 8, 2004, the Oilers traded goalie Tommy Salo and a 2005 sixth-round pick (Justin Mercier) to the Colorado Avalanche for defenceman Tom Gilbert.

On June 25, 2005, the NHL awarded the Oilers a compensatory selection for the loss of free agent Petr Nedved. The pick was No. 120, Vyacheslav Trukhno.

THE 2006 DRAFT

The 2005–06 season was the most exciting for Oilers fans since 1990, when the club won its fifth Stanley Cup. In Craig MacTavish's fifth season as head coach, Edmonton made the playoffs for the third time with him at the helm. The team won the first-round matchup against the Detroit Red Wings and then kept on going, all the way to the seventh game of the Stanley Cup Final, before falling to the Carolina Hurricanes.

General manager Kevin Lowe had an inspired season, acquiring Chris Pronger (impact defenceman) and Michael Peca (shutdown centre) in the summer, then addressing all other roster weaknesses at the trade deadline. Goalie Dwayne Roloson, defencemen Jaroslav Spacek and Dick Tarnstrom, and winger Sergei Samsonov made Edmonton a strong team across the board.

For one shining season, the glory Oilers were back in business with a new All-Star cast.

Part of the cost was a long list of draft picks, including the first-round selection sent to the Minnesota Wild for Roloson. It meant a short list of draft picks in 2006.

Prendergast and his team drafted just five men in 2006.

Patrick Thoresen was signed out of the SHL, Sweden's top league, in the summer of 2006. Although he came from Norway, Thoresen had established himself as a player of interest with his work with Djurgarden in Stockholm. In 2005–06, he scored 17–19–36 in 50 games and showed good speed and two-way play. He would spend very little time in the minors during 2006–07.

PROSPECT SPOTLIGHT
NO. 45 OVERALL: RD JEFF PETRY, DES MOINES BUCCANEERS (USHL)

Ranked No. 36 on the North American Central Scouting list, Petry didn't get a lot of pre-draft hype. He was the whole package at the junior level, including power play, and spiked during the playoffs in his draft year. At the time of the draft,

Prendergast told media the team had Petry as a high first-round pick on its list.

Scouting report and legacy: Jeff Petry ranks as one of Prendergast's best picks despite being chosen in the second round. As a mature NHL defenceman he was mobile, played an intelligent game, and was effective in both ends of the rink.

For many years after he was drafted, Petry was the most valuable player drafted after the first round by the organization.

He played heavy minutes at even strength and showed puck-moving and passing ability. Although Petry didn't produce much on the power play until being dealt to the Montreal Canadiens, his skill was obvious even as an Oilers rookie.

NO. 75 OVERALL: LD THEO PECKHAM
Owen Sound Attack (OHL)

Peckham's draft-day scouting report was positively glowing. A rugged defender with no fear, he was 6'1", 216 pounds on draft day and took 236 minutes in penalties during his draft season.

Peckham was a fast skater coming out of junior and he could defend. The elements were there for a long career in a shutdown role.

He turned pro in 2007–08 and played most of his entry deal in the minors, improving incrementally over those three years.

In 2010–11 he was ready for a full NHL season and delivered 71 games, 3–10–13, and 198 penalty minutes. He also had a five-on-five goal differential of 36–48 (minus-12), which was about average for Oilers defencemen that season (Petry was 17–28, minus-11). He was effective with partner Tom Gilbert. At that point, Peckham's future looked promising.

In 2011–12, he was most successful with Petry and Corey Potter, but was less decisive than he had been as a rookie. His five-on-five ice time fell by two minutes, and he played a reduced role after taking a puck in the face in February.

Entering training camp in 2012–13, he would be a third-pairing option and fighting for a job. That was the year of the lockout, so the season began late. He showed up at training camp at less than 100 percent fitness, forcing the Oilers to trade for Mark Fistric.

Edmonton flushed him; Peckham signed a two-way deal with the Chicago Blackhawks and did not see the NHL again. It was a difficult end to a promising career.

NO. 133 OVERALL: G BRYAN PITTON
Brampton Battalion (OHL)

Pitton was a curious choice because he didn't play much in his draft season. A backup in the OHL, his numbers (24 games, 3.43 goals-against average, .904 save percentage) didn't stand out. At 6'1", 168 pounds, he was average in height and slender in build. In his second season with the Battalion, he played a lot (61 games) but struggled (.879 save percentage) in front of a weak team. His final junior season (39 games, .911 save percentage) things appeared to kick in and he received a pro contract from Edmonton. He played mostly in the ECHL and was never a threat to take anyone's NHL job, but he did carve out a career in lower levels of pro hockey.

NO. 140 OVERALL: LD CODY WILD
Providence College (NCAA)

Wild kept showing up in a good way when Oilers scouts would drop in to view 2003 draft pick Colin McDonald play for Providence. Wild's numbers in his draft year (36 games, 6–15–21) stood out for a freshman on the defence-first Friars, especially considering he was just 18. He played two more years at Providence, turning pro with some promise despite his low draft number. Wild performed well in the AHL but got lost in the flood of young defencemen entering the system (Jeff Petry, Taylor Chorney) and was dealt to the Boston Bruins in the spring of 2010. He did not make the NHL but was a solid AHL defender for several years.

NO. 170 OVERALL: LC ALEXANDER BUMAGIN
Tolyatti Lada (RSL)

Drafted out of Russia's top league, where he was already playing as a regular (40 games, 9–14–23), Bumagin had periods of his career during which coming over to North America would have made sense. He never did, playing in Russia's top league through 2018–19.

2006 Draft Summary

In Oilers draft history, the team had never drafted so few players. The previous record was six, in 1979, a year that saw Edmonton draft three Hall of Famers. For Prendergast and his group, it would mean making every selection count. Here's what the math said. (Number in parentheses is points per game.)

- Jeff Petry (USHL) age 17: 48 games, 1–14–15 (0.31)
- Theo Peckham (OHL) age 17: 67 games, 6–9–15 (0.22)

- Bryan Pitton (OHL) age 17: 24 games, 3.43 goals-against average, .904 save percentage
- Cody Wild (NCAA) age 18: 36 games, 6–15–21 (0.58)
- Alexander Bumagin (RSL) age 18: 49 games, 9–14–23 (0.47)

It was a strange draft year. Edmonton had no first-round selection, and the first player chosen (Petry) didn't show up as an offensive contributor. However, his play (2–5–7 in 11 games) in the USHL showed potential. The only other player who showed some offensive promise was Bumagin, chosen late in the draft. Edmonton did well despite the lack of picks and the mediocre offence from the group.

NHL Career Games Played

1. Jeff Petry: 735
2. Theo Peckham: 160

Here's how the 2006 draft class compares to the preceding decade in terms of total NHL games played:

1. 2003 (1,905 games)
2. 2002 (1,579 games)
3. 2005 (1,569 games)
4. 1998 (1,214 games)
5. 1997 (1,126 games)
6. 2001 (1,043 games)
7. 1999 (937 games)
8. 2000 (928 games)
9. **2006 (895 games)**
10. 2004 (773 games)

Technically, the 2006 draft is a fail, but the five picks delivered 895 games and that's an impressive total. Petry remains active and it's possible he alone will push the final total past 1,000. Either way, I count 2006 as a pass for Edmonton.

Trades That Involved Draft Picks

On August 1, 2005, the Oilers traded Brad Isbister to the Boston Bruins for a 2006 fourth-round pick (James Delory).

On August 3, 2005, the Oilers traded Mike York and a fourth-round pick (Kevin Mongtomery) to the New York Islanders for Michael Peca.

On August 30, 2005, the Oilers traded a 2006 fourth-round pick to the Boston Bruins for Yan Stastny.

On November 19, 2005, the Oilers traded Alexei Semenov to the Florida Panthers for a fifth-round pick (No. 133 overall Bryan Pitton).

On March 8, 2006, the Oilers traded a 2006 first-round pick (Trevor Lewis) and a third-round pick (Spencer Machacek) to the Minnesota Wild for goalie Dwayne Roloson.

On March 9, 2006, the Oilers traded Marty Reasoner, Yan Stastny, and a 2006 second-round pick (Milan Lucic) for left winger Sergei Samsonov.

On June 24, 2006, the NHL awarded Edmonton a compensatory pick for Jesse Niinimaki not signing a pro contract. That selection was No. 45 (Jeff Petry).

On June 24, 2006, the Oilers traded a 2006 third-round pick (Michael Forney) and a 2006 seventh-round pick (Arturs Kulda) to the Atlanta Thrashers for selection No. 75 overall (Theo Peckham).

9

THE DECADE OF
DARKNESS BEGINS

THE 2007 DRAFT

ONE OF THE most difficult summers in Oilers history quickly followed the Game 7 loss in the Stanley Cup Final to the Carolina Hurricanes.

Edmonton's best player, Chris Pronger, asked for a trade during the spring. General manager Kevin Lowe obliged, and in doing so did not replace Pronger's minutes in the deal. What's more, free agency was unkind to the team, meaning players like Jaroslav Spacek and Sergei Samsonov were true rentals (signing elsewhere when the free-agent window opened).

Lowe's summer was already going to be busy, as high-performance youngsters such as Ales Hemsky, Shawn Horcoff, Fernando Pisani, and Jarret Stoll were looking for healthy salary increases.

Through the summer, Lowe was able to sign those youngsters, but heart-and-soul veteran Ryan Smyth stated he was unwilling to take a hometown discount. It set the stage for his exit at the 2007 trade deadline.

Lowe declined options for some players (Ty Conklin, Todd Harvey) and was able to retain goalie Dwayne Roloson, who had been acquired before the deadline in the spring.

Pronger was dealt to the Anaheim Ducks on July 3 for a package that included prospects, picks, and scoring right winger Joffrey Lupul.

The club could afford a couple of smaller free agents (Marty Reasoner, Daniel Tjarnqvist) but was in real trouble on defence due to the trade of Pronger and Spacek signing with the Buffalo Sabres.

In late August, the team signed winger Petr Sykora in an inspired move to add veteran skill.

It was a devastating season. Edmonton's win total fell from 41 to 32, points from 95 to 71, and goal differential from 256–251 (plus-5) to 195–248 (minus-53) in a shambles of a season.

Edmonton was left with a pile of draft picks and several interesting 2006–07 rookies:

- Patrick Thoresen: 68 games, 4–12–16
- Marc Pouliot: 46 games, 4–7–11
- Ladislav Smid: 77 games, 3–7–10
- Brad Winchester: 59 games, 4–5–9
- Tom Gilbert: 12 games, 1–5–6
- Mathieu Roy: 16 games, 2–0–2
- Zack Stortini: 29 games, 1–0–1
- Kyle Brodziak: 6 games, 1–0–1
- Danny Syvret: 16 games, 0–1–1

- Jean-Francois Jacques: 37 games, 0–0–0
- Bryan Young: 15 games, 0–0–0
- Alexei Mikhnov: 2 games, 0–0–0
- Sebastian Bisaillion: 2 games, 0–0–0
- Rob Schremp: 1 game, 0–0–0

Sebastian Bisaillon was signed in September of 2006 with the Oilers in an emergency situation defensively. He would play two games during 2006–07 with the Oilers (March 19 and 21, 2007). The Oilers did employ him in the minors during the 2007–08 and 2008–09 seasons before he settled in for a career in France.

The pressure was on Prendergast and his scouting staff in 2007. Various trades and a poor finish meant four high selections for Edmonton. It was imperative for Prendergast to deliver quality.

NO. 6 OVERALL: RC SAM GAGNER
London Knights (OHL)

Gagner had exceptional vision and passing ability, which made him a compelling draft option for Edmonton. The son of former NHL player Dave Gagner, his offensive instinct and touch passes were breathtaking.

At 5'11", 200 pounds, he wasn't a big player and his foot speed was not a plus. Although he was a centre, his instincts in this area were not strong. There was also the worry over the fact his linemate in London was Patrick Kane, the No. 1 overall pick in the draft. Kane was zooming Gagner's numbers, but by how much?

Gagner came to the NHL right away, partly because the Oilers needed good stories to excite the fan base. He delivered 49 points as a rookie and would score at least 40 in every full season he played in Edmonton during his first turn with the Oilers.

Gagner had coverage problems, which were significant. He did not progress as a player in outscoring at five on five, a key tenet for the Oilers over many years. Here are his on-ice goal differentials at five on five over his first seven NHL seasons:

- 2007–08: 38–49 (minus-11)
- 2008–09: 42–37 (plus-5)
- 2009–10: 35–38 (minus-3)
- 2010–11: 42–56 (minus-14)
- 2011–12: 47–39 (plus-8)
- 2012–13: 28–33 (minus-5)
- 2013–14: 32–56 (minus-22)

In 2013–14, he played centre against the second-toughest opposition available, and his line was overwhelmed by the task. Added to that, his offence and career length at an early age made him a very expensive player (he raced through his entry deal).

Gagner had extreme positives, but they were married to defensive coverage issues, and it cost him his role in Edmonton. The Oilers traded him, and the pick would have to be considered less than a complete success despite his long and offensively productive NHL career.

NO. 15 OVERALL: RD ALEX PLANTE
Calgary Hitmen (WHL)

The second player chosen by the Prendergast team remains controversial to this day, and I believe this selection was central in the Oilers' decision to replace him as scouting director.

Plante was regarded as a good skill player (58 games, 8–30–38) and a two-way defender with good size (6'3", 225 pounds). There were speed concerns; I spoke to a scout on draft weekend who was shocked Edmonton took him in the first round because of his lack of mobility. At the time, however, the Oilers suggested his speed would be NHL quality when he arrived.

Plante spent most of the next season dealing with injuries (mostly back problems) and his offence (36 games, 1–1–2) disappeared. Plante's career derailed before he reached the pros and his 10 NHL games are a severe disappointment. Injuries had a big impact on his career, and it's likely the organization had an incorrect grade on his skating.

In the meantime, there was a media uproar over the Oilers passing on two forwards—Alexei Cherepanov and Angelo Esposito. In mid-September, the club announced Stu MacGregor was the new chief scout and Prendergast had been bumped upstairs.

NO. 21 OVERALL: RC RILEY NASH
Salmon Arm Silverbacks (BCHL)

Nash had a nice range of skills, including a strong reputation for being a two-way centre who could score well enough to play a second-line role.

General manager Kevin Lowe traded two picks to move up in the draft, and most Oilers fans identified Mikael Backlund as a likely target. When the club added a Tier 2 centre who wasn't an explosive offensive threat, fans were angry. Even worse for fans, Backlund was drafted by the rival Calgary Flames three picks later.

Nash developed into the two-way centre he was expected to become and has played more than 500 NHL games. He is also shy as an offensive player, more of a bottom-six solution than a middle-six centre.

He was a fine, if early, selection.

NO. 97 OVERALL: LW LINUS OMARK
Lulea (SEL)

A truly delightful skill winger, Omark had ridiculous puck skills that rivaled 2003 pick Rob Schremp in creativity.

He lacked size (5'9", 168 pounds) and was not a physical player. His two-way skills were not strong. He was also 20 on draft day, meaning there was increased urgency surrounding getting him to the NHL.

Omark didn't come over until 2010, and by that time the Oilers had high-end skill wingers everywhere. If he had signed in 2008 or 2009, I think he might have had a much stronger NHL career. As it was, he played 79 electric NHL games before heading to Europe and entertaining hockey fans for a decade plus. As of 2020–21, he was playing in Switzerland and posting more than a point per game.

NO. 127 OVERALL: LC MILAN KYTNAR
Topolcany (Slovakia)

Kytnar was a two-way centre prospect who blew up his junior league, but scouts needed to see him in a higher league. In his draft-plus-one season, he arrived in the WHL and settled into a checking role. Checking centres in junior rarely spend much time in the NHL, and for Kytnar it was a single game in 2011–12. He found his way back to Slovakia, where he remains a productive player.

NO. 157 OVERALL: LW WILLIAM QUIST

Tingsryds (Sweden Jr.)

Oilers fans who like order were cheering for Quist, as the team has never dressed a player whose last name starts with a "Q" in an NHL game. It was not to be, as the big power winger remained in Europe, mostly Sweden, for his playing career.

2007 Draft Summary

Prendergast and his scouting staff had six first-round opportunities in their first six drafts, then were gifted three picks in 2007. What did the math think of the selections? (Number in parentheses is points per game.)

- Sam Gagner (OHL) age 17: 53 games, 35–83–118 (2.23)
- Alex Plante (WHL) age 17: 58 games, 8–30–38 (0.66)
- Riley Nash (BCHL) age 17: 55 games, 38–46–84 (1.53)
- Linus Omark (SEL) age 19: 50 games, 8–9–17 (0.34)
- Milan Kytnar (Slovakia U-18) age 17: 53 games, 37–54–91 (1.72)
- William Quist (U-20 Sweden Elite) age 17: 20 games, 8–15–23 (1.15)

Edmonton drafted an impact offensive prospect in Gagner, whose numbers were zoomed by linemate Patrick Kane in London. Plante was drafted with impressive offensive forwards still on the board (including Russian Alexei Cherepanov), and Nash was drafted with Mikael Backlund still available, making the Oilers' draft choices curious.

Those decisions had an impact on Prendergast's future.

That isn't hyperbole. *Team 1260 Radio* (now *TSN 1260 Edmonton*) hosted a draft show at Schanks in Edmonton that year with Bob Stauffer (now an Oilers employee who works on television and radio broadcasts for the team) and Guy Flaming (a prospects expert in the Edmonton market for the last two decades).

Stauffer specifically questioned those choices with so much pure offensive talent still available, mentioning both Cherapanov and Backlund as superior options. He was correct.

Math supported the Gagner pick, but it was less enamored with Plante and Nash. Cherepanov (47 games, 18–11–29 in Russia's top pro league, the second-best hockey league in the world at that time) was a spectacular talent whose death a couple of years later devastated the hockey world. Based on his talent and numbers, he would have been an impact player in the NHL.

It was a strange year at the draft table. Edmonton went into the weekend with four picks in the top 36 overall, including a top-10 selection. More was expected than what was delivered.

NHL Career Games Played

1. Sam Gagner: 886
2. Riley Nash: 578
3. Linus Omark: 79
4. Alex Plante: 10
5. Milan Kytnar: 1

Gagner and Nash remain active NHL players, and Omark continues to slice and dice defencemen in Europe. This is a difficult draft to judge because the 1,000-game marker is satisfied, but little else was accomplished.

Here's how the 2007 draft class compares to the preceding decade in terms of total NHL games played:

1. 2003 (1,905 games)
2. 2002 (1,579 games)
3. 2005 (1,569 games)
4. **2007 (1,554 games)**
5. 1998 (1,214 games)
6. 2001 (1,043 games)
7. 1999 (937 games)
8. 2000 (928 games)
9. 2006 (895 games)
10. 2004 (773 games)

In seven drafts, the Prendergast group had five that produced more than 1,000 games and two that should be fails. I noted the 2004 draft included a terrific goaltender, so I gave it a pass. The 2007 draft also passes, but with an explanation. I'm not certain Prendergast earned his fate—after all, the picks traded (more below) would have been Kevin Lowe's responsibility—but there's no doubt the draft fell well short of expectations.

Trades That Involved Draft Picks

On March 8, 2006, the Oilers traded a 2006 first-round pick (Trevor Lewis) and a 2007 third-round pick (Spencer Machacek) to the Minnesota Wild for Dwayne Roloson.

On July 3, 2006, the Oilers traded Chris Pronger to the Anaheim Ducks for Joffrey Lupul and Ladislav Smith, a first-round pick in the 2007 draft (Nick Ross), a 2008 second-round pick (Travis Hamonic), and a conditional 2008 first-round pick (Jordan Eberle).

On July 10, 2006, the Oilers traded a 2007 seventh-round pick (Nick Eno) to the Buffalo Sabres for Jan Hejda.

On February 27, 2007, the Oilers traded winger Ryan Smyth to the New York Islanders for Robert Nilsson, Ryan O'Marra, and the No. 15 overall selection in the 2007 draft (Alex Plante).

On June 22, 2007, the Oilers traded picks No. 30 (Nick Ross) and No. 36 (Joel Gistedt) in the 2007 draft to the Phoenix Coyotes for the No. 21 overall pick (Riley Nash) in the 2007 draft.

EVALUATION
KEVIN PRENDERGAST, SCOUTING DIRECTOR (2001-07)

SUCCESS IN THE FIRST 30 SELECTIONS OF EACH DRAFT

Prendergast was scouting director for seven years, drafting nine players in the top 30 overall. During his time in the head job, Edmonton enjoyed just one top-10 overall selection (Sam Gagner). His first pick, Ales Hemsky, enjoyed a solid career, as did Devan Dubnyk, Andrew Cogliano, Riley Nash, and Gagner. Of the nine men drafted by Prendergast in the first 30 picks, five (56 percent) played 500-plus NHL games. Prendergast produced NHL players, but only Hemsky could push the river and drive results on his own. Dubnyk was also a difference-maker at the other end of the ice.

SUCCESS IN THE FIRST 100 SELECTIONS OF EACH DRAFT

Prendergast and his scouts chose 24 players between picks No. 31 and 100 during his seven seasons. The best in the group (Jarret Stoll, Matt Greene, Jeff Petry) rival the first-round picks in terms of quality. A couple others (Zack Stortini, Chris

VandeVelde) found roles that allowed them to stay in the league for extended periods. Three men (Stoll, Greene, Petry) played 500-plus NHL games (12.5 percent).

SUCCESS AFTER THE FIRST 100 SELECTIONS OF EACH DRAFT

Edmonton chose 38 men after selection No. 100 during the Prendergast era. Kyle Brodziak was a home-run pick at No. 214 overall in 2003, going on to play in 917 NHL games. He's one of the best value picks in team history. Productive players included Jussi Markanen and Troy Bodie. One player (Brodziak) played in more than 500 NHL games (2.6 percent).

SUCCESS IN WHAT DEVELLANO CALLS "PROJECTING"

The Hemsky pick was inspired, and full credit is due the scouting staff for landing a top-line player in the middle of the first round. Prendergast and his staff also found two productive goaltenders (Dubnyk and Markkanen) and a fine two-way defender in Petry, who came a long way after his draft day.

SUCCESS IN ADDRESSING TEAM NEEDS

The Oilers were shy on high-level skill when Prendgerast took over the big job, so Hemsky was exactly what the team needed. The emphasis on goaltending also represented an attempt to shore up an area of need.

BEST FIRST-ROUND PICK

Ales Hemsky played during a difficult period in the organization's history, so his breathtaking skills lacked a consistent partner to help build a dominant line. He is easily Prendergast's best pick.

LEAST SUCCESSFUL FIRST-ROUND PICK

Jesse Niinimaki wins in a tough competition. The big Finn was injured in the months immediately following the draft and never got close to the NHL. Alex Plante was also injured after the draft, but he found his way to the NHL for a few games.

BEST PICK AFTER THE FIRST ROUND

In a tight race between Brodziak, Greene, Stoll, and Petry, the edge belongs to Petry for his strong two-way play and durability.

WHAT STYLE DID PRENDERGAST EMPLOY?

Coming out of the Fraser era, there's plenty of evidence to suggest Prendergast trusted his scouts and the list created by the draft process. An example would be Hemsky, who was never at his best when Prendergast dropped in to view him play. In this way, the Prendergast era would have been very different for scouts than their experience in Fraser's time. How much that hurt or harmed is an open question.

WHAT PLAYER TYPE DID PRENDERGAST LOOK FOR AT THE DRAFT?

After hitting a home run with the high-skill Hemsky, the scouting staff proved effective in finding two-way types. Stoll, Greene, Brodziak, and Petry all fit the bill, and even Cogliano would find his way as a player with a nice range of skills. It's perhaps a reason the Prendergast team had as much success in the second round as it enjoyed in the top 30 overall picks.

THE PRENDERGAST RECORD

Here is the tale of the tape from 2001 to '07 for Prendergast:
- Players drafted by Prendergast: 67
- Players who made the NHL: 33 (49.2 percent)
- Players who were in 200-plus NHL games: 11 (16.4 percent)
- Players who were in 500-plus NHL games: 9 (13.4 percent)
- Impact players: Ales Hemsky

Prendergast's best draft pick was his first, a trend that would continue for some time among chief scouts in Edmonton. Ales Hemsky would have pushed for the Hall of Fame if he had stayed healthy. Here are Fraser's numbers in the same categories:
- Players drafted by Fraser: 233
- Players who made the NHL: 96 (41.2 percent)

- Players who were in 200-plus NHL games: 40 (17.2 percent)
- Players who were in 500-plus NHL games: 29 (12.4 percent)
- Impact players (11): Andy Moog, Esa Tikkanen, Jason Arnott, Miro Satan, Ryan Smyth, and the Hall of Famers (see below)
- Hall of Fame (6): Kevin Lowe, Mark Messier, Glenn Anderson, Paul Coffey, Jari Kurri, Grant Fuhr

The obvious difference comes in the number of impact players Fraser was able to deliver (one every two seasons). The Oilers would move Prendergast out of the organization with another shuffle just a few years later.

THE 2008 DRAFT

After the 2006 Stanley Cup run and the trades of Chris Pronger and Ryan Smyth, coach Craig MacTavish had a difficult time getting his team to play as a unit. It was an inexperienced team in most areas and 2006–07 was a trying season for the coach.

In 2007–08, the Oilers missed the playoffs, but MacT had things going in a good direction. Edmonton improved by nine wins and 17 points, and the goal differential went from minus-53 to minus-16. It was an impressive recovery, despite missing the playoffs.

Although cracks would form defensively in the years that followed, several rookies were impressive in 2007–08:

- Sam Gagner: 79 games, 13–36–49
- Andrew Cogliano: 82 games, 18–27–45
- Tom Gilbert: 82 games, 13–20–33

- Curtis Glencross: 26 games, 9–4–13
- Mathieu Roy: 13 games, 0–1–1
- Rob Schremp: 2 games, 0–0–0
- Bryan Young: 2 games, 0–0–0
- Liam Reddox: 1 game, 0–0–0
- Theo Peckham: 1 game, 0–0–0

Gagner, Cogliano, and Gilbert would enjoy long NHL careers, and Glencross was a productive player for several seasons. Among Oilers rookie crops in their rookie seasons, the 2007–08 group was impressive.

Bryan Lerg was signed in April 2008 as a college free agent from Michigan State. He had offensive ability, scoring 20 goals in each of his final two seasons in university. He was a fine bet and did play eight games with the San Jose Sharks between 2014 and '16, but he was strictly a minor leaguer with the Oilers organization.

Stu MacGregor was the new scouting director, taking over from Kevin Prendergast. MacGregor was the third chief scout in Oilers history and his style was more in line with Prendergast (a consensus leader) than Fraser, whose style was forged when entire scouting staffs could fit in the front seat of a car.

PROSPECT SPOTLIGHT
NO. 22 OVERALL: RW JORDAN EBERLE, REGINA PATS (WHL)

Eberle was a centre on draft day but quickly established himself as a quality scoring prospect from right wing.

Scouting report and legacy: He scored 155 goals in four seasons with the Pats, including a 50-goal season in his final junior campaign. He also dominated two World Junior Championships and scored one of the biggest goals in WJ history. In the 2009 semifinal he scored with mere seconds left to tie the game against Russia, with Canada eventually winning and securing a gold medal.

Eberle had fast hands and a quick release that allowed him to score goals from range and in close. He was perhaps most dangerous driving toward the net with the puck on his stick. Through 2020, he averaged 25.5 goals per 82 games.

In the spring of 2017, the Oilers made the playoffs and went deep into the second round before losing in seven games. Eberle did not enjoy a strong playoff and was traded that summer to the New York Islanders.

He remains one of the most impressive draft picks in team history, chosen No. 22 overall and delivering strong offence for many years.

NO. 103 OVERALL: RD JOHAN MOTIN
Bofors (Swe–I)

Motin was a big, right-handed defenceman who had a solid if unspectacular résumé on draft day. A defence-first player, his size (6'2", 211 pounds) was a big selling point. Edmonton didn't have a second- or third-round pick, so Motin was viewed as a safe selection who had a chance to make the NHL. He played in just one game with the Oilers but was solid in his three-year AHL audition in the organization. Edmonton's RHD pipeline, which included Tom Gilbert, Jeff Petry, and Alex Plante, left Motin out in the cold. He would return to Sweden and five seasons in the SHL before moving to Finland (Liiga) and playing a significant role for HIFK Helsinki.

NO. 133 OVERALL: LW PHILIPPE CORNET
Rimouski Oceanic (QMJHL)

Cornet's scouting report read like a pure tweener. He was skilled but not fast. He would work to get to scoring areas but wasn't a winger with size (6'0", 196 pounds) or a great deal of grit. Cornet did play in two NHL games, getting an assist on a Jordan Eberle goal. In the AHL, he scored 24 goals in his second season, and he was productive in parts of five seasons in the minors. Cornet would sign in Finland and play three seasons in the Liiga beginning in 2016.

NO. 163 OVERALL: LW TEEMU HARTIKAINEN
KalPa (Finland Jr.)

At 6'1" and 233 pounds, Hartikainen was a big man with skill and slightly below-average foot speed. He adapted quickly to every new league he encountered. In his first full Liiga season in Finland, he scored 17 goals. In his first AHL season, he scored 17 goals. In his first 12 NHL games, he scored three goals.

Hartikainen was unable to establish himself under coach Tom Renney in Edmonton and then couldn't deliver much offence during a half season in the NHL under Ralph Krueger in 2012–13. A new manager meant changes and Hartikainen's rights were dealt to Toronto in January 2014. By that time Hartikainen was scoring well in Russia's KHL, for Ufa. As of 2020–21, he had scored more than 130 goals in eight seasons.

Among Oilers picks over 40-plus years, Hartikainen is one of several who had NHL ability but was crossed up by management/coaching changes and he fell through the cracks. Bad timing, that's all.

NO. 193 OVERALL: RD JORDAN BENDFELD
Medicine Hat Tigers (WHL)

A tough-as-nails defender with size (6'2", 218 pounds) who was 20 on his birthday, Bendfeld turned pro right away but played only three seasons in the pros, mostly in the ECHL.

2008 Draft Summary

Stu MacGregor was part of the Prendergast staff, and based on anecdotal evidence, he continued the democratic style employed by his predecessor. In MacGregor's first draft, it was difficult to get much of a feel for what he valued. The club had just one selection in the top 100, and the staff hit a home run. Here's what the math looked like in 2008. (Number in parentheses is points per game.)

- Jordan Eberle (WHL) age 17: 70 games, 42–33–75 (1.07)
- Johan Motin (Allsvenskan) age 17: 15 games, 2–3–5 (0.33)
- Philippe Cornet (QMJHL) age 17: 61 games, 23–26–49 (0.80)
- Teemu Hartikainen (Jr. Liiga) age 17: 37 games, 10–7–17 (0.46)

- Jordan Bendfeld (WHL) age 19: 72 games, 6–19–25 (0.35)

Eberle's goal-scoring prowess was the biggest bullet point highlight, and Hartikainen showed some pop in Finland. It was a difficult first draft on which to read the new scouting director, but the first pick was a home run for the new director for the third time in three tries (Fraser = Kevin Lowe, Prendergast = Ales Hemsky).

We have reached the point in the book where careers remain in full swing and are several years from reaching conclusion. As of this writing, Jordan Eberle is 11 years into a career with at least five more seasons likely to come. So, although the 2008 draft doesn't currently have 1,000 games amassed, it receives a passing grade due to Eberle's impressive decade.

NHL Career Games Played

1. Jordan Eberle: 779
2. Teemu Hartikainen: 52
3. Philippe Cornet: 2
4. Johan Motin: 1
5. Jordan Bendfeld: 0

Edmonton once again had five selections, matching 2006 as the lowest total for one season.

Here's how the 2008 draft class compares to the preceding decade in terms of total NHL games played:

1. 2003 (1,905 games)
2. 2002 (1,579 games)
3. 2005 (1,569 games)

4. 2007 (1,554 games)
5. 2001 (1,043 games)
6. 1999 (937 games)
7. 2000 (928 games)
8. 2006 (895 games)
9. **2008 (834 games)**
10. 2004 (773 games)

This was the first draft with Stu MacGregor as scouting director, and the success of the Eberle pick ensured success. I also give the scouts credit for Hartikainen, who was an excellent find but had bad timing with the organization. It was similar to Prendergast's first draft, with Ales Hemsky being the centrepiece.

Trades That Involved Draft Picks

On July 3, 2006, the Oilers traded Chris Pronger to the Anaheim Ducks for Joffrey Lupul, Ladislav Smid, a 2007 first-round pick (Nick Ross), the No. 22 overall pick in the 2008 draft (Jordan Eberle), and a 2008 second-round pick (Travis Hamonic).

On February 18, 2007, the Oilers traded Marc-Andre Bergeron and a 2008 third-round pick (Kirill Petrov) to the New York Islanders for Denis Grebeshkov.

On July 5, 2007, the Oilers traded a 2008 second-round pick (Travis Hamonic) to the New York Islanders for Allan Rourke and a 2008 third-round pick (Kirill Petrov).

On August 2, 2007, the Oilers successfully signed Dustin Penner of the Anaheim Ducks to an offer sheet. Compensation included 2008 No. 12 overall pick Tyler Myers, No. 43 overall pick Justin Schultz, and No. 73 overall pick Kirill Petrov.

THE 2009 DRAFT

The 2008–09 season would be the final one for Craig MacTavish as Oilers coach. A decision by Kevin Lowe to hire Steve Tambellini for the general manager's job may have contributed, as the Lowe-MacT combination neared a decade with just one deep playoff run.

MacTavish's final team posted just 85 points and missed the playoffs, but the goal differential (234–248, minus-14) improved slightly year over year.

Tambellini would bring in legendary coach Pat Quinn as head coach and Tom Renney as associate coach to try and pry five (or so) more wins from the roster.

NO. 10 OVERALL: LW MAGNUS PAAJARVI
Timra (SEL)

Paajarvi had a complete skill set on draft day, although his scoring (50 games, 7-10-17) was a little shy. Paajarvi's strongest assets were blazing speed and strong two-way acumen. He was an excellent passer and his shot was viewed as a positive but would become more of an issue as his career rolled out.

In his draft season, Paajarvi was a regular in the SHL, a fine league and a very good indicator for the player. The one concern surrounded his shooting percentage (seven goals on 103 shots, 6.8 percent), which is very low for a player projected as a future contributor on a skill line.

As his career progressed, the shot percentage story had peaks and valleys but remained a worry:

- Age 18: 7 goals on 103 shots, 6.8 percent (SEL)
- Age 19: 12 goals on 160 shots, 7.5 percent (SEL)

- Age 20: 15 goals on 180 shots, 8.3 percent (NHL)
- Age 21: 2 goals on 79 shots, 2.5 percent (NHL)
- Age 22: 9 goals on 75 shots, 12.0 percent (NHL)

The Oilers traded him in the summer of 2013 in a big deal for winger David Perron. Trading such a young player has risks, but in this case, Perron was a perfect fit and Paajarvi began to drift. He would play in the NHL for most of the decade, signing in the KHL for the 2019–20 season.

The scouting reports were correct save for the shot quality. Paajarvi's lack of a shot turned him from a top-six contributor into a fast-checking winger who brought inconsistent offence.

NO. 40 OVERALL: LC ANTON LANDER
Timra (SEL)

Born 12 days apart and in hospitals separated by about six hours' drive, Paajarvi and second-round pick Anton Lander played for Timra together and appeared destined to play many years with the Oilers in the NHL.

Lander was a centre, a leader who played with some edge to his game. He lacked Paajarvi's brilliant speed and was not projected to score at the heights expected of Edmonton's first-round selection.

He played well after the draft, improving in both seasons (still in Timra) before coming over to North America. He was projected to play in the AHL until ready, important for a player who needed to figure out where the goals were scored. New head coach Tom Renney loved his smart play and his character at Oilers camp, and his speed had improved. Lander made the Oilers in the fall of 2011.

He didn't play much, mostly penalty kill, but the Oilers kept him on the roster for most of the season. Lander took the rest of his entry contract to find his scoring touch in the AHL, eventually posting a strong year (46 games, 18–34–52 for the Oklahoma City Barons) in 2013–14.

Lander flourished at the NHL level in 2014–15 when his AHL coach (Todd Nelson) replaced Dallas Eakins in Edmonton. When Nelson wasn't hired the following season, Lander went back to being a fringe player.

He signed in the KHL in time for the 2017–18 season and has been a productive player since.

Lander had a wide range of skills and was not far from an NHL career. If he had been chosen by an organization with more patience, or if his skating were a half-step faster, his NHL career might have been longer than 215 games.

A quick note: 215 games from a second-round pick is a successful career.

NO. 71 OVERALL: LD TROY HESKETH
Minnetonka High School (USHS, Minnesota)

A tall, lean two-way defender who was reportedly on his way to Wisconsin (a fine college program), Hesketh caught the eye of Oilers scouts, who reportedly drafted him early to keep him away from other interested teams.

He did not develop as hoped. In his first 22 USHL games with the Chicago Steel, he did not score a point and was not effective defensively. Hesketh didn't remain in hockey for long.

There are times when players peak in their draft seasons and don't make any progress beyond that point. It's disappointing for player and team both.

NO. 82 OVERALL: RW CAMERON ABNEY
Everett Silvertips (WHL)

Edmonton drafted Abney, an enforcer, when there was still abundant skill on the draft board. (Cody Eakin was chosen a few picks later.)

Abney was a big player (6'5", 205 pounds) and a good skater, but his main claim to fame was as a fighter. He broke his hand while still in junior and it made him less effective. Abney did sign and turn pro in the Edmonton system, peaking out at 18 AHL games.

NO. 99 OVERALL: RD KYLE BIGOS
Vernon Vipers (BCHL)

Bigos turned 20 a little over one month before the draft and was on his way to Merrimack College (NCAA), where he would play four years. He was a big defenceman, 6'5" and 235 pounds. A big hitter with a big shot, speed was a worry but rumours at the time had the New Jersey Devils interested. When he turned pro, Bigos played in the ECHL for a few years and peaked with eight AHL games.

NO. 101 OVERALL: LW TONI RAJALA
Ilves (Finland Jr.)

At 5'10", 163 pounds, Rajala was a small winger with big skill. He scored 19 points in six games at the U-18 World Junior Championships, and spent his draft-plus-one season in the WHL with the Brandon Wheat Kings (60 games, 26–36–73). He went back to Finland for a couple years and arrived in North America in time for the 2012–13 season. He was strong in the AHL (46 games, 17–28–45) and in the ECHL (29 games, 18–20–38) and looked like a strong candidate for an NHL audition. It never came. Rajala signed in Sweden, then the KHL, and is currently a feature player for Biel in the top Swiss league.

NO. 133 OVERALL: G OLIVIER ROY
Cape Breton Screaming Eagles (QMJHL)

A famous junior goalie, Roy fell on draft day and Edmonton picked him in Round 5. He posted some strong numbers early in the low minors but was never able to grab a foothold on an AHL job. He signed in Austria and then Germany, playing almost a decade in the pros.

2009 Draft Summary

The 2008 draft didn't allow Stu MacGregor and his staff much of a chance to show what they could do, as they possessed just one pick in the top 100. The 2009 draft saw the team use five picks in the first 100, and the math had a strong reaction. (Number in parentheses is points per game.)

- Magnus Paajarvi (SHL) age 17: 50 games, 7–10–17 (0.340)
- Anton Lander (SHL) age 17: 47 games, 4–6–10 (0.21)
- Troy Hesketh (USHS) age 17: numbers are unavailable
- Cameron Abney (WHL) age 17: 48 games, 1–3–4 (0.08)
- Kyle Bigos (BCHL) age 19: 58 games, 8–25–33 (0.57)
- Toni Rajala (Jr. Liiga) age 17: 31 games, 14–17–31 (1.00)
- Olivier Roy (QMJHL) age 17: 54 games, 2.84 goals-against average, .905 save percentage

The change to appointing MacGregor as scouting director offered hope in 2008, but much of 2009 resembles Edmonton's old bad habits. Drafting a very raw high school defenceman (Hesketh) in the third round plus a pure enforcer in the top 100 (Abney) are not high-percentage moves.

On the other hand, Rajala is great value in the fourth round and Roy was a potentially major find in the fifth round. Only two men made the NHL.

NHL Career Games Played

1. Magnus Paajarvi: 467
2. Anton Lander: 215

Paajarvi and Lander were both reasonable bets, but both men had flaws the scouting staff needed to identify. Despite all the speed Paajarvi possessed and Lander's two-way play, there were areas of the game that kept both from enjoying long careers. Paajarvi's ability to score goals and Lander's foot speed were enough to drive them from the league as young men.

Here's how the 2009 draft class compares to the preceding decade in terms of total NHL games played:

1. 2003 (1,905 games)
2. 2002 (1,579 games)
3. 2005 (1,569 games)
4. 2007 (1,554 games)
5. 2001 (1,043 games)
6. 2000 (928 games)
7. 2006 (895 games)
8. 2008 (834 games)
9. 2004 (773 games)
10. **2009 (682 games)**

Although the 2008 class—MacGregor's first draft—has amassed fewer than 1,000 games, Jordan Eberle will one day (barring injury) pass that total on his own. It was a success.

MacGregor's second draft, 2009, ranks among the poorest in the team's history. Not getting it right in later rounds (Hesketh, Abney) is a concern, but the Paajarvi and Lander issues are the kinds of mistakes scouting staffs cannot make. Paajarvi didn't have a plus shot and Lander's boots were slow enough to keep him from an NHL career.

Trades That Involved Draft Picks

On July 1, 2007, the Oilers traded Jason Smith and Joffrey Lupul to the Philadelphia Flyers for Joni Pitkanen, Geoff Sanderson, and the No. 82 pick in the 2009 entry draft (Cameron Abney).

On March 4, 2009, the Oilers traded Erik Cole and a 2009 fifth-round pick (Matt Kennedy) to the Carolina Hurricanes for Patrick O'Sullivan and a 2009 second-round pick (Jesse Blacker).

On March 4, 2009, the Oilers traded a 2009 second-round pick (Jesse Blacker) to the Buffalo Sabres for Ales Kotalik.

On June 27, 2009, the Oilers traded Kyle Brodziak and a 2009 sixth-round pick (Darcy Kuemper) to the Minnesota Wild for the No. 99 overall pick (Kyle Bigos) and No. 132 overall (Olivier Roy) selection.

On June 27, 2009, the Oilers traded a 2009 seventh-round pick (Michael Sdao) to the Ottawa Senators for a 2010 sixth-round pick (Drew Czwerwonka).

Junior Points per Game

The first decade of the century saw the Oilers draft a productive group from the CHL in the first round.

When viewing the numbers below, it's important to put them in historical context.

Mid-80s junior forwards delivering a point per game were playing in a far more offensive league than the men who played 2000–09. Kim Issel's points-per-game draft season (1.00 point per game) came in a year when his team scored 5.89 goals a game during 1985–86.

Jordan Eberle scored his 1.07 points per game in 2007–08, when his team scored 3.01 goals a game.

PLAYER	YEAR	LGE	AGE	PTS/ GAME	NLGP	NHL PTS/ GAME
SAM GAGNER	2007	OHL	17	2.23	886	0.53
ALES HEMSKY	2001	QMJHL	17	1.47	845	0.68
ROB SCHREMP	2004	OHL	17	1.19	114	0.47
MARC POULIOT	2003	QMJHL	17	1.12	192	0.30
JORDAN EBERLE	2008	WHL	17	1.07	779	0.71

Three of five have enjoyed productive NHL careers, and all five men played more than one season in the NHL. Eberle's WHL points per game is the lowest on the list, but he has delivered the highest points-per-game total during his career. Hemsky may eventually hold the highest number, as some of Eberle's lower-point seasons will likely arrive in the final years of his career.

10

A FALSE SPRING

THE 2010 DRAFT

THE **2009-10 SEASON** under coach Pat Quinn was the second worst in the history of the Oilers to this point in time. Just 62 points in an 82-game season and a goal differential of minus-70 (214–284) gave fans and management a good idea about just how good Craig MacTavish was behind the bench. His final season saw the team gather 85 points and post a goal differential of minus-14.

Legend has it that Daryl Katz, Edmonton's owner, used the word "rebuild" in the early hours of January 2010, and from that point on the organization focused its attention on the June draft and optimizing return.

The 2009–10 season had an interesting group of rookies, including two goaltenders, who received a total of 64 starts:

- Ryan Stone: 27 games, 0–6–6
- Taylor Chorney: 42 games, 0–3–3
- Theo Peckham: 15 games, 0–1–1

- Alex Plante: 4 games, 0–1–1
- Ryan O'Marra: 3 games, 0–1–1
- Colin McDonald: 2 games, 1–0–1
- Johan Motin: 1 game, 0–0–0
- Jeff Deslauriers: 48 games, 3.26 goals-against average, .901 save percentage
- Devan Dubnyk: 16 games, 3.57 goals-against average, .889 save percentage

PROSPECT SPOTLIGHT
NO. 1 OVERALL: LW TAYLOR HALL, WINDSOR SPITFIRES (OHL)

Edmonton finished last and won the lottery, meaning it secured the first overall selection. It was the first time in team history that had happened, and the scouting staff took painstaking care to make the right choice.

It came down to winger Taylor Hall of the Windsor Spitfires and centre Tyler Seguin of the Plymouth Whalers. Scouting director MacGregor said he went back and forth over the year, ranking Hall first early, then Seguin, and then finally decided on Hall. A decade later, both men would have been quality choices.

Scouting report and legacy: Hall was the most dynamic young player to arrive in Edmonton in many years. He combined great speed with exceptional stickhandling and passing ability. One of his true gifts was an ability to gain the zone under control and allow the Oilers to set up offensively.

Hall's arrival coincided with some advanced statistics that allowed fans to get a clearer view of what he was accomplishing on the ice. One of the statistics is IPP, defined as "measuring a player's individual points percentage while he's on the ice." So, if the Oilers scored 50 goals while Hall was on the ice, and he had 25 points, then his IPP would be 50 percent.

As a rookie, Hall scored 67 percent IPP and then 75 and then two seasons in the 90s. He has long been a champion of the individual points percentage, which is good, but also means if offence is going to happen, it has to run through Hall.

His linemates were less talented and the teams he played on took a big step down when Hall and his line were off the ice. In 2015–16, when Hall was on the ice, Edmonton's five-on-five goal differential was 58–53 (plus-5). With Hall off the ice at five on five, the total was 76–117 (minus-41).

Based on his six seasons in Edmonton, Hall earned a position in the heart of the order for the Oilers. Per 82 games with the Oilers, Hall scored 28–43–71 and was the most dangerous outscorer on the team.

A change in management over the spring and summer of 2015 set the stage for one of the most lopsided trades in NHL history. New general manager Peter Chiarelli sent Hall (who would win a Hart Trophy in the years to come as NHL MVP) to the New Jersey Devils for shutdown defenceman Adam Larsson. Larsson was a fine defender, but the value on the trade favoured New Jersey in a big way. The deal came in the summer of 2016.

As of this writing, Hall begins his second decade of NHL play as one of the most dangerous wingers in the game.

NO. 31 OVERALL: RW TYLER PITLICK
Minnesota State–Mankato (NCAA)

Pitlick had good size (6'2", 195 pounds) and speed, while also scoring 50 goals in 43 games over two high school seasons before heading to college.

A right-shot centre, he scored 11 goals in 38 games in his first college season. The scouting organization International Scouting Services said Pitlick could play "with finesse and power" and that's what the Oilers liked in him.

Pitlick spent his draft-plus-one season with the Medicine Hat Tigers, posting 27 goals in 56 games—another good, not great,

In 2010, Edmonton finished last and won the lottery, meaning it secured the first overall selection in the draft. It was the first time in team history that had happened, and the pressure was on the scouts to make the right choice. They succeeded by taking left winger Taylor Hall. *(AP Photo/The Canadian Press, John Ulan)*

offensive season. During his entry-contract season with the AHL Oklahoma City Barons, Pitlick was often injured and couldn't build any momentum at that level.

Pitlick spent all or part of five seasons in the AHL, finally making the NHL grade for good in 2016–17 (31 games, 8–3–11). Ironically, Pitlick's injury that season allowed him to become an unrestricted free agent years earlier than would have been normal. He signed with the Dallas Stars and then the Philadelphia Flyers, having finally emerged as a productive middle-six winger with size and some scoring ability. He continues to play a successful role as an NHL journeyman.

NO. 46 OVERALL: LHD MARTIN MARINCIN
Slovakia U-20 (Slovakia)

A gigantic defenceman (6'4", 210 pounds) with a massive wingspan, Marincin was a good skater and had most of the assets needed to become a strong shutdown defenceman. As a young player he was inconsistent and that probably kept him out of the first round.

Marincin used all three years of his entry deal to make the NHL, and management change in the summer of 2015 meant he was part of a trade to Toronto in a three-way deal to acquire veteran shutdown defender Eric Gryba from the Ottawa Senators.

Marincin played 227 games in the NHL over seven seasons but was relegated to the AHL in 2020–21.

NO. 48 OVERALL: LW CURTIS HAMILTON
Saskatoon Blades (WHL)

An intelligent two-way player with good offensive skills, Hamilton's issue early and late was injury. In his draft year, he had to deal with breaking his collarbone (twice) as well as separating his shoulder.

He had good speed and in his draft-plus-one season scored 82 points in 62 games with Saskatoon, seemingly putting the injuries behind him.

He would spend four seasons in the AHL battling injury and a lack of offensive output in climbing to the NHL. He would eventually play in just one NHL game before heading to Europe. Injuries had a major impact on his career and, like Marc Pouliot in 2003, some of those injuries happened before his NHL draft day.

NO. 61 OVERALL: LC RYAN MARTINDALE
Ottawa 67's (OHL)

Martindale was a tall centre with skill, scoring 60 points in 61 games in his draft season. His strength came from speed and size (6'2", 207 pounds). NHL teams love skill centres who are bigger bodies. The downbeat involved inconsistent play and that seemed to plague him during his three years in Oklahoma City with the Barons. Playing in 79 AHL games over those three years, he scored 9–17–26 and Edmonton dealt him to the Florida Panthers organization. He improved slightly but did not play in the NHL.

NO. 91 OVERALL: RD JEREMIE BLAIN
Acadie-Bathurst Titan (QMJHL)

Blain had good size and some offensive ability, and at this point in the draft teams had picked clean the legit prospects. Said general manager Steve Tambellini on draft weekend, "He's 6'3", they think he'll play around 220. He's a right-hand shot, and he plays with the edge, he's a hard guy to play against and he scored 40 points last year. Not a lot of people talked about him, but Oiler scout Bill Dandy was passionate about him. We waited a little, one extra pick, but we got him. I'm happy about this pick."

Blain continued to make progress through junior, but the Oilers didn't sign him and he caught on with the Vancouver and then Detroit organizations. He signed in Austria and then in the Czech Republic, where he played in 2020–21.

NO. 121 OVERALL: G TYLER BUNZ
Medicine Hat Tigers (WHL)

Bunz had a promising career but concussion issues derailed him. On his draft day, Stu MacGregor said Bunz "carried the mail in Medicine Hat all year. Willie Desjardins said he was one of the big reasons they were able to defeat Kootenay in the first round. He's got some battle in his game, he needs to smooth things out a little in his technique."

Bunz posted save percentages of .919 and .921 with the Tigers in the years after he was drafted, but he couldn't establish himself in pro partly due to injury. He did play one NHL game in the 2014–15 season.

NO. 162 OVERALL: LD BRANDON DAVIDSON
Regina Pats (WHL)

Davidson is a great story and he emerged as a true NHL player several years after he was drafted. Growing up in Taber, Alberta, Davidson got a late start in hockey because he couldn't afford to play AAA level. He finally got noticed and made the leap to the Regina Pats of the WHL (a massive step up) and contributed immediately.

Still, his scouting reports had skating as an issue and that's a limiting assessment. Scouts loved his hockey sense and ability to move the puck, so Edmonton drafted him deep in the 2010 draft.

He stayed in junior an extra year to have the game settle for him and then played three full seasons with the Oklahoma City Barons of the AHL. He improved each season under the watchful eye of coach Todd Nelson and assistants Rocky Thompson and Gerry Fleming.

There was a moment when the Oilers considered waiving Davidson; legend has it they were tipped that he would be claimed. The decision to keep Davidson turned out to be an astute move, as he helped the Oilers with the smart play and strong puck-moving ability scouts saw on the prairies years ago.

As a rookie, he showed a great ability to help his team win the shot and goal share while he was on the ice. This is a difficult thing to accomplish, and Davidson was not a spectacular player in any way, but he played an intelligent game and used his passing ability to send the puck in a good direction.

Puck IQ is a site that tracks time on ice against elite talent, and as a rookie in 2015–16 Davidson faced top competition 34 percent of the time. He won the dangerous shot battle (Puck IQ measures the danger of each shot) and the goal battle 12–8 against elites.

It was a fantastic accomplishment and suggested Davidson might have a major NHL future. As often happens with young defencemen, injuries derailed his development and kept him out of the lineup for months at a time. The Oilers ended up trading him, getting him back, and trading him again. All the while,

Davidson showed enough value to stay in the league most of the time. On the eve of the 2021–22 season, he had played in 180 NHL games.

NO. 166 OVERALL: LW DREW CZERWONKA
Kootenay Ice (WHL)

Czerwonka was a big winger who was very tough and had some skill. At 6'2", 203 pounds, he brought a lot to any battle. Unfortunately, injuries forced him out of hockey before he could turn pro.

NO. 181 OVERALL: LW KRISTIANS PELSS
Dynamo (Belarus Jr.)

Pelss was drafted from an obscure league, but the Oilers liked him. Scouting director MacGregor said, "We saw him at the U-18 World Championships when we were in Belarus. He played extremely well; he has some talent. He's not a big body, but he is a guy we feel has real offensive talent."

In his two post-draft seasons, he flourished with the Edmonton Oil Kings of the WHL and divided his first pro season between the AHL and the ECHL. The summer after that season, Pelss returned home and celebrated with friends after a long winter away. He took a late-night swim at a favourite old spot and drowned in mid-June 2013. It devastated the hockey world, and his teammates on the Oil Kings would later dedicate their 2014 Memorial Cup victory to his memory.

NO. 202 OVERALL: LW KELLEN JONES
Vernon Vipers (BCHL)

Jones was almost 20 on his draft day. His twin, Connor, would join Kellen for all four years at Quinnipiac (NCAA) University. Both men landed in Oklahoma City (AHL) and played together often, forming a substantial penalty-killing duo and showing skill. It was Connor who made the NHL, for four games with the New York Islanders.

2010 Draft Summary

The Oilers loaded up for a big draft, copying the Chicago Blackhawks and Pittsburgh Penguins in the early 2000s. Edmonton had 11 picks, four in the top 50, and the math had a roller-coaster ride. (Number in parentheses is points per game.)

- Taylor Hall (OHL) age 17: 57 games, 40–66–106 (1.86)
- Tyler Pitlick (NCAA) age 17: 38 games, 11–8–19 (0.50)
- Martin Marincin (Slovak) age 17: 36 games, 2–4–6 (0.17)
- Curtis Hamilton (WHL) age 17: 26 games, 7–9–16 (0.62)
- Ryan Martindale (OHL) age 17: 61 games, 19–41–60 (0.98)
- Jeremie Blain (QMJHL) age 17: 64 games, 4–34–38 (0.59)
- Tyler Bunz (WHL) age 17: 57 games, 2.91 goals-against average, .898 save percentage
- Brandon Davidson (WHL) age 18: 59 games, 1–33–34 (0.58)
- Drew Czerwonka (WHL) age 17: 54 games, 4–9–13 (0.24)
- Krisitans Pelss (Belarus) age 17: 46 games, 6–3–9 (0.196)
- Kellen Jones (BCHL) age 19: 41 games, 12–41–53 (1.29)

The Pitlick, Martindale, Hamilton, and Martindale selections didn't deliver any outstanding offensive prospects despite those players being available. Tyler Toffoli, who scored more than a point per game in the OHL in 2009–10, was the player chosen between Marincin and Hamilton. The Oilers needed the MacGregor group to deliver value, and it was there, but the choices were something other than the best player available.

The Oilers drafted four men who have played a significant amount but hit just one home run, and that was at No. 1 overall. Despite several players covering the draft bet (Brandon Davidson was splendid value where he was chosen), a decade later the draft is a disappointment.

NHL Career Games Played

1. Taylor Hall: 680
2. Tyler Pitlick: 286
3. Martin Marincin: 227
4. Brandon Davidson: 180
5. Curtis Hamilton: 1
6. Tyler Bunz: 1

The Hall pick should have changed fortunes by year three, but the Oilers couldn't gather enough talent to support him. As time went on, the pressure from the lack of success would land on Hall, one of the distinctive features of losing teams. Pitlick, Marincin, and Davidson enjoyed some NHL success, but the 2010 draft must be viewed as a missed opportunity.

Here's how the 2010 draft class compares to the preceding decade in terms of total NHL games played:

1. 2003 (1,905 games)

2. 2002 (1,579 games)
3. 2005 (1,569 games)
4. 2007 (1,554 games)
5. **2010 (1,375 games)**
6. 2001 (1,043 games)
7. 2006 (895 games)
8. 2008 (834 games)
9. 2004 (773 games)
10. 2009 (682 games)

Trades That Involved Draft Picks

On June 27, 2009, the Oilers traded a 2009 seventh-round pick (Michael Sdao) to the Ottawa Senators for a 2010 sixth-round pick (Drew Czwerwonka).

On March 1, 2010, the Oilers traded Denis Grebeshkov to the Nashville Predators for the No. 48 overall pick in the 2010 draft (Curtis Hamilton).

On March 3, 2010, the Oilers traded Lubomir Visnovsky to the Anaheim Ducks for Ryan Whitney and the No. 162 overall pick in the 2010 draft (Brandon Davidson).

On June 24, 2010, the Oilers traded a sixth-round pick (Mirko Hoefflin) to the Chicago Blackhawks for Colin Fraser.

On June 26, 2010, the Oilers traded the rights to Riley Nash to the Carolina Hurricanes for the No. 46 overall pick in the 2010 draft (Martin Marincin).

On June 26, 2010, the Oilers traded a sixth-round pick in the 2011 draft (David Broll) for the No. 202 pick in the 2010 draft (Kellen Jones).

THE 2011 DRAFT

The 2010–11 season was expected to show improvement, but the Oilers ended the year with the same point total as 2009–10 (62). The goal differential was 193–269 (minus-76), even more ghastly than the previous season's minus-70.

Taylor Hall showed well but was injured, and the team when he was off the ice was beyond brutal. Older players such as Ales Hemsky and Shawn Horcoff were becoming injury prone, and the men who were old enough to take on an increased role (Sam Gagner, Dustin Penner) struggled and failed in the feature minutes.

The one area that was encouraging came from the rookie crop of 2010–11, one of the best in team history:

- Jordan Eberle: 69 games, 18–25–43
- Taylor Hall: 65 games, 22–20–42
- Magnus Paajarvi: 80 games, 15–19–34
- Linus Omark: 51 games, 5–22–27
- Ryan O'Marra: 21 games, 1–4–5
- Teemu Hartikainen: 12 games, 3–2–5
- Jeff Petry: 35 games, 1–4–5
- Chris VandeVelde: 12 games, 0–2–2
- Shawn Belle: 5 games, 0–0–0
- Alex Plante: 3 games, 0–0–0
- Devan Dubnyk: 35 games, 2.71 goals-against average, .916 save percentage

In Hall, Eberle, Petry, and Dubnyk, the Oilers brought into the league some of the finest talent at their positions over the next decade. Regrettably, none of them would remain with the club for the balance of the 2010s.

Mark Arcobello signed with the Oilers in April of 2011. He exited college hockey and signed an ECHL-AHL deal with the Oklahoma City Barons, starting his pro career with the Stockton Thunder of the ECHL. He dominated, then flourished in the AHL and Edmonton signed him after one pro season. He made his NHL debut in February 2013 and played 139 productive games as a smart centre with skill and utility. He was rarely out of position and was often referred to as a coach's dream.

On March 8, 2011, the Oilers signed free-agent defenceman Taylor Fedun. He played in the AJHL with the Fort Saskatchewan Traders and Spruce Grove Saints, so he would have been known to Oilers scouts by 2006. Fedun attended Princeton University for four years and established himself as a solid two-way defenceman with impressive passing skills. Edmonton signed him in the spring of 2011. Oilers executive Rick Olczyk said, "We've been targeting Taylor for a couple of years. A strong kid, fierce competitor, good leadership on and off the ice. And he's obviously a smart kid."

That fall, in Oilers training camp, Fedun was injured by Minnesota Wild winger Eric Nystrom on a dangerous hit (it was a "race for icing" event) that resulted in a broken right leg. He would miss the 2011–12 season.

Fedun would play in the AHL the following year and showed quality two-way acumen. He got into two games before the Oilers lost him to free agency, and Fedun has been playing NHL and AHL games since. As of this writing, he has 127 games on his résumé, most recently with the Dallas Stars.

PROSPECT SPOTLIGHT
NO. 1 OVERALL: LC RYAN NUGENT-HOPKINS, RED DEER REBELS (WHL)

Nugent-Hopkins offered a great deal of skill and utility on draft day. He was a power-play wizard and a quality positional centre, and he was so good on his edges he was constantly involved in the play.

Scouting report and legacy: Red Line Report nailed the résumé, saying Nugent-Hopkins had "the highest offensive upside and is the most potent playmaker of the bunch. He'll struggle to handle the physicality of the NHL over a grueling 82-game season since his current walking around weight is a slightly built 163 pounds. But he is gritty and willing to battle in traffic and stand up for himself, so he'll eventually get there."

Nugent-Hopkins has been part of two brilliant youth movements in Edmonton, the Hall–Eberle and McDavid–Draisaitl eras. He brings solid two-way play and significant offence to the dance and has been the most consistently aware defensive forward among the top players in Edmonton during the decade.

Puck IQ shows him playing monster minutes against elites from 2014 to '20 while outscoring the league's best players 87–75 in those seasons.

Per 82 games since he arrived in the NHL, Nugent-Hopkins has averaged 23–37–60. It is less than Hall's per 82 games (28–44–72 points), but Nuge is a centre with a range of skills.

In the Hall–Eberle era, Nugent-Hopkins played centre on the top line, meaning he was facing much bigger and more mature players (like Anze Kopitar of the Los Angeles Kings) even as a teenager. As the decade wore along and Edmonton added more strong centres, the load was shared more and allowed Nugent-Hopkins to wheel more.

Perhaps the highest compliment available to Nugent-Hopkins comes in his five-on-five play from 2011 to 2020. This is an interesting statistic that can only be applied to Nuge among the high picks from the early part of the decade:

- Edmonton Oilers five-on-five goal differential: 1,227–1,438 (minus-211)
- Nugent-Hopkins five-on-five goal differential: 369–377 (minus-8)
- Edmonton Oilers without Nuge five on five: 858–1061 (minus-203)

That's an amazing number over nine seasons. Perhaps Nugent-Hopkins' most impressive feat is that he survived five general managers and eight coaches from 2011 to '20. He is the last player from the 2011–12 Oilers remaining in Edmonton.

NO. 19 OVERALL: LD OSCAR KLEFBOM
Farjestads (SHL)

The scouting reports on Klefbom were very strong, but the statistics on the ice didn't match the résumé for some time. Only when Klefbom entered the NHL did we see the complete picture of this player.

The scouting reports gushed about Klefbom's passing ability and offensive instincts, along with quality foot speed. He had size, at 6'3" and 196 pounds, and had good defensive coverage along with the offensive potential scouts kept hammering.

He also had injuries. Concussions, shoulders, and later infections and knees. There's little doubt his potential as a player was affected by various maladies early and late.

Even with those things understood, Klefbom was Edmonton's best defenceman by 2017 and would remain so when healthy through the end of the decade. In 2020, during the offseason, it was revealed that Klefbom's shoulder was so bad that his 2020–21 season was in peril and his career was in some doubt.

NO. 31 OVERALL: LD DAVID MUSIL
Vancouver Giants (WHL)

Musil to the Oilers had a special (and negative) impact because his father (Frank, a fine defenceman in his own right) was part of the amateur scouting staff. The risks were great, but the organization made sure everyone knew Musil the elder wasn't part of the evaluation process.

Musil was ranked at the end of the first round on some lists and Bob McKenzie's TSN list (the draft bible) had him No. 41. Musil was a shutdown defender who peaked as a teenager (he was dominant at several U-18 World Junior tournaments) and did not offer the kind of dynamic skill set Klefbom would bring.

Musil's skating wouldn't have been an issue five or 10 years earlier, but it was on draft day 2011. He did have elements to his game that gave him value—he was a rugged, physical player and a punishing hitter; he had size and strength and read defensive plays well.

Musil would play in only four NHL games and hang around the AHL for a time before finally landing as an effective defender in the Czech league.

NO. 62 OVERALL: G SAMU PERHONEN
JYP (Finland Jr.)

At 6'5", 196 pounds, Perhonen had the perfect size NHL teams look for in goaltenders. The downside for Perhonen was what Red Line called "hyper and wasted movement" in net. Perhonen has played in Finland for the entire decade, save for a brief period in 2013–14 when he struggled in the USHL, and is a regular in the top league (Liiga) since 2014. He is still in search of consistency.

NO. 74 OVERALL: LC TRAVIS EWANYK
Edmonton Oil Kings (WHL)

Ewanyk was described by Red Line Report as the quintessential power-checking centre and was highly regarded (No. 64 at Red Line), but there was very little offence at the junior level. That became even more pronounced in the AHL, and Edmonton dealt him to the Ottawa organization in 2015. The Oilers, who drafted many offensively shy forwards under both Fraser and Prendergast, were doing the same under MacGregor. The difference was the picks were taking place outside the first round under MacGregor.

NO. 92 OVERALL: LD DILLON SIMPSON
North Dakota (NCAA)

Evaluating Simpson was difficult, as he was 17 and playing NCAA hockey. Most college teams have players in their early to mid-twenties, so Simpson was giving up a lot in years and strength as a freshman. His skating was described as sluggish and his offence as tentative. It's possible the Oilers drafted him on the strength of a terrific AJHL season with the Spruce Grove Saints. Either way, he improved in each season of college and graduated to pros as a promising two-way prospect. He played four seasons in Edmonton's system, getting into three NHL games, before signing with the Columbus Blue Jackets. He remains a solid two-way defenceman just shy of the NHL.

NO. 114 OVERALL: RW TOBIAS RIEDER
Kitchener Rangers (OHL)

Rieder was a little undersized (5'11", 186 pounds) but had plus skills and played a smart game. He didn't have great speed, but he could keep up and his shot was just average. His assets offensively were great hands and anticipation. Rieder was ranked as a late second- or third-round pick but lasted all the way to the fourth round. He grew into a fine two-way player who excelled on the penalty kill and was effective at even strength. So far, he has played in 478 NHL games.

NO. 122 OVERALL: LD MARTIN GERNAT
Kosice (Czech Jr.)

Gernat was 6'4", 205 pounds, and had good offensive instincts, meaning he had a chance if he developed in the years after he was drafted. He played well in his two seasons after he was drafted, and his first year as a pro was impressive. After that, he drifted, and Edmonton traded him at the trade deadline in 2016. Gernat is back in the Czech Republic playing big minutes and delivering impressive offence.

NO. 182 OVERALL: G FRANS TUOHIMAA
Jokerit (Finland Jr.)

A second Finnish goalie, Tuohimaa was 6'2", 194 pounds, and calmer in net than Perhonen. He was 20 on his draft day. The Oilers signed him in 2013, but he didn't show enough to stay and returned to Finland. He has played in the Liiga since with uneven results.

2011 Draft Summary

The math of MacGregor's drafts showed solid work in the first round; in the second round, the scouting staff tended once again to reach early on players who didn't bring enough offence to project as NHL players. The MacGregor group went against the grain with a later pick in 2011—Tobias Rieder's points-per-game total was impressive compared to Ewanyk, who was chosen 40 spots earlier. (Number in parentheses is points per game.)

- Ryan Nugent-Hopkins (WHL) age 17: 69 games, 31–75–106 (1.54)
- Oscar Klefbom (SHL) age 17: 23 games, 1–1–2 (0.09)
- David Musil (WHL) age 17: 62 games, 6–19–25 (0.40)
- Samu Perhonen (Jr. Liiga) age 17: 29 games, 2.71 goals-against average, .922 save percentage
- Travis Ewanyk (WHL) age 17: 72 games, 16–11–27 (0.38)
- Dillon Simpson (NCAA) age 17: 30 games, 2–8–10 (0.33)
- Tobias Rieder (OHL) age 17: 65 games, 23–26–59 (0.91)
- Martin Gernat (Slovak U-20) age 17: 28 games, 3–15–18 (0.64)

- Frans Tuohimaa (Jr. Liiga) age 19: 37 games, 2.14 goals-against average, .931 save percentage

Edmonton had the No. 1 overall pick in the first round and another at No. 19 and chose wisely twice. The late pick of Rieder was inspired, and the word of the scouts in 2010–11 delivered quality return in career NHL games.

NHL Career Games Played
1. Ryan Nugent-Hopkins: 656
2. Tobias Rieder: 478
3. Oscar Klefbom: 378
4. David Musil: 4
5. Dillon Simpson: 3

With three more pieces to the puzzle added to Hall, Eberle, Petry, and Dubnyk, Edmonton was building a strong foundation for a contender built to last.

The 2011 draft did give the team two long-term solutions, and both Nuge and Klefbom have been part of the team's vital infrastructure for years. It was MacGregor's strongest draft.

Here's how the 2011 draft class compares to the preceding decade in terms of total NHL games played:
1. 2003 (1,905 games)
2. 2002 (1,579 games)
3. 2005 (1,569 games)
4. 2007 (1,554 games)
5. **2011 (1,519 games)**
6. 2010 (1,375 games)
7. 2006 (895 games)

8. 2008 (834 games)
9. 2004 (773 games)
10. 2009 (682 games)

The 2011 draft is already a success, and with two men still playing as regulars, it will be one of the best of the decade when all is said and done.

Trades That Involved Draft Picks

On January 17, 2009, the Oilers traded Mathieu Garon to the Pittsburgh Penguins for Ryan Stone, Dany Sabourin, and the No. 113 overall pick in the 2011 draft (Tobias Rieder).

On March 3, 2010, the Oilers traded Steve Staios to the Calgary Flames for Aaron Johnson and the No. 73 overall pick in the 2011 draft (Travis Ewanyk).

On June 26, 2010, the Oilers traded a sixth-round pick in the 2011 draft (David Broll) for the No. 202 pick in the 2010 draft (Kellen Jones).

On February 28, 2011, the Oilers traded Dustin Penner to the Los Angeles Kings for Colton Teubert, the No. 19 pick in the 2011 draft (Oscar Klefbom), and a third-round pick in the 2012 draft.

THE 2012 DRAFT

In 2011–12, the Oilers improved. Unfortunately, it was not enough for the team to make the playoffs.

The team's goal differential improved markedly:

- 2009–10: 214–284 (minus-70)
- 2010–11: 193–269 (minus-76)
- 2011–12: 212–239 (minus-27)

That's a lot of progress, and the team's young players (Hall, Eberle, Petry, Dubyk) who were rookies in 2010–11 welcomed another impressive newcomer in Ryan Nugent-Hopkins.

- Ryan Nugent-Hopkins: 62 games, 18–34–52
- Anton Lander: 56 games, 2–4–6
- Teemu Hartikainen: 17 games, 2–3–5
- Chris VandeVelde: 5 games, 1–0–1
- Colten Teubert: 24 games, 0–1–1
- Philippe Cornet: 2 games, 0–1–1
- Ryan O'Marra: 7 games, 0–1–1
- Alex Plante: 3 games, 0–1–1
- Milan Kytnar: 1 game, 0–0–0

Entering the 2012 offseason, the club was heading in a good direction under coach Tom Renney. He had the young players flourishing and the incumbent veterans were solid. Tambellini's free-agent bets (Eric Belanger, Cam Barker, Ben Eager) didn't work out, but the coach and his young players were progressing.

Tambellini moved on from Renney and hired Ralph Krueger, who had impressed everyone with his approach to the game and his rapport with young players. The constant churn in management and coaching continued.

Edmonton drafted first overall for the third year in a row, this time moving up (past the Columbus Blue Jackets) to pick No. 1. The New Jersey Devils won in 2011, moving up four spots but allowing Edmonton to retain No. 1 overall.

It was a mixed blessing for MacGregor and the scouts. Several years later, Mark Spector got the story on paper for Sportsnet, and it was a classic tale of indecision at the top.

The scouts preferred Ryan Murray (in a 9–2 vote over Yakupov based on Spector's reporting), but management (Tambellini, Kevin Lowe, the newly hired Craig MacTavish, and owner Darryl Katz) seemed to agree with Oilers fans—Russian winger Yakupov was a dynamic talent in junior and ranked No. 1 on most draft lists.

On July 1, 2012, the Oilers landed college free agent Justin Schultz, one of the most prized free agents of his kind in the cap era. A brilliant offensive defenceman, Schultz was considered a major prize and a fantastic win for the Oilers organization. General manager Steve Tambellini was thrilled to add another key piece to a growing cluster of impressive young talent that began with the selection of Taylor Hall at the 2010 draft.

Schultz had enormous talent but struggled on a young team with a rookie coach and general manager. He would play just 248 games in Edmonton before blossoming after a trade to the Pittsburgh Penguins. He was part of two Stanley Cup championships and established himself as an NHL defenceman.

NO. 1 OVERALL: RW NAIL YAKUPOV
Sarnia Sting (OHL)

Yakupov's scouting report was strong—good skater, volume shooter, dynamic. ISS called him a gifted goal scorer. Yakupov suffered a knee injury in his draft year, and it had a significant impact on his season:

- Before injury: 26, 21–32–53 (2.04 points per game)
- After injury: 16, 10–6–16 (1.00 points per game)

Injuries tend to get forgotten, but they can sometimes have a major impact on a career. Yakupov didn't have a normal training camp in the fall of 2012, as the NHL locked out players in October.

The season started a shortened schedule in January, and Yakupov delivered a solid offensive campaign (48 games, 17–14–31) while causing much chaos without the puck. At five on five he scored 2.20 points per 60, good for third among Oilers forwards. Krueger appeared to be a rookie whisperer, getting top results offensively from a player who was very raw for the NHL game. He also rode plenty of luck, reflected in out-of-this-world 21 percent shooting success.

At the end of the season, Coach Krueger raved about his rookie, saying, "He's been getting smarter with the puck and more patient. He's understanding the difference between simple plays versus opportunity and that's all showing up. We're excited for a kid that age, what he's done here in these two and a half months, it certainly shows us that we have an exciting future with Nail."

In Yakupov's second season, his shooting percentage halved and new coach Dallas Eakins began the hard work of having the youngster learn to play without the puck. It was a painful process, and the Oilers were not a winning team. Somewhere along the way, player and team lost each other and in October of 2016 he was sent to St. Louis in a minor trade.

When he laced them up for the Blues, he was 22 and 98 games from the end of his career. He left for the KHL in 2018–19 and remains a regular in that league.

What went wrong? Many blame the player, but the management and coaching staffs must share in the result. Yakupov was a fan favourite due to his winning smile and generosity, but it was not a match.

Not getting a decade of quality from a No. 1 overall pick represents professional death. Many men who were on the stage when Yakupov was chosen are no longer in the NHL.

NO. 32 OVERALL: LW MITCHELL MOROZ
Edmonton Oil Kings (WHL)

Moroz was a huge (6'3", 220 pounds) winger who had success on a checking line with the Oil Kings as a rookie. He had a power forward's attitude and delivered crushing body checks all over the ice while scoring 16 goals. Like Travis Ewanyk in the 2011 draft, Moroz was chosen too early for the offence he was able to deliver.

As an Oilers draft pick playing junior hockey in Edmonton, the pressure on him was immense, but Moroz was able to flourish and posted seasons with 13 and then 35 goals with the team. In 2014 he was one of the contributors to the Oil Kings winning the WHL championship and Memorial Cup. He devoted the win to fallen teammate Kristians Pelss on national television after the win.

When he hit pro hockey, Moroz didn't have enough offence to play on a feature line in the AHL. Like his teammate Ewanyk, Moroz faded from the AHL soon after his entry deal expired.

NO. 63 OVERALL: LC JUJHAR KHAIRA
Prince George Spruce Kings (BCHL)

Khaira was 6'2", 182 pounds on his draft day but would play in the NHL at 6'4", 212 pounds. He is one of the strongest men to play for the Oilers and has a mean streak that can be useful. He had a powerful stride and scored well in the BCHL (29–50–79 in 54 games), offering some hope he could make it to the NHL as a two-way player.

Khaira hit college (Michigan Tech) and the WHL (Everett Silvertips) and scored enough to earn an entry deal. In the AHL, he started slowly but in his second AHL season scored enough

(10–17–27 in 49 games) to get an NHL look. He became a regular in 2017–18, scoring 11 goals in his NHL rookie season. His offence has been an issue, but he's a dynamite penalty killer and he's physically intimidating. He has played in 257 NHL games through 2020–21, making him a successful third-round pick.

NO. 91 OVERALL: LW DANIIL ZHARKOV
Belleville Bulls (OHL)

Russian winger Zharkov was drafted out of the Belleville Bulls (OHL) and had a nice résumé. He struggled in his draft-plus-one season, trying to add to his two-way abilities while improving offensively without success. He played in Russia season two after the draft and played measured minutes in the KHL (49 games, 2–3–5) and then in the VHL (39 games, 4–5–9). He attended training camp with the Bakersfield Condors in fall 2015, where he suffered a significant injury. He has played in the VHL (second Russian league) since 2016.

NO. 93 OVERALL: LD ERIK GUSTAFSSON
Djurgardens (SEL)

Gustafsson was a tall, thin, puck-moving defenceman on draft day. He had pro experience, and in the seasons that followed he continued to post strong numbers in the top Swedish league. The Oilers eventually lost his rights, and he was signed by the Chicago Blackhawks in 2015. He spent a couple of seasons in the AHL before emerging as an effective NHL player. His career high is 60 points and Gustafsson has played in 250 NHL games.

NO. 123 OVERALL: LD JOEY LALEGGIA
Denver (NCAA)

A 5'10", 180-pound puck mover, he was also 20 on draft day and boasted some impressive college numbers (43 games, 11–27–38 at the University of Denver). A fine skater and an intelligent offensive player, Laleggia turned pro and delivered more solid offence in the AHL. He played left wing for a time and in July of 2018 signed with the St. Louis Blues. He has never played in the NHL and at 28, his window may have closed. There's no doubt he had enough talent to play NHL hockey, but the opportunity never presented itself.

NO. 153 OVERALL: RW JOHN MCCARRON
Cornell (NCAA)

McCarron was 20 on his draft day and a big winger (6'3", 220 pounds) with enough skill to be worth a late draft pick. The Oilers liked his shot and strength, plus his aggression around the net. He would not sign with Edmonton and eventually peaked at the AHL level.

2012 Draft Summary

The Oilers didn't get much from the 2012 draft, but it has turned out to be a disappointing year for many teams. The issues of the MacGregor era are perfectly described in the first two picks: Yakupov, who scored well but had an injury that affected him, and Moroz, who was the physical player the Oilers coveted but was shy offensively. (Number in parentheses is points per game.)

- Nail Yakupov (OHL) age 17: 42 games, 31–38–69 (1.64)
- Mitch Moroz (WHL) age 17: 66 games, 16–9–25 (0.38)

- Jujhar Khaira (BCHL) age 17: 54 games, 29–50–79 (1.46)
- Daniil Zharkov (OHL) age 17: 50 games, 23–13–36 (0.72)
- Erik Gustafsson (SEL) age 19: 41 games, 3–4–7 (0.17)
- Joey Laleggia (NCAA) age 19: 43 games, 11–27–38 (0.88)
- John McCarron (NCAA) age 19: 35 games, 6–13–19 (0.54)

There's no one at fault for the Yakupov pick; he was the best player available. The math adored him on draft day. His speed, trumpeted on draft day, was not enough to separate in the NHL, and his shot rarely found the range.

Moroz was chosen two rounds early based on his offence. Khaira delivered promising offence in a Tier 2 league. After that, Gustafsson and the two college men showed offensive promise. As it turned out, the two forwards who posted more than a point per game in their draft year and the Swedish defenceman emerged as NHL players of note.

NHL Career Games Played

1. Nail Yakupov: 350
2. Jujhar Khaira: 258
3. Erik Gustafsson: 250

If you didn't know the Oilers owned the No. 1 overall pick, and Yakupov was still in the league, then this draft class could be defended. However, the combination of Yakupov not landing a feature role in the NHL, the offensively shy picks, and not signing Gustafsson means 2012 was a mess.

What fans hoped is that interference from above wouldn't affect the scouting decisions moving forward.

Here's how the 2012 draft class compares to the preceding decade in terms of total NHL games played:

1. 2003 (1,905 games)
2. 2005 (1,569 games)
3. 2007 (1,554 games)
4. 2011 (1,519 games)
5. 2010 (1,375 games)
6. 2006 (895 games)
7. **2012 (858 games)**
8. 2008 (834 games)
9. 2004 (773 games)
10. 2009 (682 games)

The 2012 draft has a good chance to finish last among the drafts of the decade that began in 2010.

Trades That Involved Draft Picks

On February 28, 2011, the Oilers traded Dustin Penner to the Los Angeles Kings for Colton Teubert, the No. 19 pick in the 2011 draft (Oscar Klefbom), and the No. 91 pick in the 2012 draft (Daniil Zharkov).

On June 26, 2011, the Oilers traded Colin Fraser and a 2012 seventh-round selection (Dmitri Sinitsyn).

THE 2013 DRAFT

The 2013 season was a short one because of the lockout. The Oilers were buyers at the deadline and dead in the water a few days later. The goal differential was minus-9 (in 48 games), so progress continued but change was in the wind.

The Oilers fired Steve Tambellini as general manager in April 2013, replacing him with Craig MacTavish. MacTavish wanted to get a strong assistant for Krueger and went shopping. During the process he came across young coach Dallas Eakins, who impressed MacTavish with his passion and enthusiasm. MacTavish called him "relentless" several times. Krueger was fired, and Eakins was hired as the new head coach in June 2013.

The NHL rookies for 2012–13:

- Nail Yakupov: 48 games, 17–14–31
- Justin Schultz: 48 games, 8–19–27
- Chris VandeVelde: 11 games, 0–0–0
- Mark Arcobello: 1 game, 0–0–0

Two of the rookies were among the most successful in the league. Yakupov led freshmen in goals and points, while Schultz would lead the league in rookie assists under coach Ralph Krueger. For both, it would be their best season with the Oilers.

PROSPECT SPOTLIGHT
NO. 7 OVERALL: LD DARNELL NURSE, SAULT STE. MARIE GREYHOUNDS (OHL)

Nurse was the initial first-round draft pick under general manager Craig MacTavish and the seventh under Stu MacGregor as scouting director.

MacTavish was more hands-on than any previous general manager since Glen Sather, and was very strong on Nurse as his first draft pick.

"He gives us an element we're sorely lacking," MacTavish said. "He's a guy who, over time, if we're patient with him, is going to provide us with toughness. He's a guy that will ride shotgun for a lot of our first overall picks and our skilled players for a lot of years. But our overriding draft philosophy is still to draft the player who is going to have the greatest impact on our team over time. Based on that philosophy, I still thought Darnell was the player who is going to have the greatest impact on our team."

Nurse delivered impressive junior numbers across the board and was a rock defensively. Kyle Dubas, the Greyhounds' general manager, talked at length about Nurse as an impact shutdown player at the junior level and Oilers fans dreamed of having a difference-maker on the blue line.

Scouting report and legacy: Scouts projected Nurse as a two-way type with tremendous mobility, with more of his value on the defensive side of the puck. He performed well in junior and was part of Canada's gold medal–winning World Junior team in 2015.

Nurse turned pro in the fall of 2015 with time in the AHL with the Bakersfield Condors planned. He lasted just nine games before being recalled to the NHL. As a rookie, he was used heavily against elite opposition due to injury and he survived (outscored opponents 19–11) in a difficult situation.

In his second and third seasons Nurse settled in, and the Oilers won more than 50 percent of the shot and goal differential. By 2019–20 he and rookie partner Ethan Bear took on the most difficult minutes when Oscar Klefbom and partner Adam Larsson faltered due to injury.

After six NHL seasons, Nurse is firmly established as a strong two-way defender, playing top-four defensive minutes and posting strong offensive numbers at five on five (24–27 points in the last three seasons).

NO. 56 OVERALL: LC MARCO ROY
Blainville-Boisbriand Armada (QMJHL)

Roy was a good skater who could grind along the way and earned a two-way reputation in his draft year. He posted just a little over a point per game in his draft year (65 games, 29–38–67) and projected as a middle-six forward if he continued to develop as a prospect.

Roy didn't progress offensively in his two post-draft seasons but remained a fairly complete prospect with some offensive potential. The Oilers signed him to an AHL contract, and he played fourth line and penalty kill in 2015–16, all the while outscoring more prominent prospects and showing more range as a player. Roy played in the AHL and ECHL through the end of the decade, never grabbing an NHL contract.

NO. 83 OVERALL: LC BOGDAN YAKIMOV
Nizhnekamsk (Russia Jr.)

A huge centre (6'5", 200 pounds) described by one scouting service as "a thickly constructed specimen," Yakimov was a load with the puck on his stick. Strong along the wall and effective at puck retrieval, he was more power forward than finesse pivot, but he scored 7–6–13 in 11 junior games in his draft year.

Yakimov played in the KHL in his draft-plus-one year (33 games, 7–5–12) and then in the AHL (Oklahoma City Barons) in 2015–16 (57 games, 12–16–28). He was a solid outscorer but didn't bring enough offence, and his foot speed was a concern. He played in one NHL game and returned to the KHL, where he is delivering an uneven career.

NO. 88 OVERALL: LW ANTON SLEPYSHEV
Ufa (KHL)

The most offensively talented forward chosen by Edmonton in the 2013 draft, Slepyshev scored 4–2–6 in 11 KHL games in his draft year (he was 19 on draft day). A fine skater with a plus shot, he was also elusive and could wire the puck from distance and beat the goalie clean. His downsides included his play away from the puck (normal for teenagers) and poor passing skills. Slepyshev played just over 50 AHL games then found his way to the NHL, where he showed flashes of brilliance but could not sustain his momentum. He went back to the KHL after 102 NHL games and some impressive moments with the Oilers.

NO. 94 OVERALL: RW JACKSON HOUCK
Vancouver Giants (WHL)

Houck scored well in his draft season (69 games, 23–34–57). A physical winger with good skills, foot speed and his small size were his main issues (6'0", 186 pounds). His father Paul was drafted by the Oilers in 1981. Houck was a "tweener," a player with enough skill to get drafted but not enough to make the next step to the NHL. He did not sign with the Oilers.

NO. 94 OVERALL: RC KYLE PLATZER
London Knights (OHL)

Platzer didn't play much in his draft year (65 games, 5–17–22) and didn't have any one skill that made him a strong draft option. He had good speed and some offensive potential but was considered a long shot. He delivered a strong final season in junior but sputtered offensively through his entry deal with the Bakersfield Condors (AHL). Platzer has been productive in the Liiga since signing there in 2019.

NO. 113 OVERALL: LW AIDAN MUIR
Victory Honda Midget (MWEHL)

Muir played in a college feeder league in his draft year. He was a project selection heading for Western Michigan. He had size (6'4", 211 pounds) and scored well (37 games, 17–23–40) but at a very low level, making him a long shot. He attended Western Michigan for four years but didn't earn a pro contract.

NO. 128 OVERALL: LW EVAN CAMPBELL
Langley Rivermen (BCHL)

Campbell was 20 years old on draft day and headed to UMass Lowell. He had one good season in college and was a regular for most of his four seasons with the Rivermen. The Oilers didn't sign him but did add teammate Joe Gambardella as a college free agent in 2016.

NO. 158 OVERALL: LD BEN BETKER
Everett Silvertips (WHL)

A big defenceman with a massive wingspan, Betker had below-average speed and not much offence. That made him an extreme long shot, but he landed a pro contract and played his entry deal in the AHL (Bakersfield). Betker signed in Slovakia in 2018 and is currently playing there.

NO. 188 OVERALL: RC GREG CHASE
Calgary Hitmen (WHL)

A terrific value pick this late in the draft, Chase had real NHL potential. He posted 17–32–49 in 69 games in his draft year and improved in year two. Chase plateaued in his final junior season and spent his first year as a pro in the ECHL. He could not score enough at the AHL level to gain any traction and spent much of the decade in the AHL.

2013 Draft Summary

MacTavish employed some analytics expertise in 2013, the first time in Oilers history that the organization acknowledged the use of numbers to help compile a draft list. Here are the results in terms of draft season boxcar numbers by the players chosen. (Number in parentheses is points per game.)

- Darnell Nurse (OHL) age 17: 68 games, 12–29–41 (0.60)
- Marco Roy (QMJHL) age 17: 65 games, 29–38–67 (1.03)
- Bogdan Yakimov (VHL) age 17: 31 games, 8–14–22 (0.71)
- Anton Slepyshev (KHL) age 18: 25 games, 7–2–9 (0.36)
- Jackson Houck (WHL) age 17: 69 games, 23–34–57 (0.83)
- Kyle Platzer (OHL) age 17: 65 games, 7–12–19 (0.29)
- Aidan Muir (MWEHL) age 17: 37 games, 17–23–40 (1.08)
- Evan Campbell (BCHL) age 19: 51 games, 20–46–66 (1.29)
- Ben Betker (WHL) age 17: 68 games, 1–5–6 (0.09)
- Greg Chase (WHL) age 17: 69 games, 17–32–49 (0.71)

The top four picks all had solid numbers. Nurse was a strong two-way defenceman, Roy had substantial offence in the QMJHL and a two-way reputation, and both Russians had offensive ability. As late as the final choice (Greg Chase), Edmonton was selecting players who could reasonably be projected as successful pro players based on their junior offensive output. Although the draft did not result in multiple NHL players, the bets were excellent.

A quick note about draft analytics and math as adopted by the Oilers—in 2013, the Oilers announced a public contest (Hackathon) welcoming contestants to submit their own analyses and present a compelling case to help the club win games.

The contest winner, Michael Parkatti, was well known in the Oilers public analytics community and would later publish much of his thinking about the draft.

The news surrounding Parkatti's win uncovered Edmonton's involvement with Darkhorse Analytics and Daniel Haight.

It was the first real confirmation that the Edmonton Oilers were involved in analytics as it pertained to the game. Although nothing about the draft was specifically mentioned, unusual things began to happen about this time.

I interviewed Parkatti a couple years later, and he discussed his model as it pertained to the Oilers and their selection of Marco Roy in the second round of the 2013 draft.

Per Parkatti, "The model really liked Marco Roy. There's a lot of things to like about the player outwardly, and if you look at the statistics diagnostically it's not just the point production but also the situation he found himself in. The team he played for this year was very good, but it was one of those situations where he wasn't being dragged along by anybody. The way I like to look at it was he was the good player on the team, he played an integral part on that team. And you really saw that in the playoffs."

From the Roy selection forward, clues would drop in each draft summer that aligned with advanced thinking by the organization.

MacT's analytics people were telling him additional third-round picks could bring the organization more value. The general manager made two deals.

First trade: Edmonton trades No. 37 overall (Valentin Zykov) to Los Angeles for No. 57 overall (William Carrier), No. 88 overall (Anton Slephyshev), and No. 96 overall (Kyle Platzer).

Second trade: Edmonton trades No. 57 overall (William Carrier) to St. Louis for No. 83 overall (Bogdan Yakimov), No. 94 overall (Jackson Houck), and No. 113 overall (Aidan Muir).

William Carrier (255 NHL games), Slepyshev (102), Valentin Zykov (55), and Yakimov (1) all played in the NHL. It didn't work out as a smash hit for any team, but it was more than worth the risk for Edmonton. MacT grabbed five picks for one in the two deals.

NHL Career Games Played

1. Darnell Nurse: 406
2. Anton Slepyshev: 102
3. Bogdan Yakimov: 1

Nurse is going to play in more than 1,000 games based on his first six seasons, so the draft will be a success in due time. I don't have a major criticism of this draft, although not signing Marco Roy was a curious decision. The big bet was the trade, and it was a solid risk that didn't work out. MacTavish didn't spend a lot of time learning the general manager job, and I believe that cost him the job when the 2015 lottery went down, but his instincts were excellent.

Here's how the 2013 draft class compares to the preceding decade in terms of total NHL games played:

1. 2005 (1,569 games)
2. 2007 (1,554 games)
3. 2011 (1,519 games)
4. 2010 (1,375 games)
5. 2006 (895 games)
6. 2012 (858 games)

7.   2008 (834 games)
8.   2004 (773 games)
9.   2009 (682 games)
10. **2013 (509 games)**

Trades That Involved Draft Picks

On July 12, 2011, the Oilers traded Andrew Cogliano to the Anaheim Ducks for the No. 56 overall pick in the 2013 draft (Marco Roy).

On January 14, 2013, the Oilers traded a third-round pick (Niklas Hansson) to the Dallas Stars for Mark Fistric.

On April 3, 2013, the Oilers traded a fourth-round pick (Matt Buckles) to the Florida Panthers for Jerred Smithson.

On June 30, 2013, the Oilers traded No. 37 overall (Valentin Zykov) to Los Angeles for No. 57 overall (William Carrier), No. 88 overall (Anton Slephyshev), and No. 96 overall (Kyle Platzer). All picks were in the 2013 draft.

On June 30, 2013, the Oilers traded No. 57 overall (William Carrier) to St. Louis for No. 83 overall (Bogdan Yakimov), No. 94 overall (Jackson Houck), and No. 113 overall (Aidan Muir). All picks were in the 2013 draft.

THE 2014 DRAFT

The 2013–14 season was a tough one for the Oilers, as a rookie coach (Dallas Eakins) and a rookie general manager (Craig MacTavish) were forced to navigate the rapids with sharks circling and ready to pillage the roster. Edmonton's goal differential (203–270, minus-67) reflected a team slow to adjust to changes by the coach and unable to gain any traction during the year.

MacTavish offloaded Devan Dubnyk and Ladislav Smid in a mad dash to fix the goaltending, but the only move that anyone remembers is Edmonton dealing Dubnyk for less than 100 cents on the dollar. Rookie general managers are vulnerable, no matter how smart they are.

There are advantages to employing intelligent managers, and the Oilers would benefit from MacTavish's knowledge of the game in the first round of the 2014 draft.

The 2013–14 rookies were an interesting group:

- Mark Arcobello: 41 games, 4–14–18
- Martin Marincin: 44 games, 0–6–6
- Luke Gazdic: 67 games, 2–2–4
- Oscar Klefbom: 17 games, 1–2–3
- Taylor Fedun: 4 games, 2–0–2
- Tyler Pitlick: 10 games, 1–0–1
- Brad Hunt: 3 games, 0–0–0

There was plenty of talent bubbling up to the NHL in 2013–14, but none of the players was ready to have an immediate impact. It's clear years later that the Oilers rebuild was split into two parts due to management, coaching change, and trades by incoming management people. So, the Hall-Eberle-Petry-Dubnyk talent cluster was sent away before the impact players of 2014–15 could grow into feature roles in support.

On March 31, 2014, the Oilers signed college free agent Jordan Oesterle out of Western Michigan. A fast skater with skill, Oesterle quickly established himself as a quality AHL player with the Oklahoma City Barons in 2014–15 and then the Bakersfield Condors in the following two seasons. Oesterle played 25 games with the Oilers, reached free agency, and has been in the NHL since with the Chicago Blackhawks and Arizona Coyotes. He was a productive NHL player in those seasons.

PROSPECT SPOTLIGHT
NO. 3 OVERALL: LC LEON DRAISAITL, PRINCE ALBERT RAIDERS (WHL)

A year after drafting his stud enforcer-defenceman in Darnell Nurse, general manager Craig MacTavish continued to build up the middle with big centre Draisaitl.

Scouting report and legacy: There are two parts to the Draisaitl story. The first is the player he was on draft day. He was ranked No. 4 by Bob McKenzie and Craig Button at TSN, both respected lists by the industry.

Draisaitl's scouting report was grand; Red Line Report called him "tenacious in puck pursuit with his relentless forecheck often creating chances for linemates. Dominates the game down low with outstanding puck protection. Constantly outthinks the opposition and knows where his outlets are at all times. Has learned to use his size to carve out space for himself and effectively separate opponents from the puck. Strong hockey sense in all three zones leads to good positioning. Traditional playmaking centre finds 'mates with crisp, accurate passes. Intelligent, two-way, classically schooled centre."

There were scouting reports that suggested he needed to get quicker and that his first-step stride was a little slow, and others that talked about shift length and ability to sustain tempo later in shifts. He was known to slow down the play in the neutral zone, making him an easier target for checkers.

When MacTavish took Draisaitl at No. 3 overall, Oilers fans were thrilled. A big, skilled centre was a need from the day Jason Arnott was traded 16 years previously. At the time he was drafted, Edmonton had a plethora of young scoring wingers (Hall, Eberle, Yakupov) with whom to match the big pivot as soon as he was NHL ready.

The club kept him to start the 2014–15 season, but he struggled to score and eventually went back to junior (where he won a WHL Championship with the Kelowna Rockets). He would end his amateur career by winning MVP honours at the 2015 Memorial Cup.

Draisaitl was recalled in late October of 2015 and has been in the NHL since. His improvement from the early days to the pinnacle of the game (he won the Hart Trophy in 2020) is the stuff of legends.

That brings us to the second part of the story. Draisaitl is the rare player who overcame all the challenges mentioned by scouting reports on draft day. His skating is impressive, his stamina is improved, and he became more disciplined in shift length.

Draisaitl moved to wing during long periods of his career but found a home at centre in January of 2020 and helped unleash a dynamic outscoring line with Nugent-Hopkins.

Beginning in 2018–19, Draisaitl emerged as one of the best forwards in the NHL.

NO. 91 OVERALL: LD WILLIAM LAGESSON
Frolunda (Sweden Jr.)

Lagesson was a solid two-way prospect who brought the elements of a shutdown defenceman at a young age. An unusual skater, he's fast enough to play at the highest levels efficiently. He made stops in Swedish junior and the USHL, NCAA, SHL, AHL, and NHL in the six years after he was drafted, improving at each stop.

His on-ice goal differentials at even strength in the AHL were top quality, and he received his first NHL action (eight games) during the 2019–20 season. He has a long career ahead of him and much of it could be in the NHL, but there are no guarantees.

NO. 111 OVERALL: G ZACH NAGELVOORT
Michigan (NCAA)

At 6'1", 209 pounds, Nagelvoort had a good reputation on draft day. Former NHL goaltender Phil Myre, a scout for International Scouting Services, said, "Good size goalie. Very competitive and excellent focus. Excellent quickness and recovery. Catches very well. Has a chance to become a #1 NHL goalie." He did not grab the starting role with the Wolverines and did not progress after his draft day. Nagelvoort would complete four years of college and then play three ECHL games to complete his story.

NO. 130 OVERALL: LW LIAM COUGHLIN
Vernon Vipers (BCHL)

Coughlin was an obscure but talented pick. Kirk Luedeke, at the time a scout and now working in the USHL in procurement, assessed him as such: "Big kid, can skate, industrious." He played well in the BCHL in 2014–15 and the Oilers traded him to the Chicago Blackhawks in the summer of 2015. He played four years in Vermont and played 2019–20 in the ECHL.

NO. 153 OVERALL: RW TYLER VESEL
Omaha Lancers (USHL)

Vesel was 20 on his draft day and coming off a strong year (33 goals in 49 games) in the USHL. He scored well at Nebraska-Omaha in four years of NCAA play, getting close to a point per game in his junior and senior years. He didn't get to pro hockey until age 24 and had a very small window to prove himself. Vesel has been in the Allsvenskan (second Swedish league) since 2019.

NO. 183 OVERALL: G KEVEN BOUCHARD
Val d'Or Foreurs (QMJHL)

Bouchard would be Stu MacGregor's final selection as Oilers scouting director, as he would be replaced by the 2015 draft. He liked the goalie, saying, "It's always difficult with goaltenders when they don't play a lot but we had an eye on him from the previous year and I happened to be at a game this season where he did play and had a period at the Memorial Cup. He's a guy with potential. He's very fit and strong and he's willing to put in the work. [Goalie coaches] Freddie Chabot and Sylvain Rodrique know him really well and have worked with him."

Bouchard would play junior through 2016–17 but did not sign with Edmonton and did not turn pro.

2014 Draft Summary
Craig MacTavish and Stu MacGregor were a team at the draft table twice, and I would argue it was a very productive partnership. In 2014, the scouting staff chose Leon Draisaitl when real quality remained. It was a franchise-altering move and would make the 2015 draft even more substantial. Here are the boxcar totals for each player chosen in the 2014 draft by Edmonton. (Number in parentheses is points per game.)

- Leon Draisaitl (WHL) age 17: 64 games, 38–67–105 (1.64)

- William Lagesson (SuperElite U-20) age 17: 44 games, 8–12–20 (0.45)
- Zach Nagelvoort (NCAA) age 19: 24 games, 2.20 goals-against average, .929 save percentage
- Liam Coughlin (BCHL) age 18: 53 games, 18–27–45 (0.85)
- Tyler Vesel (USHL) age 19: 49 games, 33–38–71 (1.45)
- Keven Bouchard (QMJHL) age 17: 27 games, 2.95 goals-against average, .887 save percentage

The Draisaitl selection may one day eclipse all other first-round picks chosen during the MacGregor draft era, and his selection at No. 3 overall certainly represents the best draft strategy by the team in MacGregor's time. Lagesson and Nagelvoort were reasonable bets. The team went shopping for two successful overages and then (curiously) added another goalie among just six picks. It would be MacGregor's final draft. Draisaitl is already a dominant player from this draft, as his career NHL games total proves.

NHL Career Games Played
1. Leon Draisaitl: 478
2. William Lagesson: 27

Draisaitl has scored 50 goals in a season and won the Hart Trophy as NHL MVP in 2020. He alone makes the 2014 draft a success. In Oilers draft history, very few players have had the kind of impact Draisaitl delivered in his first six seasons.

Here's how the 2014 draft class compares to the preceding decade in terms of total NHL games played:
1. 2005 (1,569 games)
2. 2007 (1,554 games)

3. 2011 (1,519 games)
4. 2010 (1,375 games)
5. 2006 (895 games)
6. 2012 (858 games)
7. 2008 (834 games)
8. 2009 (682 games)
9. 2013 (509 games)
10. **2014 (505 games)**

The drafts from 2012 to 2020 haven't seen enough seasons to be properly graded in this fashion. It's clear Draisaitl will single-handedly carry this draft, with William Lagesson possibly emerging with an NHL career.

Trades That Involved Draft Picks

On March 4, 2013, the Oilers traded a 2014 fourth-round pick (Nicholas Magyar) to the Toronto Maple Leafs for Mike Brown.

On July 10, 2013, the Oilers traded Magnus Paajarvi, a 2014 second-round pick (Ivan Barbashev), and a 2015 fourth-round pick (Adam Musil) to the St. Louis Blues for David Perron and a 2015 third-round pick (Mike Robinson).

On October 21, 2013, the Oilers traded Mike Brown to the San Jose Sharks for the No. 111 overall pick in the 2014 draft (Zach Nagelvoort).

January 15, 2014, the Oilers traded a 2014 third-round pick (Dominic Turgeon) to the Los Angeles Kings for Ben Scrivens.

On March 4, 2014, the Oilers traded a 2014 fifth-round pick (Matthew Berkovitz) and a 2015 fifth-round pick (Dennis Yan) in the 2015 draft to Anaheim for Viktor Fasth.

On March 5, 2014, the Oilers traded Ales Hemsky to the Ottawa Senators for the No. 130 pick in the 2014 draft (Liam Coughlin) and a 2015 third-round pick.

On March 5, 2014, the Oilers traded Nick Schultz to the Columbus Blue Jackets for a 2014 fifth-round pick (Tyler Bird).

On June 25, 2014, the Oilers traded a 2014 fifth-round pick (Tyler Bird) to the Columbus Blue Jackets for Nikita Nikitin.

EVALUATION
STU MACGREGOR, SCOUTING
DIRECTOR (2008-14)

SUCCESS IN THE FIRST 30 SELECTIONS OF EACH DRAFT

No Oilers scouting director had more success in his early picks as a percentage of overall success than MacGregor. His first selection in 2008 (Jordan Eberle) delivered top-10 value at No. 22 overall. It was a pure home-run pick.

MacGregor enjoyed a string of No. 1 overall selections between 2010 and '12 and cashed in twice with Taylor Hall and Ryan Nugent-Hopkins. In 2011, the team also delivered a strong return with the No. 19 overall pick in Oscar Klefbom.

Darnell Nurse was a top-10 pick in 2013 and Leon Draisaitl was a top-five overall pick in 2014. MacGregor enjoyed tremendous fortune because he picked so high in most of his drafts (a reflection of the poor product on the ice) and he delivered quality often.

Of the eight men drafted by MacGregor in the top 30 overall during these seasons, five have played or will play more than 500 NHL games in their career. They are Eberle,

Hall, Nugent-Hopkins, Nurse, and Draisaitl. Klefbom (injury) and Nail Yakupov (no longer in the NHL) are both currently shy, but that could change in the years to come. That's a 62.5 percent success rate, with several impact players and award winners in the group.

Looking back, the Oilers might have been better off keeping Craig MacTavish as general manager through the 2015 draft and beyond. He was on an interesting and productive path.

SUCCESS IN THE FIRST 100 SELECTIONS OF EACH DRAFT

MacGregor and his scouts chose 23 players between Nos. 31 and 100 in the group's seven seasons together. The best of them (Tyler Pitlick, Martin Marincin, Erik Gustafsson, Jujhar Khaira, and Anton Lander) were productive for three seasons or more in the NHL and some are still playing in the league.

None have played in 500 games yet, but that's a reflection of this era of drafting being so recent. When all is said and done, two or three of these names should make the grade: Pitlick (286), Marincin (227), Gustafsson (250), Khaira (258), and Lander (215).

SUCCESS AFTER THE FIRST 100
SELECTIONS OF EACH DRAFT

The Oilers enjoyed 24 picks after No. 100 in this era. Tobias Rieder (478 NHL games) was the big success, but Brandon Davidson (180) also forged an interesting career.

SUCCESS IN WHAT DEVELLANO CALLS "PROJECTING"

Eberle was a talented scorer, but no one knew he would score 225 NHL goals before his 30th birthday or he would have gone long before No. 22 overall in 2008. Klefbom had wheels and potential, but projecting him to become the complete player the Oilers have deployed for several years took scouting ability. Finally, we have Draisaitl. He was a big centre and talented on his draft day, but what he has become is so much more than was implied by his skill set and draft-year numbers.

SUCCESS IN ADDRESSING TEAM NEEDS

MacGregor was drafting first overall often so was able to address centre (Nuge, Draisaitl), wing (Hall, Eberle), and even defence (Klefbom). Among all scouting directors, he had the least success in picking goalies. Tyler Bunz' single NHL game represents the sum for six goaltenders selected.

BEST FIRST-ROUND PICK

Hall and Draisaitl can both lay claim to the title; either choice is brilliant. Eberle gets an honourary mention for being chosen so late in the first round.

LEAST SUCCESSFUL FIRST-ROUND PICK

Magnus Paajarvi had speed and two-way acumen but couldn't score enough goals to play on a skill line. That's a disappointing career for such a talented player. Yakupov, selected No. 1 overall in 2012, did not work out as hoped, but I don't believe the scouting department was to blame. Yakupov was in fact the best player in 2012 based on available information.

BEST PICK AFTER THE FIRST ROUND

Rieder has enjoyed a productive career as a middle-six winger with scoring ability and an uncanny ability to get scoring chances while killing penalties.

WHAT STYLE DID MACGREGOR EMPLOY?

Even more than Kevin Prendergast, and certainly more than Barry Fraser, MacGregor appears to have been open to passionate arguments from his area scouts. Some of the team's early work under MacGregor saw the Oilers spend precious early picks on absolute long shots (Troy Hesketh, Cameron Abney). Based on media reports at the time, there is evidence an area scout successfully argued for a player who was drafted out of order based on his skill set. This happened early, in the third and fourth rounds. MacGregor's short term with the team as scouting director was likely the result of his open, democratic style. He also appears to have been vulnerable to interference from upper management.

The Yakupov selection and the story surrounding it speaks to the general manager, consultant, and possibly owner all getting involved to make the pick. That is not a template for draft success.

WHAT PLAYER TYPE DID MACGREGOR LOOK FOR AT THE DRAFT?

Likely due to draft position, MacGregor's record shows a preference for skilled, dynamic, and entertaining players. He also took a pile of Russian players in 2012 and 2013, which stands out for an organization that has traditionally avoided the area.

11

THE HOCKEY GODS SHINE A LIGHT, AGAIN

THE 2015 DRAFT

IN THE HISTORY of any sports franchise, there are relatively few earth-shattering moments. Most historic events, like the acquisition of Wayne Gretzky by the Edmonton Oilers, are not completely recognized in the moment they happen, then begin a rewrite of franchise fortunes in the days that follow.

The five Stanley Cups and Gretzky acquisition by the WHA Oilers aside, no event in Oilers history had a bigger impact than the 2015 draft lottery. It was instant euphoria for Oilers fans, the city of Edmonton, management, and ownership—the impossible dream made real.

On April 18, 2015, the Oilers moved up from No. 3 to No. 1 overall, meaning the team would draft first for the fourth time in six years (2010, 2011, 2012, and 2015).

That's only part of the story. The top pick in 2015 was a generational talent, far beyond the previous gems brought in by the organization. Connor McDavid was touted as the best draft pick since Sidney Crosby a decade previously and would deliver on that promise and then some.

It was the biggest draft event in Oilers history. Great scouting and luck brought Mark Messier, Jari Kurri, Paul Coffey, Glenn Anderson, Grant Fuhr, and Kevin Lowe to the Oilers via the draft. The No. 1 overall pick landed Taylor Hall, Ryan Nugent-Hopkins, and Nail Yakupov in Edmonton.

But a No. 1 overall selection guaranteed to be the best, or close to the best, player in the game? It was barely believable and set off a gigantic celebration in Edmonton.

The 2014–15 Oilers got their coach and general manager fired. Dallas Eakins was replaced midseason by Craig MacTavish (also the GM) for a brief period before Todd Nelson took the reins.

Nelson had the most success, delivering 66 percent of the team's 62 points in 56 percent of the games. After the season and just days after the lottery victory, MacTavish was moved out of the general manager's job and former Boston Bruins GM Peter Chiarelli took over in April 2015.

Chiarelli would fire chief scout Stu MacGregor in the days leading to the draft, elevating Bob Green, who had been in the scouting department in a modified amateur/pro/college role. MacGregor had company out the door: pro scout Morey Gare, amateur scouts Brad Davis and Kent Hawley, and pro scout Dave Semenko were also relieved of their duties.

This was a period of great upheaval in the organization, and my suspicion is that the McDavid lottery win was the genesis for the moves. MacTavish out, Chiarelli in, Green replaces MacGregor, Todd McLellan hired as head coach. However, MacTavish wasn't all the way out, as he appeared onstage at the draft with McDavid, Chiarelli, Green, owner Darryl Katz, new coach McLellan, and executive Scott Howson.

The 2014–15 rookies:

- Oscar Klefbom: 60 games, 2–18–20
- Leon Draisaitl: 37 games, 2–7–9
- Andrew Miller: 9 games, 1–5–6
- Iiro Pakarinen: 17 games, 1–2–3
- Tyler Pitlick: 17 games, 2–0–2
- David Musil: 4 games, 0–2–2
- Brandon Davidson: 12 games, 1–0–1
- Jordan Oesterle: 6 games, 0–1–1
- Darnell Nurse: 2 games, 0–0–0
- Curtis Hamilton: 1 game, 0–0–0
- Bogdan Yakimov: 1 game, 0–0–0
- Laurent Brossoit: 1 game, 2.01 goals-against average, .961 save percentage
- Tyler Bunz: 1 game, 9.00 goals-against average, .750 save percentage

The organization built enormous young talent in the early portion of the decade (Hall, Eberle, Petry, Dubnyk), but by the 2015 draft Dubnyk and Petry were gone and new management didn't have the same connection to Hall and Eberle.

When management changes, the connection to players currently on the roster is not strong. Brothers become cousins.

Entering the 2015 draft, the Oilers had terrific prospects (Draisaitl, Klefbom, Nurse) added to Nugent-Hopkins, Hall, Eberle, and Justin Schultz. This group would have one year together.

PROSPECT SPOTLIGHT
NO. 1 OVERALL: LC CONNOR McDAVID, ERIE OTTERS (OHL)

The scouting reports were incredible. Craig Button, former NHL general manager: "Two words: unprecedented speed. Skating speed, hand quickness and mental processing that he executes simultaneously to threaten defenders and create opportunities. He would be the first pick at every draft since Sidney Crosby in 2005, perhaps even in Crosby's draft year."

Red Line Report: "Is the kind of player on the ice, and the kind of person off the ice, that you want associated with your franchise."

Scouting report and legacy: McDavid's speed is breathtaking. At first blush, it's not believable. It shocks the eye and delights the mind, and you're left wondering if you can trust what appeared before you.

The first time I saw Connor McDavid was at Oilers orientation camp right after the 2015 draft. It was at Northlands Coliseum, a building I'd been to many times. In those visits, the best players of the 1980s through 2010s had been in action, many of them playing for the home side.

Nothing prepared me for his speed and quickness. In short order, NHL fans would witness NHL defencemen who were also not ready for his speed and quickness, and

McDavid would shock the hockey world with his brilliance and talent.

He did not win the Calder Trophy (he got hurt and played just 45 games, 16–32–48) in his rookie season. He blossomed in 2016–17 (second year), scoring 100 points and winning the Art Ross, Hart, and Lindsay Trophies. He would win the Art Ross and Lindsay Trophies the following year.

Perhaps his biggest contribution to the Oilers is his urgency. McDavid is not satisfied with a season out of the playoffs and the Oilers missed three times in his first six years. Edmonton has overhauled management and coaching twice during the first portion of his career with the Oilers; that desire to win that McDavid possesses is the driver for the organization.

NO. 117 OVERALL: LD CALEB JONES
U.S. National Development Team (USHL)

Jones wasn't a highly rated player entering the draft, but he was given credit for being a good skater with a strong first pass. Jones, brother of NHL defender Seth Jones, had size and played a rugged style but his calling card was moving the puck. Jones played his draft-plus-one season in the WHL, flourishing and emerging as a bona fide NHL prospect. His second season with the Portland Winterhawks was even better, so Jones arrived in pro hockey with a solid reputation.

His first AHL campaign was difficult. Jones had trouble in coverage and missed some games. His second year with the Bakersfield Condors showed real growth across the board and earned Jones an NHL recall. In 2019–20, he received a midseason recall and established himself as a solid NHL player. Jones has the look of a defenceman who is going to be around a long time. He was dealt to the Chicago Blackhawks in the summer of 2021.

NO. 124 OVERALL: RD ETHAN BEAR
Seattle Thunderbirds (WHL)

Bear was a two-way defensive prospect with a plus shot and outstanding outlet passing ability. A good skater and a solid hitter, all of his skills were good, but much would depend on his development.

Bear had two strong post-draft seasons in Seattle and then impressed immediately in the pros with the Bakersfield Condors. He earned a recall to the Oilers in his first year but spent most of his first two pro seasons in the AHL.

Selecting centre and generational talent Connor McDavid at No. 1 overall in 2015 was the biggest draft event in Oilers history. (AP Photo/Alan Diaz)

Bear trained all summer in 2019, preparing to make an impression on new coach Dave Tippett at training camp that September. He showed up faster, quicker, and deadly effective, winning an NHL job and moving up the depth chart to the top pairing with Darnell Nurse.

After a strong debut season, he was less consistent in his second year, and the club dealt Bear to the Carolina Hurricanes.

NO. 154 OVERALL: RD JOHN MARINO
South Shore Kings (USPHL)

Marino was another under-the-radar pick, but he progressed during one USHL season and three more at Harvard University. A mobile defender with good two-way skills and a strong skater, he did not sign with the Oilers and forced a trade to the Pittsburgh Penguins. He was a quality rookie defenceman in 2019–20 for Pittsburgh and is now an NHL regular.

NO. 208 OVERALL: G MIROSLAV SVOBODA
Trinec (Czech Jr.)

There wasn't much on him on draft day, but Svoboda had size (6'3", 192 pounds) and some nice progression through his junior career in the Czech Republic. He posted strong numbers in the top Czech league, but the Oilers passed on signing him. The Nashville Predators signed Svodoba and he spent some time in the ECHL, but has made his mark back home with consistent seasons in the Czech league.

NO. 209 OVERALL: LD ZIYAT PAIGIN

Kazan Akbars (KHL)

Paigin was 20 on draft day, so there was more urgency in his development timeline. Paigin had size (6'5", 213 pounds) and a monster shot. He loved physical play. His foot speed kept him from thriving in North America, but Paigin has been a consistent scoring defenceman in the KHL.

2015 Draft Summary

It's difficult to credit Bob Green for the work of an entire season by Stu MacGregor, but Green and staff were at the draft table when the selections were made, so Green is our official scouting director of record. (Number in parentheses is points per game.)

- Connor McDavid (OHL) age 17: 47 games, 44–76–120 (2.55)
- Caleb Jones (USHL) age 17: 25 games, 2–6–8 (0.32)
- Ethan Bear (WHL) age 17: 69 games, 13–25–38 (0.55)
- John Marino (USPHL) age 17: 49 games, 4–24–28 (0.57)
- Miroslav Svoboda (Czech U-20) age 19: 33 games, 2.72 goals-against average, .917 save percentage
- Ziyat Paigin (KHL) age 19: 33 games, 1–1–2 (0.06)

McDavid's numbers were unreal. He lost some games to injury, or the boxcar totals might have been historic. Jones and Bear showed well as two-way types and Marino played in an obscure league, so it was difficult to get a read on him. Edmonton drafted two older players (19) to round out the proceedings. Even though many of the prospects were later traded, the club's scouts identified four tremendous talents. Only the first one was easy.

Four players drafted in 2015 are going to play a long time, and this draft has a chance to be one of the best in Oilers history.

NHL Career Games Played

1. Connor McDavid: 407
2. Ethan Bear: 132
3. John Marino: 108
4. Caleb Jones: 93

The last time Edmonton had four regulars emerge this quickly after draft was 1980.

Here's how the 2015 draft class compares to the preceding decade in terms of total NHL games played:

1. 2007 (1,554 games)
2. 2011 (1,519 games)
3. 2010 (1,375 games)
4. 2006 (895 games)
5. 2012 (858 games)
6. 2008 (834 games)
7. **2015 (740 games)**
8. 2009 (682 games)
9. 2013 (509 games)
10. 2014 (505 games)

The four picks by Edmonton that made the NHL so quickly will eventually overtake most of the Oilers' drafts dating back to 1979. It's possible the 2015 draft will eventually pass all but the 1979–81 Edmonton drafts.

Trades That Involved Draft Picks

Peter Chiarelli traded away enormous riches in 2015, a deep draft that has delivered exceptional return five years on. If the Oilers had kept the picks, it's extremely likely the club would be much closer to a Stanley Cup than it is today.

On July 10, 2013, the Oilers traded Magnus Paajarvi, a 2014 second-round pick (Ivan Barbashev), and a 2015 fourth-round pick (Adam Musil) to the St. Louis Blues for David Perron and a 2015 third-round pick (Mike Robinson).

On March 4, 2014, the Oilers traded a 2014 fifth-round pick (Matthew Berkovitz) and a 2015 fifth-round pick (Dennis Yan) in the 2015 draft to the Anaheim Ducks for Viktor Fasth.

On March 5, 2014, the Oilers traded Ales Hemsky to the Ottawa Senators for the No. 130 pick in the 2014 draft (Liam Coughlin) and a 2015 third-round pick (Sergey Zborovskiy).

On January 2, 2015, the Oilers traded David Perron to the Pittsburgh Penguins for Rob Klinkhammer and a first-round pick (Mathew Barzal).

On March 2, 2015, the Oilers traded Jeff Petry to the Montreal Canadiens for a 2015 second-round pick (Jonas Siegenthaler) and the No. 117 pick in the 2015 draft (Caleb Jones).

On June 26, 2015, the Oilers traded the No. 16 overall pick in the 2015 draft (Mathew Barzal) and the No. 33 overall selection in the 2015 draft (Mitchell Stephens) to the New York Islanders for Griffin Reinhart.

On June 27, 2015, the Oilers traded No. 57 overall (Jonas Siegenthaler), No. 79 overall (Sergey Zborovskiy), and No. 184 overall (Adam Huska), all 2015 picks, to the New York Rangers for Cam Talbot and No. 209 overall (Ziyat Paigin).

On June 27, 2015, the Oilers traded a third-round pick (Mike Robinson) to the San Jose Sharks for coach Todd McLellan.

On June 27, 2015, the Oilers traded Martin Marincin to the Toronto Maple Leafs for Brad Ross and the No. 107 pick (Craig Wolanin).

On June 27, 2015, the Oilers traded the No. 107 pick in the 2015 draft to the Ottawa Senators for Eric Gryba.

On June 27, 2015, the Oilers traded a 2016 seventh-round pick (Otto Somppi) to the Tampa Bay Lightning for the No. 208 overall pick (Miroslav Svoboda) in the 2015 draft.

12

BALL OF CONFUSION

THE 2016 DRAFT

THE OILERS WERE new top-to-bottom in management (Peter Chiarelli) and coaching (head coach Todd McLelan) and had a new scouting director (Bob Green) in 2015–16.

The on-ice performance improved, with Edmonton winning 31 games (24 the previous season) and cutting the shot-differential gap in half. In 2014–15, Edmonton's goals for–against (198–283) gave the team a minus-85 goal differential. McLellan increased the offence and had a major impact on the defence (203–245, minus-42) in year one despite missing the playoffs.

Connor McDavid missed 37 games and still finished third in team scoring. Taylor Hall and Leon Draisaitl had a good run, but Hall's scoring in the final 32 games (8–9–17) ruined a strong start (50 games, 18–30–48) to the year. Hall played well during the time McDavid was out, but a lot of attention postseason was focused on how he finished.

The 2015–16 rookies:

- Connor McDavid: 45 games, 16–32–48
- Iiro Pakarinen: 63 games, 5–8–13
- Brandon Davidson: 51 games, 4–7–11
- Darnell Nurse: 69 games, 3–7–10
- Adam Clendening: 20 games, 1–5–6
- Jordan Oesterle: 17 games, 0–5–5
- Jujhar Khaira: 15 games, 0–2–2
- Griffin Reinhart: 29 games, 0–1–1
- Anton Slepyshev: 11 games, 0–1–1
- Anders Nilsson: 26 games, 3.14 goals-against average, .901 save percentage
- Laurent Brossoit: 5 games, 3.61 goals-against average, .873 save percentage

In May 2016, Drake Caggiula signed with Edmonton as a college free agent. A skilled winger with two-way ability, Caggiula would make the team out of his first camp and spend the first four seasons of his pro career playing in the NHL. Caggiula had chemistry with Connor McDavid at five on five, scoring 2.36 points per 60 (anything over 2.00 is quality) in his time with Edmonton. GM Peter Chiarelli sent Caggiula to the Chicago Blackhawks in December 2018, as Edmonton was looking for physical defenceman.

In August of 2016, the Oilers signed defenceman Matt Benning as a college free agent. Originally drafted by the Boston Bruins when Chiarelli was the GM for the team, his move to Edmonton (Benning's hometown) was a coincidence that benefited the Oilers. After a very short stint in the AHL, Benning emerged as a productive third-pairing defenceman in the NHL. His outscoring at five on five over four seasons was notable. Benning would sign in Nashville to play for the Predators in 2020–21.

NO. 4 OVERALL: RW JESSE PULJUJARVI
Karpat (Liiga)

Puljujarvi was universally regarded as the No. 3 prospect in the draft, so there was an audible gasp at the First Niagara Centre in Buffalo, New York, when the Columbus Blue Jackets chose Pierre-Luc Dubois at No. 3 overall.

Red Line Report suggested Puljujarvi was a "big horse [who] looks and plays like a Mats Sundin clone. Has the four S's': size, skills, skating, shot. Has all the tools to be a dominant power forward who combines top-notch skills with brute force."

Oilers fans were thrilled with what looked like good fortune (again!) and talked about Finland or Bakersfield as his destination, with an NHL look possible.

He made the NHL team and scored in the first game, and it looked like it would be an easy adjustment for the big Finn. Puljujarvi could disappear at times during the game, and he had a tough time with his play away from the puck. He picked up an assist in late October, but his playing time was sporadic, and he didn't play in an NHL game after January 5.

In the AHL, Puljujarvi played well and found the range offensively (39 games, 12–16–28). Based on the previous decades of prospects coming through the minors, we know those numbers are shy of NHL potential for a 20-year-old graduating from junior college or European player.

Puljujarvi was 18 when he arrived in the AHL, meaning those numbers were most promising for his offensive potential.

Right winger Jesse Puljujarvi was regarded as the No. 3 prospect in the 2016 draft, but the Columbus Blue Jackets chose Pierre-Luc Dubois with that selection instead, allowing Puljujarvi to fall to the Oilers at No. 4. *(Nathan Denette/The Canadian Press via AP)*

The Oilers should have kept him there, but by year two Chiarelli spent most of the cap room and the team needed wingers.

He played 139 NHL and 53 AHL games during his entry deal, and then signed in Liiga and enjoyed a strong season in 2019–20. The Oilers finally got him under contract again when Ken Holland signed the Finn to a two-year deal in the 2020 offseason.

In his first season back in Edmonton, Puljujarvi blossomed as a more complete player and enjoyed his strongest offensive year (15 goals and 25 points in 55 games). He was placed on Connor McDavid's line and had success, and as training camp 2021 arrived he appeared to be on track as a young two-way skill forward in the NHL.

NO. 32 OVERALL: LW TYLER BENSON
Vancouver Giants (WHL)

Benson was drafted by his hometown team after a famous run through minor hockey in the city. Benson's scouting report reflected an agitating winger with two-way ability and a fairly complete skill set. The offence was the question mark, partly because of several injuries that affected both his development and speed. Benson entered pro hockey in 2018–19 and delivered a fantastic AHL season with the Bakersfield Condors (68 games, 15–51–66), one of the best by an Oilers AHL prospect in two decades. He was unable to deliver the same quality in year two but did play in seven NHL games in 2019–20. In 2020–21, he once again delivered a strong AHL season (36 points in 36 games) and had clearly graduated from the AHL. The question remained: Could he land an NHL job?

NO. 63 OVERALL: LD MARKUS NIEMELAINEN
Saginaw Spirit (OHL)

A huge defenceman (6'5", 198 pounds), Niemelainen was highly rated and fell to No. 63 for the Oilers. Scouts mentioned his foot speed as a positive and he had some passing ability. The big appeal was the size. He signed back in Finland for the 2017–18 season and spent several years in the Liiga with mixed results. Edmonton signed him in the spring of 2020, and he played well for the Bakersfield Condors (AHL) in 2020–21. Niemelainen showed more range than expected and raised his status as a prospect after several unimpressive years in Finland.

NO. 84 OVERALL: LD MATTHEW CAIRNS
Georgetown Raiders (OJHL)

Cairns was a big defender (6'2", 202 pounds), had a strong year in the OJHL (46 games, 9–24–33), and spiked in the playoffs (22 games, 3–16–19). The scouting reports spent more time on his defensive abilities and that matched his performance after leaving the OJHL. He bounced from the USHL to the BCHL (a bad sign) in his draft-plus-one season before settling in for three years at Cornell (in a depth role). He transferred to the University of Minnesota-Duluth for 2020–21 and showed more offensive prowess. He did not sign with the Oilers.

NO. 91 OVERALL: RD FILIP BERGLUND
Skelleftea (Sweden Jr.)

Berglund was chosen in the second year of his eligibility. At 6'2", 209 pounds, and with puck-moving ability, the only down arrows for Berglund were average speed and the fact he was 18 and playing in junior. Since his draft day he has been increasing his share of ice time and performing well in the SEL. He signed with the Oilers and will come over in 2021–22. He is expected to flourish in the AHL and eventually push for NHL employment.

NO. 123 OVERALL: G DYLAN WELLS
Peterborough Petes (OHL)

Wells was brilliant playing for Canada at the summer Hlinka championships and NHL teams followed him closely as his draft season began. He was playing for a strong Peterborough team and things should have gone well, but Wells struggled all year and his draft ranking fell from No. 5 mid-term to No. 10 on the final list. Edmonton chose him late and his draft-plus-one season was improved (.916 save percentage). When he turned pro, Wells had a tough time getting to the AHL. After two pro seasons, he played 33 ECHL games (.896) and 19 AHL games (.898) but things didn't look promising entering the final year of his entry deal. He was traded to the Carolina Hurricanes organization in 2021.

NO. 149 OVERALL: LW GRAHAM MCPHEE
U.S. National Development Team (USHL)

Small for the NHL of 2016 (5'11", 172 pounds), McPhee is the son of NHL executive (and current president of hockey operations for the Vegas Golden Knights) George McPhee. Possessing good speed, average skill, and a lot of determination, he had one good season at Boston College (2017–18, 12–12–24 in 36 games) but didn't move the needle in the other seasons. Edmonton didn't sign him out of college, and he played 2020–21 in Austria.

NO. 153 OVERALL: RC AAPELI RASANEN
Tappara (Finland Jr.)

Although he was drafted late, Rasanen checked off a lot of boxes scouts look for in prospects. He was a good skater, played centre, and had enough skill to project to the highest levels. He was still a long shot, but at No. 153, all the obvious impact prospects are gone. Rasanen had a solid year in the USHL (38 games, 7–18–25) in his draft-plus-one season and then headed for Boston College. After two pedestrian seasons in college, he blossomed offensively in his junior season, scoring 11–13–24 in 34 games. He left college to return to Finland (Liiga), where he played well. He has a résumé that suggests he might have NHL ability but has not signed with Edmonton.

NO. 183 OVERALL: RD VINCENT DESHARNAIS
Providence (NCAA)

Desharnais was 6'7", 228 pounds on draft day and coming off his freshman (19, 1–1–2) college season. He was an awkward skater who was mostly about the defensive game but did make a good first pass. He played four seasons with Providence, the best his senior year at age 22. He has been a solid player for Edmonton's AHL affiliate since turning pro but does not have an NHL contract.

2016 Draft Summary
The 2016 draft is six years old and has been slow developing. Ironically, it looks more promising now than it has in years. (Number in parentheses is points per game.)

- Jesse Puljujarvi (Liiga) age 17: 50 games, 13–15–28 (0.56)
- Tyler Benson (WHL) age 17: 30 games, 9–19–28 (0.93)
- Markus Niemelainen (OHL) age 17: 65 games, 1–25–26 (0.40)
- Matt Cairns (OJHL) age 17: 46 games, 9–24–33 (0.72)
- Filip Berglund (SuperElite J-20) age 18: 43 games, 19–22–41 (0.95)
- Dylan Wells (OHL) age 17: 27 games, 4.59 goals-against average, .871 save percentage
- Graham McPhee (USHL) age 17: 20 games, 5–0–5 (0.25)
- Aapeli Rasanen (Finland Jr.) age 17: 50 games, 19–19–38 (0.76)
- Vincent Desharnais (NCAA) age 19: 19 games, 1–1–2 (0.11)

Puljujarvi's points-per-game total was shy of fellow Finn Patrik Laine (0.72) and Puljujarvi's teammate Sebastian Aho pushed the river in the Liiga and at the World Junior Championships on Puljujarvi's line. Edmonton mishandled the young man's entry-level career, but there were signs that the big winger was not going to be Laine's equal on draft day. The draft turns on Puljujarvi, a top-five overall pick.

NHL Career Games Played

1. Jesse Puljujarvi: 194
2. Tyler Benson: 7

Here's how the 2016 draft class compares to the preceding decade in terms of total NHL games played:

1. 2007 (1,554 games)
2. 2011 (1,519 games)
3. 2010 (1,375 games)
4. 2012 (858 games)
5. 2008 (834 games)
6. 2015 (740 games)
7. 2009 (682 games)
8. 2013 (509 games)
9. 2014 (505 games)
10. **2016 (201 games)**

The re-emergence of Puljujarvi may save the 2016 draft, and the fact that Benson, Niemelainen, and Berglund are still developing gives a hint of promise for a draft that has been the wayward wind since draft weekend.

Trades That Involved Draft Picks

On July 4, 2013, the Oilers traded Shawn Horcoff to the Dallas Stars for Philip Larsen and a seventh-round pick in the 2016 draft (Otto Somppi).

On June 27, 2015, the Oilers traded a 2016 seventh-round pick (Otto Somppi) to the Tampa Bay Lightning for the No. 208 overall pick (Miroslv Svoboda) in the 2015 draft.

On February 27, 2016, the Oilers traded Teddy Purcell to the Florida Panthers for No. 84 overall (Matthew Cairns).

On February 27, 2016, the Oilers traded Justin Schultz to the Pittsburgh Penguins for the No. 91 overall pick in the 2016 draft (Filip Berglund).

On February 27, 2016, the Oilers traded Anders Nilsson to the St. Louis Blues for Niklas Lundstrom and the No. 149 pick in the 2016 draft (Graham McPhee).

On February 29, 2016, the Oilers traded Martin Gernat and a 2016 fourth-round pick (Jack Kopacka) to the Anaheim Ducks for Patrick Maroon.

THE 2017 DRAFT

The 2016–17 season was a watershed for the Edmonton Oilers. The team finished with 103 points, 47 wins, and a plus-35 goal differential and came within two points of winning the division.

The team was not balanced but won behind the brilliance of Connor McDavid (who swept the regular season awards) and fine goaltending of Cam Talbot.

The defence was heavily reliant on two Swedes (Oscar Klefbom and Adam Larsson) plus Slovakian Andrej Sekera. In the playoffs, the Oilers rolled past the San Jose Sharks in a hard-fought series that went six games (with each team winning once in overtime).

Against the Anaheim Ducks in the second round, the Oilers looked strong, but the mistakes of youth and a devastating injury to Sekera (which would bleed into the following season) led to a heartbreaking seven-game series loss.

Rookies in 2016–17:

- Drake Caggiula: 60 games, 7–11–18
- Matt Benning: 62 games, 3–12–15
- Anton Slepyshev: 41 games, 4–6–10
- Jesse Puljujarvi: 28 games, 1–7–8
- Jujhar Khaira: 10 games, 1–0–1
- Dillon Simpson: 3 games, 0–0–0
- Laurent Brossoit: 8 games, 1.99 goals-against average, .928 save percentage

The Oilers had been on quite a run of rookies over the 2014–15 and 2015–16 seasons, bringing in Connor McDavid, Leon Draisaitl, Oscar Klefbom, and Darnell Nurse. The Jacks and Kings were there, just as they were in 2011 when Ryan Nugent-Hopkins joined Taylor Hall, Jordan Eberle, Jeff Petry, and Devan Dubnyk.

The 2016–17 rookie class had so much promise, but as of 2021 the group above was either playing in other NHL cities or hanging on in Edmonton. Jesse Puljuarvi's resurgence in 2020–21 represented the only good news for the group.

PROSPECT SPOTLIGHT
NO. 22 OVERALL: RW KAILER YAMAMOTO, SPOKANE CHIEFS (WHL)

Yamamoto famously told Peter Chiarelli, "You gotta draft me, otherwise I'm gonna come back and haunt you." His intelligent play with and without the puck is the key to his success.

Scouting report and legacy: The Yamamoto selection, no matter how it turns out, is a historic one for the Oilers. For almost 40 years, through periods when skill was king and through periods when size was the priority, the team shied away from players as small as Yamamoto (5'8",153 pounds) in the first round, no matter how many goals they produced.

HockeyProspect.com's *NHL Draft Black Book* called Yamamoto "an electric player with dynamic offensive ability, easily some of highest skill of any forward I watched this year, he's just so small and at times took some big contact when I was viewing him. Love his aggressive nature and how he attacks puck carries from all angles, it puts players on edge."

Yamamoto auditioned well in the first two training camps, 2017 and 2018, making the team both times. He struggled when the competition got stronger and was sent out on each occasion.

In 2019, under new manager Ken Holland and coach Dave Tippett, Yamamoto spent training camp on the sidelines, recovering from wrist surgery. He played in the AHL with the Bakersfield Condors until New Year's, and then caught fire when placed on a line with Leon Draisaitl and Ryan Nugent-Hopkins. In the final 27 games of the year, he posted 11–15–26 to establish himself as an NHL skill winger. In 2020–21, he posted lesser numbers (52 games,

8–13–21) but remained an effective skill winger with Draisaitl as his centre.

After decades of passing on small skill in the first round, the Oilers finally gave in and drafted Yamamoto. He was the smallest first-round pick by the organization in team history.

NO. 78 OVERALL: G STUART SKINNER
Lethbridge Hurricanes (WHL)

The Oilers were very high on Skinner, trading up to make sure they could secure his rights. He had great size (6'4", 206 pounds) and lateral movement, along with a quick glove. Skinner had a strong WHL career after his draft, leading the Swift Current Broncos to the 2018 WHL Championship and a Memorial Cup appearance. Once he turned pro, Skinner had difficulty establishing himself and entered the 2020–21 season with a lot of pressure to show the promise of his junior career at the pro level. He made his NHL debut and won, and then delivered a strong performance for the AHL Bakersfield Condors. As the 2021–22 training camp approached, Skinner was in the mix for the top job in Bakersfield and first recall to the NHL.

NO. 84 OVERALL: LD DMITRI SAMORUKOV
Guelph Storm (OHL)

Samorukov was a big Russian (6'3", 197 pounds) with a mean streak playing in Canadian junior. A two-way type, he had moments of complete chaos in his draft year and fell down the draft lists (Bob McKenzie had him at No. 76, Craig Button at No. 53) due to midseason struggles.

Right winger Kailer Yamamoto, drafted No. 22 overall in 2017, was the smallest first-round pick by the Oilers in team history. Edmonton, which had long prioritized size, could not deny his offensive skill. *(AP Photo/Nam Y. Huh)*

After he was drafted, Samorukov's game grew across the board. He showed impressive growth as a passer and puck mover and even spent time on the power play. He became a feared defender and punishing hitter, using his impressive wingspan to great effect.

When Samorukov turned pro with the Bakersfield Condors, his game faded and the chaos returned. The Oilers were still high on the player's future, but new general manager Ken Holland took an unusual step: Edmonton loaned Samorukov to KHL CSKA Moscow for the entire season plus playoffs. And as happened in his post-draft seasons in the OHL, the light went on again and Samorukov emerged as a strong NHL prospect with a fairly complete skill set.

NO. 115 OVERALL: RW OSTAP SAFIN
Sparta Praha (Czech Jr.)

Safin was a mid-second-round projection but fell on draft day. A big man with skill and agility, he came to North America in his draft-plus-one season and scored well for the Saint John Sea Dogs of the QMJHL (61 games, 26–32–58). It looked like Edmonton found a scorer in the later rounds of the draft. In his final junior season, Safin was badly injured and hasn't returned to previous levels. His first pro season (2019–20) was spent in the ECHL, where he scored just 35 points in 54 games. His time with Bakersfield in 2020–21 (22 games, 4–2–6) featured some flashes but lacked consistency.

NO. 146 OVERALL: RW KIRILL MAKSIMOV
Niagara Ice Dogs (OHL)

A big winger with good speed and hands, Maksimov caught fire midway through his draft season after a trade in the OHL. He scored 19 goals in the final 33 games (regular season and play-offs) and then hammered OHL goalies for 74 goals in his final two junior seasons. The Russian struggled in his first pro season with the Bakersfield Condors, although he did show great utility by playing effectively on the penalty kill. He spent 2020–21 in Russian leagues, scoring few goals and raising concern about his future. No one doubts his talent, but he will need to deliver more.

NO. 177 OVERALL: LC SKYLER BRIND'AMOUR
U.S. National Development Team (USHL)

The son of former NHL star Rod Brind'Amour, Skyler was a raw talent with some distinct positives on his résumé. He is a good skater and a calm decision-maker and able to help in puck possession with his stick handling. He is not a natural scorer, but more of a two-way type who can be effective in all three zones. He began his post-draft career in the BCHL, where he played well in a defined role. It continued upon his arrival with Quinnipiac (NCAA) beginning in 2019–20. Brind'Amour is building a solid if unspectacular résumé.

NO. 208 OVERALL: RD PHIL KEMP
U.S. National Development Team (USHL)

An interesting prospect, Kemp is a good skater who plays defence first and blocks a lot of shots. He made several U.S. national teams during his junior career as the shutdown defender, making a famous sweep save of a sure goal at the 2019 World Junior Championships. At Yale, he showed great range defensively, and in his junior year the offence came alive and gave him a more complete résumé. He signed with Edmonton in 2020 and began his pro career in the Allsvenskan (Sweden) playing a two-way style. Later in 2020–21, he played for the Bakersfield Condors (AHL) and showed good shutdown skills.

2017 Draft Summary

By 2017, NHL teams were using analytics to identify draft inefficiencies and take advantage of them. Yamamoto is a great example, as he delivered terrific offence despite being undersized. It signaled a new day for Edmonton at the draft.

- Kailer Yamamoto (WHL) age 17: 65 games, 42–57–99 (1.52)
- Stuart Skinner (WHL) age 17: 60 games, 3.26 goals-against average, .905 save percentage
- Dmitri Samorukov (OHL) age 17: 67 games, 4–16–20 (0.29)
- Ostap Safin (Czech U-20) age 17: 24 games, 6–12–18 (0.75)
- Kirill Maksimov (OHL): age 17: 66 games, 21–17–38 (0.58)
- Skyler Brind'Amour (USHL) age 17: 8 games, 1–0–1 (0.13)
- Phil Kemp (USHL) age 17: 25 games, 2–2–4 (0.16)

What isn't known is just how much the math of the draft factors into the team's decisions.

The perception post-draft was that Bob Green and his Oilers scouts had delivered less talent than in 2016. A couple of years later, the 2017 edition looks better. We'll know by 2025.

Keith Gretzky was hired by the Oilers to be assistant general manager in August 2016. His heavy background in amateur scouting meant he worked closely with Green and his staff in assessing the 2017 (and later) drafts.

NHL Career Games Played

1. Kailer Yamamoto: 107
2. Stuart Skinner: 1

Here's how the 2017 draft class compares to the preceding decade in terms of total NHL games played:

1. 2011 (1,519 games)
2. 2010 (1,375 games)
3. 2012 (858 games)
4. 2008 (834 games)
5. 2015 (740 games)
6. 2009 (682 games)
7. 2013 (509 games)
8. 2014 (505 games)
9. 2016 (201 games)
10. **2017 (106 games)**

Trades That Involved Draft Picks

On February 24, 2016, the Oilers traded Philip Larsen to the Vancouver Canucks for a 2017 fifth-round pick (Michael Karow).

On October 7, 2016, the Oilers traded Nail Yakupov to the St. Louis Blues for Zach Pochiro and a 2017 third-round pick (Cameron Crotty).

On April 24, 2017, the Oilers traded a 2017 second-round pick (Jack Studnicka) to the Boston Bruins in exchange for hiring Peter Chiarelli.

On June 24, 2017, the Oilers traded a 2017 third-round pick (Cameron Crotty) and fifth-round pick (Michael Karow) to the Arizona Coyotes for the No. 78 overall pick (Stuart Skinner).

THE 2018 DRAFT

The promise of spring 2017 was replaced by another season of disappointment. A goal differential that was brilliant in 2016–17 (247–212, plus-35) fell to earth (234–263, minus-29) in a heartbeat. Andrej Sekera's loss was massive, and general manager Peter Chiarelli spent the last available cap money signing Kris Russell, meaning the badly needed scoring winger position would have to be solved internally.

Time was running out for Chiarelli and head coach Todd McLellan.

Top rookies in 2017–18:

- Pontus Aberg: 16 games, 6–2–8
- Ethan Bear: 18 games, 1–3–4
- Kailer Yamamoto: 9 games, 0–3–3
- Keegan Lowe: 2 games, 0–0–0
- Nathan Walker: 2 games, 0–0–0
- Laurent Brossoit: 14 games, 3.24 goals-against average, .883 save percentage

Bear emerged as a quality top-four defenceman with a strong year in 2019–20 and Yamamoto, who also took his time, showed the talent he possesses in the same season Bear emerged.

In May 2018, the Oilers signed defenceman Joel Persson. He came out of nowhere in the Swedish leagues and established himself as an intriguing puck mover. It was determined that he would wait a year before coming to North America.

In July of 2018, the Oilers signed Josh Currie to an NHL deal. He spent three seasons on an AHL deal with the Bakersfield Condors before signing the contract and would play in the NHL during 2018–19.

NO. 10 OVERALL: RD EVAN BOUCHARD
London Knights (OHL)

Bouchard was the 12th selection by Edmonton from the London Knights and has a chance to be the best one of all. Sam Gagner (844) and Steve Smith (804) are the most successful Oilers picks from London through 2021.

Bouchard's passing touch is exceptional. His vision is fantastic and in the offensive zone he can slide down and find open lanes beautifully. As an offensive defenceman, he's special with the puck on his stick. He has the potential to be the best offensive defenceman drafted by Edmonton since Paul Coffey.

He came right to the NHL for seven games but wasn't ready in the same way that Jesse Puljujrvi and Kailer Yamamoto weren't ready. He completed his junior career, played well (and improved) with Bakersfield of the AHL, and spent the first portion of 2020–21 playing in Sweden's second league (Allsvenskan) and flourished. Bouchard was used sparingly in the 2020–21 NHL season, getting into just 14 games (2–3–5) and showing his potential in every game. He has a bright future.

NO. 40 OVERALL: LC RYAN MCLEOD
Mississauga Steelheads (OHL)

A speedy centre who was projected on some lists to be a first-round pick, McLeod fell to Edmonton in the second round. His offence projected him to middle-six as opposed to top-six forward potential, as he finished his draft season (68 games, 26–44–70) at just over a point per game. He finished strong in junior and then showed solid two-way play and posted 5–18–23 in 56 games as a rookie pro in the AHL. In 2020–21, he played well in Swiss-A, and then produced a point per game in 28 AHL contests. Finally, in 2020–21 he played in his first NHL games (10, 0–1–1), showing great speed and puck retrieval. His story is just getting started.

NO. 62 OVERALL: G OLIVIER RODRIGUE
Drummondville Voltigeurs (QMJHL)

Rodrigue is a quick, athletic goaltender who was slightly under-sized (6'1", 156 pounds) on draft day. Red Line Report wrote that he "makes every first save and doesn't give up softies—shooters have to earn every goal. Outstanding reflexes and quickness around the crease. Lightning fast moving cross-crease, and always under control. Very quick feet and glove." He played a pedestrian post-draft season and a half in junior and then caught fire and was as good as anyone in the last half of his final season in the QMJHL. At the beginning of 2020–21, he was playing well in the Austrian league, then he came back to the AHL and posted inconsistent numbers (11 games, .894 save percentage) with Bakersfield.

NO. 164 OVERALL: RD MIKE KESSELRING
New Hampton School (USHS, New Hampshire)

Kellselring was a raw talent on his draft day and a flier pick by Edmonton. He had size (6'4", 185 pounds) and an awkward but effective stride, with impressive offensive instincts. High school defencemen are hit-or-miss, but the hits (Edmonton landed Tom Poti) are unique and valuable. Kesselring is still building his résumé but is an intriguing talent. He turned pro with the Bakersfield Condors in 2020–21, showing raw talent (21 games, 1–2–3, plus three points in six playoff games) in an intriguing AHL run.

NO. 195 OVERALL: LW PATRIK SIIKANEN
Blues (Finland Jr.)

Siikanen was the 11th player drafted by Edmonton out of Finnish junior, with the only NHL player so far being Teemu Hartikainen. On the other hand, Finland's top league (Liiga) has been a fantastic resource for the Oilers (see: Jari Kurri, Esa Tikkanen, Raimo Summanen, Jussi Markkanen, and Jesse Puljujarvi). Siikanen was an obscure selection who had some offensive acumen but as of 2021 was having a hard time making it as a regular in the Liiga.

2018 Draft Summary

As was the case with the 2017 draft, Edmonton's first-round selection was an analytics star. This appeared to confirm the team's placing increasing value on the math of the draft. (Number in parentheses is points per game.)

- Evan Bouchard (OHL) age 17: 67 games, 25–62–87 (1.30)
- Ryan McLeod (OHL) age 17: 68 games, 26–44–70 (1.03)
- Olivier Rodrigue (QMJHL) age 17: 53 games, 2.54 goals-against average, .903 save percentage
- Mike Kesselring (USHL) age 17: 12 games, 0–2–2 (0.17)
- Patrik Siikanen (Finland Jr.) age 17: 24 games, 10–7–17 (0.71)

Bouchard's numbers were outstanding, inspiring Scott Wheeler of The Athletic to compare him to Nashville Predators star Ryan Ellis. Second-round selection McLeod also showed well, scoring more than a point per game in his draft year.

Evan Bouchard's 21 NHL games and Ryan McLeod's 10 are the sum total of 2018 selections' time in the world's best league.

Trades That Involved Draft Picks

On January 4, 2018, the Oilers traded a fourth-round pick in 2018 (Jasper Weatherby) for goalie Al Montoya.

On June 23, 2018, the Oilers traded a 2018 third-round pick (Jordan Harris) and a 2018 fifth-round pick (Samuel Houde) to the Montreal Canadiens for the No. 62 overall pick (Olivier Rodrigue).

13

A MEASURED APPROACH

THE 2019 DRAFT

THE 2018-19 OILERS ran in place, and it cost jobs in high places. Peter Chiarelli and Todd McLellan were the big names to go, replaced on an interim basis by Keith Gretzky (GM) and Ken Hitchcock (coach). The team's goal differential in 2018–19 (232–274, minus-42) was a slight downgrade from 2017–18 (234–263, minus-29) and for an organization that employed Connor McDavid, going the wrong way was unacceptable.

At the end of the 2018–19 season, McDavid said he was "not happy," which sent a tremor through the Alberta capital and led to changes.

Ken Holland would be the new general manager by draft day and Dave Tippett would take over as coach. Bob Green remained amateur scouting director.

Rookies on the team:

- Caleb Jones: 17 games, 1–5–6
- Josh Currie: 21 games, 2–3–5
- Colby Cave: 33 games, 2–1–3
- Joe Gambardella: 15 games, 0–3–3
- Kailer Yamamoto: 17 games, 1–1–2
- Evan Bouchard: 7 games, 1–0–1
- Cooper Marody: 6 games, 0–0–0
- Valentin Zykov: 5 games, 0–0–0
- Patrick Russell: 6 games, 0–0–0
- Anthony Stolarz: 6 games, 3.77 goals-against average, .897 save percentage

The rookies represent a watershed of young names who will likely populate NHL rosters in the future, the most promising being Jones, Yamamoto, and Bouchard. None had a major impact in 2018–19.

Bob Green retained his title as scouting director, but with Ken Holland being named the new general manager in May, the overall feel of Edmonton's draft was different than in the past. As an example, for the first time ever, the Oilers' 2019 draft did not include any OHL or WHL players. In the previous drafts, at least one player from one of those leagues had been selected.

NO. 8 OVERALL: LD PHILIP BROBERG
AIK (Allsvenskan)

Broberg more closely resembled a Detroit Red Wings pick than a typical Oilers selection. An outstanding skater and two-way prospect, Broberg was less of a complete product (like Bouchard) and more a project with room to grow in all areas. Craig Button from TSN: "Elite skating defenceman makes it very difficult to forecheck him and allows him to open up ice. Attributes of a modern NHL blueliner." Broberg had more risk to him but a chance to be a complete defenceman. In his first year post-draft, he contributed well to his SHL team but in 2020–21 ran in place while suffering some injuries. As 2021–22 training camp loomed, there were questions surrounding Broberg being able to deliver on his draft pedigree.

NO. 38 OVERALL: RC RAPHAEL LAVOIE
Halifax Mooseheads (QMJHL)

Lavoie had first-round talent but fell to Edmonton in the second round. A volume shooter, Lavoie was a productive player throughout his junior career. He scored 100 goals in his three full junior seasons. In his draft-plus-two season, Lavoie continued to fill the net in Sweden's Allsvenskan. As 2021 dawned, his career looked promising. Scott Wheeler from The Athletic wrote, "He gets to the net at will and he has the ability to finish plays in tight by pounding home rebounds or using some impressive stick handling to beat goalies with a deke." He finished 2020–21 in the AHL scoring 5–5–10 in 19 games with Bakersfield, adding 1–3–4 in six postseason games.

NO. 85 OVERALL: G ILYA KONOVALOV
Yaroslavl Lotomotiv (KHL)

Drafted at 20, Konovalov is undersized for an NHL goalie prospect (5'11", 196 pounds). His résumé was splendid, as his save percentages are .933, .930, .912, and, as of this writing, .927 for 2020–21. Corey Pronman from The Athletic wrote, "His eyes seem magnetically attracted to the puck. He's never fooled by reverse passes from behind the net or centering plays, and he stays in position even when the puck is bouncing around the crease. He has that very low panic threshold you want in a goalie." The team signed him after the 2020–21 season and he will compete for an NHL job in the seasons to come.

NO. 100 OVERALL: LW MATEJ BLUMEL
Waterloo Blackhawks (USHL)

A speedy Czech winger, Blumel was one of the final true scoring forwards available in the draft at No. 100 overall. Red Line Report wrote, "Explosive skater with the ability to fill lanes and get up the ice quickly. More than the sum of his parts—works his ass off every shift, never stops moving his feet, and outhustles defenders for loose pucks." He was pedestrian in Czech league play in his draft-plus-one year but blossomed in year two (2020–21) and is on track as a prospect. He did not sign with Edmonton.

NO. 162 OVERALL: LC TOMAS MAZURA
Kimball Union (USHS, New Hampshire)

A Czech forward, Mazura was 18 on draft day and older for a high-end high school player. Scouting reports suggested he was quite skilled and considered a top prep player for his all-around offensive potential. He was considered raw on draft day, a theme on Holland's first Oilers draft weekend. He played just three games in 2020–21, in Finland's U-20 junior league (1–2–3).

NO. 193 OVERALL: LC MAXIM BENEZHKIN
Yaroslavl (Russia Jr.)

Benezhkin has high skill and is a little undersized. Chances are he has NHL talent but may never come to North America. Corey

Pronman of The Athletic wrote, "He's a versatile forward, and has the skill and hockey sense to create offence. He's a very good passer and finisher who scores with his above-average shot but also by attacking the net hard."

2019 Draft Summary

Holland wasn't hired in time to put his stamp on the scouting department, but I've always thought he had an impact on the first selection. Swedish defenceman Philip Broberg had size and two-way ability, and he was a tremendous skater. The view of Broberg offensively was less clear. (Number in parentheses is points per game.)

- Philip Broberg (Allsvenskan) age 17: 41 games, 2–7–9 (0.22)
- Raphael Lavoie (QMJHL) age 17: 62 games, 32–41–73 (1.18)
- Ilya Konovalov (KHL) age 20: 45 games, 1.89 goals-against average, .930 save percentage
- Matej Blumel (USHL) age 18: 58 games, 30–30–60 (1.03)
- Tomas Mazura (USHS) age 18: 37 games, 14–40–54 (1.46)
- Maxim Denezhkin (MHL) age 17: 51 games, 22–17–39 (0.76)

The Broberg pick aside, Lavoie and Blumel were solid selections based on points per game in the leagues each played in. The big question after the 2019 draft concerned the direction Holland would take the amateur scouting department.

Trades That Involved Draft Picks

On February 24, 2018, the Oilers traded Brandon Davidson to the New York Islanders for the No. 85 overall pick in the 2019 draft (Ilya Konovalov).

On February 26, 2018, the Oilers traded Patrick Maroon to the New Jersey Devils for the rights to forward Joey Dudek and a 2019 third-round selection (Alexander Campbell).

On March 21, 2018, the Oilers traded a 2019 third-round pick to the Philadelphia Flyers for the rights to Cooper Marody.

On June 23, 2018, the Oilers traded a 2019 fifth-round pick (Rhett Pitlick) to the Montreal Canadiens for the rights to goalie Hayden Hawkey.

On December 30, 2018, the Oilers traded Chris Wideman and a 2019 third-round pick (John Ludvig) to the Florida Panthers for Alex Petrovic.

EVALUATION
BOB GREEN, SCOUTING DIRECTOR (2015-19)

SUCCESS IN THE FIRST 30 SELECTIONS OF EACH DRAFT

Edmonton chose five picks inside the top 30 overall during the years Green was in charge of the draft.

All five have a chance to enjoy long NHL careers. Connor McDavid is the best player in the game, Jesse Puljujarvi is a giant, toolsy winger who can make an impact in all areas, Kailer Yamamoto has played more than 100 NHL games, and two defencemen (Evan Bouchard, Philip Broberg) are developing well.

Yamamoto's selection in 2017 showed innovation by Green and the staff. A willingness to draft not just a small winger, but the smallest winger, was not a place I thought the Oilers would ever visit. Yamamoto's résumé helped; he has no fear and a great deal of skill. It was an excellent pick, especially considering where they got him.

It was the most "analytics" selection of the decade for Edmonton.

SUCCESS IN THE FIRST 100 SELECTIONS OF EACH DRAFT

The Green team drafted 11 men between Nos. 31 and 100, but it's early days on the entire group. Ryan McLeod (10), Tyler Benson (7), and Stuart Skinner (1) have already made an NHL appearance, with Dmitri Samorukov, Raphael Lavoie, and others trending in a good direction. It's an intriguing group, more skilled than in the past.

SUCCESS AFTER THE FIRST 100 SELECTIONS OF EACH DRAFT

Green's Oilers scouting staff have had great early success in this area of the draft. Ethan Bear (132), John Marino (108), and Caleb Jones (93) all arrived in the 2015 draft. The team drafted 17 men at 100-plus games between 2015 and 2019.

SUCCESS IN WHAT DEVELLANO CALLS "PROJECTING"

Green's scouting staff focused on puck movers and passing defencemen, improving the club's ability to get the puck moving north quickly. They also recognized that Yamamoto could survive using his quickness and was worth the risk.

SUCCESS IN ADDRESSING TEAM NEEDS

The Oilers drafted defencemen heavily during Green's time in the chair. Of the 33 picks between 2015 and '19, 13 were spent on defencemen. The Oilers needed to shore up the area and did so, especially during the 2015 and 2016 drafts (eight of 15 selections).

BEST FIRST-ROUND PICK

McDavid. However, that's not really fair, since the club was drafting first overall due to the lottery. McDavid aside, Puljujarvi can still be an impact player and Yamamoto has a chance to be a difference-maker on a skill line.

LEAST SUCCESSFUL FIRST-ROUND PICK

No player qualifies at this time; there hasn't been enough time to evaluate 2018–19 picks and the 2015–17 trio have been successful.

BEST PICK AFTER THE FIRST ROUND

Bear, in a surprisingly close race with Jones and Marino.

WHAT STYLE DID GREEN EMPLOY?

Green (and then Gretzky when he arrived) appeared to put in place a modern system. The scouts and Green would create the list and then Gretzky and the general manager would finalize it. I'm convinced Marino was a Chiarelli pick and Holland chose Broberg based on years of observation and anecdotal evidence.

WHAT PLAYER TYPE DID GREEN LOOK FOR AT THE DRAFT?

During Green's time, the Oilers began paying more attention to skill. The scoring rates for his forwards were superior to MacGregor's and Prendergast's eras and much of Fraser's.

THE 2020 DRAFT

The 2019–20 season was a ringing success for an organization badly in need of winning. Although COVID-19 shorted the season (Edmonton played 71 games instead of 82), the goal differential (225–217, plus-8) represented just the third time in 15 years (2005–06, 2016–17) the club scored more goals than it allowed.

Edmonton finished in second place in the Pacific Division, and Leon Draisaitl won the Art Ross Trophy, Hart Memorial Trophy, and Ted Lindsay Award. Connor McDavid, who faced a career crossroads with a potentially devastating injury at the end of 2018–19, returned and was effective for the entire season. Rookies Ethan Bear and Caleb Jones helped defensively and young Kailer Yamamoto had a monster run starting in January.

Edmonton was dismissed early in the postseason, but things were looking up for the organization after a couple of difficult campaigns.

Here are the 2019–20 rookies:
- Ethan Bear: 71 games, 5–16–21
- Caleb Jones: 43 games, 4–5–9
- Joel Persson: 13 games, 0–2–2
- Tyler Benson: 7 games, 0–1–1
- William Lagesson: 8 games, 0–0–0

Four defencemen from the group and four players drafted by the Oilers composed the rookies in 2019–20. Bear and Jones appear to be locks for regular duty on Edmonton's blue line for much of the next decade, with Lagesson and Benson still trying to establish themselves.

NO. 14 OVERALL: LC DYLAN HOLLOWAY
Wisconsin (NCAA)

Holloway's résumé suggested there were multiple ways he could make it to the NHL. After filling the net in the AJHL in 2018–19, he scored just 8–9–17 in 35 games in his freshman season with Wisconsin. Oilers scouts and the NHL industry were divided on how much offence he would bring. Holloway scored 5–4–9 in his final 10 games of 2018–19 and scored twice to begin his 2020–21 Wisconsin season after the draft. Holloway made the Oilers scouts look like geniuses with a breakout sophomore campaign for the Badgers, scoring 11–24–35 in 23 Big Ten games and dominating in all areas. He signed with Edmonton and was going to play in the AHL or NHL, but a late-season college injury postponed the opportunity. As he was heading to Oilers camp in September 2021, there were some questions about how much his injured thumb and wrist might affect his season.

NO. 100 OVERALL: LW CARTER SAVOIE
Sherwood Park Crusaders (AJHL)

A pure scorer, Savoie fell on draft day for reasons unknown. Red Line Report agreed he had first-line talent but was critical of his performances in the Top Prospects Game and World Jr. A Challenge. Savoie's first four games in his draft-plus-one season with Denver University (NCAA) saw him score five goals and six points, suggesting the Oilers may have stolen a player later in the 2020 draft. His shot is a game-changer and alone could get him to the NHL. He finished his freshman season with 13 goals in 24 games and is one of the most promising first-shot scorers in the system.

NO. 126 OVERALL: RW TYLER TULLIO
Oshawa Generals (OHL)

Tullio is a skill forward. Red Line Report noted his "excellent speed and great edge control" and compared him to Paul Byron. That's a tell that the Oilers took another skill forward who plays a determined style. In this way he is similar to Holloway in that he can make the NHL as a skill winger or a checker. He is more likely to develop into a middle-six, agitating forward with goal-scoring ability, and with that skill set he is destined to be a fan favourite in Edmonton. Tullio had a frustrating 2020–21, as he was unable to get much playing time in the Slovak Extraliga, the top league in Slovakia, but things were looking up for 2021–22 when the Oshawa Generals named him team captain in September. He signed his entry-level deal with the Oilers on September 6, 2021.

NO. 138 OVERALL: LW MAXIM BEREZKIN
Lokomotiv (KHL)

Berezkin is 6'2", 201 pounds, shoots right, and has an October 2001 birth date. He is a plus passer and has a great wrist shot, and at least one scouting report I've read suggests he displays some elements of a defensive game. Speed is his issue; his scouting report is somewhat similar to Teemu Hartikainen's on his draft day. His draft-plus-one season was divided between the KHL (he played 31 games, a large number for a teenager) and the MHL, where he scored consistently (25 games, 13–15–28). In the early days of the 2021–22 KHL season, Berezkin was once again playing, but getting limited minutes.

NO. 169 OVERALL: RC FILIP ENGARAS
University of New Hampshire (NCAA)

Engaras is an obscure name who drew some attention back in 2017 as draft eligible in Sweden's lower leagues. Like everyone on the list from Edmonton's 2020 draft, he is skilled. Through 2020–21, he had delivered two similar seasons for UNH in a two-way role.

NO. 200 OVERALL: LW JEREMIAS LINDEWALL

MoDo Jr. (Sweden)

Lindewall is 6'2", 183 pounds, and has a January 2002 birthday. He played in four games before the 2020 draft and went 4-4-8, and then moved up to the Allsvenskan (second Swedish league) and scored well there at 18. Although he was drafted very late, Lindewall's early résumé resembles prospects who have pushed much higher than originally projected.

2020 Draft Summary

Holland hired Tyler Wright as his director of scouting shortly after the 2019 draft, and the scouts (with Bob Green) did the evaluations of the 2020 draft crop. It takes time to get a feel for a scouting department, but a good guess has the Wright team being less democratic than previous incarnations after the Fraser era. (Number in parentheses is points per game.)

- Dylan Holloway (NCAA) age 17: 35 games, 8-9-17 (0.486)
- Carter Savoie (AJHL) age 17: 54 games, 53-46-99 (1.83)
- Tyler Tullio (OHL) age 17: 62 games, 27-39-66 (1.06)
- Maxim Berezkin (MHL) age 17: 51 games, 25-29-54 (1.06)
- Filip Engaras (NCAA) age 20: 25 games, 8-7-15 (0.60)
- Jeremias Lindewall (SuperElite U-20) age 17: 39 games, 11-17-28 (0.72)

Holloway, who filled the net at 16 in the AJHL (40 goals in 53 games), played in less of a feature role in college as a freshman. Savoie, Tullio, and Berezkin were all quality analytics picks, meaning the Oilers could be classified as a team whose drafting reflected math draft models.

Trades That Involved Draft Picks

On February 24, 2020, the Oilers traded Sam Gagner, a second-round pick in 2020 (Brock Faber), and a second-round pick in 2021 to the Detroit Red Wings for Andreas Athanasiou and Ryan Kuffner.

On February 24, 2020, the Oilers traded Kyle Brodziak and a fourth-round pick in the 2020 entry draft (Jan Bednar) to the Detroit Red Wings for Mike Green.

On October 7, 2020, the Oilers traded the No. 75 overall pick in the 2020 draft (Danil Gushchin) to the San Jose Sharks for No. 100 in 2020 (Carter Savoie) and No. 126 overall (Tyler Tullio) in the 2020 entry draft.

THE 2021 DRAFT

The Oilers had a strong regular season in the makeshift "Canadian" division, a one-time grouping of the Canadian teams due to Covid–19 restrictions at the border of Canada and the United States.

Edmonton finished second in the division, with a plus-29 goal differential—the highest since 2016–17. The Oilers exited the playoffs in the first round, the second year in a row with the same result under general manager Ken Holland and coach Dave Tippett.

Fans, already restless, had high expectations for a summer that left Holland with a pile of money and a bunch of roster holes. Connor McDavid swept all the awards, and the overall trajectory of the franchise was headed in a good direction (save the lack of playoff success).

Rookies in 2020–21 were a generally inconsequential group as freshmen, but held hope for big success in the future:

- RD Evan Bouchard: 14 games, 2-3-5
- LD William Lagesson: 19 games, 0-2-2
- LC Ryan McLeod: 10 games, 0-1-1
- G Stuart Skinner: 1 game, 5.03 goals-against average, .868 save percentage

NO. 22 OVERALL: RC XAVIER BOURGAULT
Shawinigan Cataractes (QMJHL)

Bourgault was the second player chosen by Edmonton from Shawinigan (Mathieu Descoteaux, 1996 first round) and is a fine offensive prospect. Red Line Report called him a "smooth fluid skater, deceptive with the puck. Soft hands for both giving and receiving passes. He's a finisher from the circles in." The selection continues a trend of drafting skill by Edmonton over several seasons. He scored 20 goals in 29 games during the shortened QMJHL regular season and posted 53 goals in 92 games over two seasons. He has an October 2002 birthday, so he could turn pro in the fall of 2022—continuing a recent tendency of choosing older picks that goes back several seasons for Edmonton.

NO. 90 OVERALL: LD LUCA MUNZENBERGER
Cologne (Germany Jr.)

After six forwards in a row were chosen by Tyler Wright at the beginning of his time with Edmonton, the club finally returned to defence with big German shutdown defender Munzenberger.

He is a throwback type, has size (6'2", 194 pounds) and good speed, and offensively has a good shot and can make a fine first pass. He'll earn his money suppressing offence and will attend Vermont (NCAA) beginning fall 2021.

NO. 116 OVERALL: RC JAKE CHIASSON
Brandon Wheat Kings (WHL)

Chiasson is a taller, lean forward (6'1", 165 pounds) who plays a PF style and has the complete range of skills. His shot is sneaky fast and he can score from range. He may land on the wing, but if he can continue to deliver offensively (23 games, 9–11–20) Edmonton may have landed a second-round talent in the fourth round.

NO. 180 OVERALL: RW MATVEI PETROV
Krylja Sovetov (Russia 2)

Another big forward (6'2", 181 pounds) with good hands, Petrov scored 22–20–42 in 58 games. A pure scorer with a quick release and a willingness to shoot often, he can also pass well. A one-dimensional player who will need to work on his defensive awareness, Petrov is another of Wright's pure scorers.

NO. 186 OVERALL: LW SHANE LACHANCE
Boston Jr. Bruins (NCDC)

Lachance has an excellent NHL pedigree: his father Scott played 819 NHL games and his grandfather (Jack Parker) was the legendary coach of the Boston University Terriers hockey club for decades. Lachance is 6'4" with great hands and shot and finds seams with passes. Speed is an issue.

NO. 212 OVERALL: RD MAXIMUS WANNER
Moose Jaw Warriors (WHL)

At 6'3", 185 pounds, Wanner is a two-way defender with good speed and excellent passing ability. He didn't get much exposure (22 games, 17 in 2020–21) due to the pandemic and should be regarded as a sleeper pick with great potential.

2021 Draft Summary

Tyler Wright's aggressive pursuit of skilled forwards continued in 2021. His first two Edmonton drafts delivered nine skill forwards and two defencemen. In 2020, two AJHL starters (Dylan Holloway and Carter Savoie) along with junior scorers Tyler Tullio and Maxim Berezkin gave the Oilers' draft a look of pure skill and impressive upside. The 2021 draft wasn't as aggressive, but the skilled talent was given priority:

- Xavier Bourgault (QMJHL) age 17: 29 games, 20–20–40 (1.38)
- Luca Munzenberger (Germany Jr.) age 17: 6 games, 1–2–3 (0.50)
- Jake Chiasson (WHL) age 17: 23 games, 9–11–20 (0.87)
- Matvey Petrov (Rus-2) age 17: 58 games, 22–20–42 (0.72)
- Shane Lachance (NCDC) age 17: 25 games, 6–9–15 (0.60)
- Max Wenner (WHL) age 17: 17 games, 0–4–4 (0.24)

The 2021 draft saw plenty of picks traded, but the ones used by the Oilers were spent on skill. This continued a trend going back to 2015 and the McDavid draft.

Trades That Involved Draft Picks

On July 19, 2019, the Oilers traded Milan Lucic and a 2021 third-round pick (Kirill Kirsanov) to the Calgary Flames for James Neal.

On July 26, 2019, the Oilers traded the rights to John Marino to the Pittsburgh Penguins for a 2021 sixth-round pick (Shane Lachance).

On February 24, 2020, the Oilers traded Sam Gagner, a second-round pick in 2020 (Brock Faber), and a second-round pick in 2021 to the Detroit Red Wings for Andreas Athanasiou and Ryan Kuffner.

On February 24, 2020, the Oilers traded a 2020 fifth-round pick (Gage Alexander) to the Ottawa Senators for Tyler Ennis.

On July 23, 2021, the Oilers traded the No. 20 overall selection (Jesper Wallstedt) to the Minnesota Wild for the No. 22 (Xavier Bourgault) and No. 90 (Luca Munzenberger) picks.

EVALUATION
TYLER WRIGHT, SCOUTING DIRECTOR (2019-PRESENT)

There are only two drafts to look at so far with Tyler Wright as the director of scouting for the Edmonton Oilers.

Wright's 2020 and 2021 drafts focused on skill forwards. There were questions about how much Dylan Holloway would deliver offensively, but the 2020 first-round pick delivered a terrific draft-plus-one season for the Wisconsin Badgers.

In 2021, Xavier Bourgault was a slight surprise, but once again offence is the calling card and Bourgault is money in the offensive zone.

Carter Savoie, Tyler Tullio, and Maxim Berezkin bring some offence, and all appear to have a chance.

14

FINAL SUMMARY

THIS BOOK ABOUT the Edmonton Oilers' draft history is also an overview of what works and what doesn't at the NHL draft. These are the conclusions:

- Drafting skill is the key to success.
- Teams who can deliver a strong "draft cluster" (Oilers 1979–81) can open a decade-long window of Stanley Cup opportunity.
- A retrospective look at Barry Fraser's early drafts suggests he discovered the "perfect storm" that modern scouting staffs are uncovering in real time. His 1979–81 drafts were exceptional because he chose skill at almost every turn. He just didn't know the value of his discovery.
- The Oilers went away from drafting skill and paid a heavy price. The first forward Edmonton drafted in the first round (Scott Metcalfe in 1985) wasn't a

strong offensive option. He was at about one point per game in his draft year, playing in a league that would see the average team score 301 goals. Metcalfe led his team in points that season, but his team scored just 239 goals. Randy Burridge was a superior player in the same league, same year, and was available through seven rounds. He would score 199 NHL goals. Fraser was looking for Dave Hunter. The parent team had Wayne Gretzky, Jari Kurri, Mark Messier, and Glenn Anderson. Why worry?

- It was an epic misstep. Replacing Gretzky was impossible, but it didn't mean they shouldn't try.
- Edmonton returned to emphasizing skill only when forced to when Gretzky and Kurri and Messier and Anderson were gone (salaries spiraling yearly).
- As soon as the scouts made it a priority, in the early 1990s the club found first-round gems (Jason Arnott, Ryan Smyth, Martin Rucinsky) but also later quality (Satan).
- By 1996, the team drafted a checking centre (Boyd Devereaux) No. 6 overall.
- Late-1990s success came via the Arnott-Smyth draft cluster and some brilliant trades by Glen Sather (Doug Weight, Curtis Joseph).
- At the end of Fraser's run as scouting director, the scouting staff struck on some interesting college players (Shawn Horcoff, Mike Comrie, Fernando Pisani) and that group sustained the organization through the early 2000s. A stunning series of trades

by general manager Kevin Lowe brought impact
defenceman Chris Pronger, goalie Dwayne Roloson,
and several other key components. Edmonton would
play in its seventh Stanley Cup Final in 2006.

• That brings us to the just-completed decade, the
2010s. Edmonton's drafting in the first half of the
decade included several top selections, but the youngsters couldn't pull the entire roster into the playoffs.

• In 2015, the Oilers won the draft lottery. That meant
Connor McDavid, the best player in a generation,
would spend his first decade (at least) in Edmonton.

• The team attempted to compete immediately and fell
flat. Fans blamed Peter Chiarelli, and he is the general
manager of record, but the pressure on ownership to
contend and fill a new arena must have been enormous. It's a good guess that pressure filtered down to
management.

All of this brings me to the final stanza in the story of Oilers
draft history—the McDavid cluster. The heart of the order (modern
edition) includes players drafted in 2013 (Darnell Nurse), 2014
(Leon Draisaitl), and of course 2015 (McDavid, Ethan Bear, Caleb
Jones).

There are signs the organization has recognized the impor-
tance of skill. The turning point, in my opinion, was the selection
of Kailer Yamamoto in 2017—a small, high-skill winger with the
intelligence to survive in a tough league and flourish because of
his skill.

In the final installment of junior points per game, we're looking at the lottery decade. These are No. 1 overall picks or top-five picks (Draisaitl), and Yamamoto:

PLAYER	YEAR	LGE	AGE	PTS/ GAME	NLGP	NHL PTS/ GAME
CONNOR McDAVID	2015	OHL	17	2.55	407	1.41
TAYLOR HALL	2010	OHL	17	1.86	680	0.88
LEON DRAISAILT	2014	WHL	17	1.64	478	1.06
NAIL YAKUPOV	2012	OHL	17	1.64	360	0.39
R NUGENT-HOPKINS	2011	WHL	17	1.54	656	0.73
KAILER YAMAMOTO	2017	WHL	17	1.52	105	0.50

That's the kind of draft list Edmonton needs to be looking at every year. A player is too small, but posted 1.50 points per 60 in any of the CHL leagues? Draft that guy.

It goes deeper, of course, but if you read through this book there does seem to be a recognition, beginning in the Stu MacGregor era and then running through Green and possibly Tyler Wright, of high-end skill being a priority.

Edmonton drafted another searing offensive talent the following year (Evan Bouchard) and have delivered some substantial talent in the years 2017–19.

The 2020 draft by new scouting director Tyler Wright featured all forwards who brought offence as a central skill.

It may signal a new era for Edmonton at the top of the NHL standings.

To compete for the Stanley Cup annually, great drafting is vital. We'll know the answer in 2025, but the players drafted between 2017 and '20 could be the support group for the McDavid–Draisaitl Oilers on a trip to a sixth Stanley Cup victory.

The emphasis on skill may have returned to Edmonton. In the past, the pursuit of offensively gifted talent has always led to better days. We wait.

10 PLAYERS WHO MISSED BUT HAD THE TALENT TO MAKE IT

Over the years, Edmonton has drafted several players whose draft-day numbers suggested a future NHL career was likely. Here are the 10 men who had great promise on draft day but failed to play in 100 NHL games.

1. **D Selmar Odelein** was a first-round pick in 1984 and displayed a range of skills. A talented player with the puck and capable defensively, an injury derailed his career just as he was starting in pro hockey.

2. **C Mike Golden** was chosen in the second round of the 1983 draft, No. 40 overall, after a fantastic season at Reading High School in Massachusetts. He started his college career at New Hampshire and then transferred to Maine, where he filled the net for three seasons and was a finalist in 1988 for the Hobey Baker award. He never played in the NHL despite a stunning amateur résumé.

3. **C Tomas Kapusta** was a skilled Czech forward drafted in 1985. He had good size and adjusted quickly to the

North American game. Kapusta was impressive as an AHL rookie in 1989–90, finishing just shy of a point per game. The timing was wrong, but he had NHL talent.

4. **LW Dan Currie** was drafted in the fourth round of the 1986 draft, No. 84 overall. He scored 21 goals in his draft year with the Soo Greyhounds of the OHL and increased his scoring to 31 and 50 goals in his two final junior seasons. During his first three AHL seasons, Currie scored 29, 36, and 47 goals, and then 50 in his fourth minor league season. In the season he scored 50 goals, Edmonton's top left wingers were Craig Simpson, Esa Tikkanen, Petr Klima, and Martin Gelinas. He played just 22 NHL games.

5. **C Gord Sherven** played in 97 NHL games, so he barely qualifies for this list. Sather traded him and then got him back. He scored well for Canada at the 1988 Olympics, but he couldn't find an NHL home. Sherven's rookie NHL season (69 games, 11-19-30) should have earned him a full second season, but he never got the chance.

6. **RW Kim Issel** had size and skill on the wings and hit 30 goals twice early in his minor league career. His résumé and early pro success should have resulted in more opportunities than he received from the Oilers.

7. **RW David Oliver** was drafted in 1991 from the Michigan Wolverines. A strong scoring winger, he arrived in the NHL in 1994–95 and would score 36 goals in his first 124 games. A scoring slump followed, and then he was lost to waivers and spent the next

decade bouncing between the minors and the NHL. He
ended up with 49 goals in 233 games, an average of 17
goals per 82 games. His scoring prowess should have
earned him more NHL time.

8. **LW Ralph Intranuovo** was drafted in 1992, No. 96
    overall. He played in just 22 NHL games, but if he
    played in the 2000s there's a good chance he would
    have enjoyed a long career. A great skater and impres-
    sive playmaker, he dominated the AHL for five seasons
    but barely got a sniff of the NHL.

9. **LD Doug Lynch** was drafted in the second round of
    the 2001 draft and progressed quickly through junior.
    He was named to the season-ending rookie All-Star
    team after a strong AHL debut. At that point Lynch
    was fairly close to a can't-miss prospect, but a wrist
    injury and the fallout from it derailed his career.

10. **LW Teemu Hartikainen** was a late pick in 2008 who
    had size and good hands but slower boots. When he
    arrived in North America, it was clear he had enough
    skill to push for an NHL job. A terrible scoring slump
    during his 2012–13 audition sealed his fate but there
    was a player there.

BEST VALUE PICKS

The Oilers have chosen wisely, gotten lucky, and used inside
knowledge to draft some of the most dominant players in the
game over the last 40 years. Here are the best of the best.

- Mark Messier, No. 48 overall in 1979 (1,756 NHL
  games)
- Jari Kurri, No. 69 overall in 1980 (1,251 NHL games)

- Glenn Anderson, No. 69 overall in 1979 (1,129 NHL games)
- Miro Satan, No. 111 overall in 1993 (1,050 NHL games)
- Esa Tikkanen, No. 80 overall in 1983 (877 NHL games)
- Shawn Horcoff, No. 99 overall in 1998 (1,008 NHL games)
- Steve Smith, No. 111 overall in 1981 (804 NHL games)
- Andy Moog, No. 132 overall in 1980 (713 NHL games)
- Jeff Petry, No. 45 overall in 2006 (735 NHL games)
- Jason Chimera, No. 121 overall in 1997 (1,107 NHL games)

APPENDIX

OILERS DRAFT LIST

1979

Round 1, Pick 21: D Kevin Lowe, Quebec Remparts (QMJHL)

Round 3, Pick 48: LW Mark Messier, Cincinnati Stingers (WHA)

Round 4, Pick 69: RW Glenn Anderson, Denver Pioneers (NCAA)

Round 4, Pick 84: LW Max Kostovich, Portland Winterhawks (WHL)

Round 5, Pick 105: C Mike Toal, Portland Winterhawks (WHL)

Round 6, Pick 126: Blair Barnes, Windsor Spitfires (OHA)

1980

Round 1, Pick 6: D Paul Coffey, Kitchener Rangers (OHA)

Round 3, Pick 48: RW Shawn Babcock, Wndsor Spitfires (OHA)

Round 4, Pick 69: RW Jari Kurri, Helsinki (Liiga)

Round 5, Pick 90: C Walt Poddubny, Kingston Canadians (OHA)

Round 6, Pick 111: LW Mike Winther, Brandon Wheat Kings (WHL)

Round 7, Pick 132: G Andy Moog, Billings Bighorns (WHL)
Round 8, Pick 153: G Rob Polman-Tuin, Michigan Tech (NCAA)
Round 9, Pick 174: LW Lars-Gunnar Pettersson, Lulea (SEL)

1981

Round 1, Pick 8: G Grant Fuhr, Victoria Cougars (WHL)
Round 2, Pick 29: C Todd Strueby, Regina Pats (WHL)
Round 4, Pick 71: RW Paul Houck, Kelowna Buckaroos (BCJHL)
Round 5, Pick 92: LW Phil Drouillard, Niagara Falls Flyers (OHL)
Round 6, Pick 111: D Steve Smith, London Knights (OHL)
Round 6, Pick 113: C Marc Habscheid, Saskatoon Blades (WHL)
Round 8, Pick 155: D Mike Sturgeon, Kelowna Buckaroos (BCJHL)
Round 9, Pick 176: D Miloslav Horava, Kladno (Czech)
Round 10, Pick 197: C Gord Sherven, Weyburn Beavers (SJHL)

1982

Round 1, Pick 20: D Jim Playfair, Portland Winterhawks (WHL)
Round 2, Pick 41: LW Steve Graves, Soo Greyhounds (OHL)
Round 3, Pick 62: LW Brent Loney, Cornwall Royals (OHL)
Round 4, Pick 83: LW Jaroslav Pouzar, Budejovice (Czech)
Round 5, Pick 104: D Dwayne Boettger, Toronto Marlboros (OHL)
Round 6, Pick 125: LW Raimo Summanen, Lahti (Liiga)
Round 7, Pick 146: RW Brian Small, Ottawa 67's (OHL)
Round 8, Pick 167: LW Dean Clark, St. Albert Saints (AJHL)
Round 9, Pick 188: G Ian Wood, Penticton Knights (BCJHL)
Round 10, Pick 209: D Grant Dion, Cowichan Capitals (BCJHL)
Round 11, Pick 230: G Chris Smith, Regina Pats (WHL)
Round 12, Pick 251: RW Jeff Crawford, Regina Pats (WHL)

1983

Round 1, Pick 19: D Jeff Beukeboom, Soo Greyhounds (OHL)

Round 2, Pick 40: C Mike Golden, Reading High School (USHS, Massachusetts)

Round 3, Pick 60: D Mike Flanagan, Acton-Boxborough High School (USHS, Massachusetts)

Round 4, Pick 80: LW Esa Tikkanen, Helsinki (Liiga)

Round 6, Pick 120: RW Don Barber, Kelowna Buckaroos (BCJHL)

Round 7, Pick 140: C Dale Derkatch, Regina Pats (WHL)

Round 8, Pick 160: LW Ralph Vos, Abbotsford Flyers (BCJHL)

Round 9, Pick 180: G Dave Roach, New Westminster Royals (BCJHL)

Round 10, Pick 200: C Warren Yadlowski, Calgary Wranglers (WHL)

Round 11, Pick 220: D John Miner, Regina Pats (WHL)

Round 12, Pick 240: D Steve Woodburn, Verdun Junior (QMJHL)

1984

Round 1, Pick 21: D Selmar Odelein, Regina Pats (WHL)

Round 2, Pick 42: G Darryl Reaugh, Kamloops Oilers (WHL)

Round 3, Pick 63: C Todd Norman, Hill-Murray High School (USHS, Minnesota)

Round 4, Pick 84: RW Richard Novak, Richmond Sockeyes (BCJHL)

Round 5, Pick 105: LW Rick Lambert, Henry Carr Crusaders (Metro Junior B Hockey League, MJBHL)

Round 6, Pick 106: D Emanuel Viveiros, Prince Albert Raiders (WHL)

Round 6, Pick 126: LW Ivan Dornic, Trencin (Czech)

Round 7, Pick 147: D Heikki Riihijarvi, Karpat Oulu (Finland Div. I)

Round 8, Pick 168: RW Todd Ewen, New Westminster Bruins (WHL)

Round 10, Pick 209: LW Joel Curtis, Oshawa Generals (OHL)

Round 11, Pick 229: C Simon Wheeldon, Victoria Cougars (WHL)

Round 12, Pick 250: D Darren Gani, Belleville Bulls (OHL)

1985

Round 1, Pick 20: C Scott Metcalfe, Kingston Canadians (OHL)

Round 2, Pick 41: D Todd Carnelley, Kamloops Blazers (WHL)

Round 3, Pick 62: RW Mike Ware, Hamilton Steelhawks (OHL)

Round 5, Pick 104: C Tomas Kapusta, Gottwaldov (Czech)

Round 6, Pick 125: G Brian Tessier, North Bay Centennials (OHL)

Round 7, Pick 146: RW Shawn Tyers, Kitchener Rangers (OHL)

Round 7, Pick 167: RW Tony Fairfield, St. Albert Saints (AJHL)

Round 9, Pick 188: RW Kelly Buchberger, Moose Jaw Warriors (WHL)

Round 10, Pick 209: D Mario Barbe, Chicoutimi Sagueneens (QMJHL)

Round 11, Pick 230: C Peter Headon, Notre Dame High School Wilcox (Saskatchewan)

Round 12, Pick 251: G John Haley, Hull High School (USHS, Massachusetts)

1986

Round 1, Pick 21: RW Kim Issel, Prince Albert Raiders (WHL)

Round 2, Pick 42: RW Jamie Nicolls, Portland Winterhawks (WHL)

Round 3, Pick 63: D Ron Shudra, Kamloops Blazers (WHL)

Round 4, Pick 84: LW Dan Currie, Soo Greyhounds (OHL)

Round 5, Pick 105: LW David Haas, London Knights (OHL)

Round 6, Pick 126: D Jim Ennis, Boston Universty (NCAA)

Round 7, Pick 147: RW Ivan Matulik, Bratislava Slovan (Slovakia)

Round 8, Pick 168: LW Nick Beaulieu, Drummondville Voltigeurs (QMJHL)

Round 9, Pick 189: G Mike Greenlay, Calgary Midgets AAA

Round 10, Pick 210: D Matt Lanza, Winthrop High School (USHS, Massachusetts)

Round 11, Pick 231: D Mojmir Bozik, Kosice (Czech)

Round 12, Pick 252: RW Tony Hand, Murrayfield Racers (BHL)

1987

Round 1, Pick 21: LW Peter Soberlak, Swift Current Broncos (WHL)

Round 2, Pick 42: D Brad Werenka, Northern Michigan University (NCAA)

Round 3, Pick 63: D Geoff Smith, St. Albert Saints (AJHL)

Round 4, Pick 64: LW Peter Eriksson, Jonkoping (SEL)

Round 5, Pick 105: C Shaun Van Allen, Saskatoon Blades (WHL)

Round 6, Pick 126: C Radek Toupal, Ceske Budejovice HC (Czech)

Round 7, Pick 147: LW Tomas Srsen, Brno (Czech)

Round 8, Pick 168: D Age Ellingsen, Storhammer (Norway)

Round 9, Pick 189: G Gavin Armstrong, RPI (NCAA)

Round 10, Pick 210: C Mike Tinkham, Newburyport High School (USHS, Massachusetts)

Round 11, Pick 231: D Jeff Pauletti, University of Minnesota (NCAA)

Round 12, Pick 241: D Jesper Duus, Rodovre (Denmark)

Round 12, Pick 252: LW Igor Vyazmikin, CSKA Moscow (RSL)

1988

Round 1, Pick 19: D Francois Leroux, St. Jean Castors (QMJHL)

Round 2, Pick 39: RW Petro Koivunen, Kiekko-Espoo (Finland Jr.)

Round 3, Pick 53: C Trevor Sim, Seattle Thunderbirds (WHL)

Round 3, Pick 61: D Collin Bauer, Saskatoon Blades (WHL)

Round 4, Pick 82: D Cam Brauer, RPI (NCAA)

Round 5, Pick 103: D Don Martin, London Knights (OHL)

Round 6, Pick 124: C Len Barrie, Victoria Cougars (WHL)

Round 7, Pick 145: RW Mike Glover, Soo Greyhounds (OHL)

Round 8, Pick 166: LW Shjon Podein, Minnesota-Duluth (NCAA)

Round 9, Pick 187: G Tom Cole, Woburn High Schoool (USHS, Massachusetts)

Round 10, Pick 208: D Vladimir Zubkov, CSKA Moscow (RSL)

Round 11, Pick 229: LW Darin MacDonald, Boston University (NCAA)

Round 12, Pick 250: C Tim Tisdale, Swift Current Broncos (WHL)

1989

Round 1, Pick 15: D Jason Soules, Niagara Falls Thunder (OHL)
Round 2, Pick 36: RW Richard Borgo, Kitchener Rangers (OHL)
Round 4, Pick 78: C Josef Beranek, Litvinoc HC (Czech)
Round 5, Pick 92: C Peter White, Michigan State University (NCAA)
Round 6, Pick 120: C Anatoli Semenov, Moscow Dynamo (RSL)
Round 7, Pick 140: RW Davis Payne, Michigan Tech (NCAA)
Round 7, Pick 141: LW Sergei Yashin, Dynamo Riga (Latvia)
Round 8, Pick 162: D Darcy Martini, Michigan Tech (NCAA)
Round 11, Pick 225: RW Roman Bozek, Ceske Budejovice HC (Czech)

1990

Round 1, Pick 17: LW Scott Allison, Prince Albert Raiders (WHL)
Round 2, Pick 38: D Alexander Legault, Boston University (NCAA)
Round 3, Pick 59: LW Joe Crowley, Lawrence Academy (USHS, Massachusetts)
Round 4, Pick 67: LW Joel Blain, Hull Olympiques (QMJHL)
Round 5, Pick 101: G Greg Louder, Cushing Academy (USHS, Massachusetts)
Round 6, Pick 122: LW Keijo Sailynoja, Jokerit-Helsinki (Liiga)
Round 7, Pick 143: G Mike Power, Western Michigan University (NCAA)
Round 8, Pick 164: RW Roman Mejzlik, Dukla Trencin (Czech)
Round 9, Pick 185: LW Richard Zemlicka, HC Sparta Praha (Czech)
Round 10, Pick 206: C Petr Korinek, Plzen (Czech)

Round 12, Pick 248: D Sami Nuutinen, Kiekko-Espoo (Finland Div. I)

1991

Round 1, Pick 12: C Tyler Wright, Swift Current Broncos (WHL)

Round 1, Pick 20: LW Martin Rucinsky, Litvinov HC (Czech)

Round 2, Pick 34: G Andrew Verner, Peterborough Petes (OHL)

Round 3, Pick 56: RW George Breen, Cushing Academy (USHS, Massachusetts)

Round 4, Pick 78: LW Mario Nobili, Longueuil College-Francais (QMJHL)

Round 5, Pick 93: LW Ryan Haggerty, Westminster High School (USHS, Connecticut)

Round 7, Pick 144: RW David Oliver, Michigan (NCAA)

Round 8, Pick 166: C Gary Kitching, Thunder Bay Flyers (USHL)

Round 10, Pick 210: F Vegar Barlie, Oslo (Norway)

Round 11, Pick 232: G Evgeny Belosheiken, CSKA Moscow (RSL)

Round 12, Pick 254: RW Juha Riihijarvi, Oulu Karpat (Liiga)

1992

Round 1, Pick 13: LW Joe Hulbig, St. Sebastian's High School (USHS, Massachusetts)

Round 2, Pick 37: LW Martin Reichel, Freiburg EHC (Ger-1)

Round 3, Pick 61: D Simon Roy, Chicoutimi Cataractes (QMJHL)

Round 3, Pick 65: LW Kirk Maltby, Owen Sound Platers (OHL)

Round 4, Pick 96: LW Ralph Intranuovo, Soo Greyhounds (OHL)

Round 5, Pick 109: G Joaquin Gage, Portland Winterhawks (WHL)

Round 7, Pick 157: LW Steve Gibson, Windsor Spitfires (OHL)

Round 8, Pick 181: LW Kyuin Shim, Sherwood Park Crusaders (AJHL)

Round 8, Pick 190: C Colin Schmidt, Regina Midgets

Round 9, Pick 205: RW Marko Tuomainen, Clarkson University (NCAA)

Round 11, Pick 253: LW Bryan Rasmussen, St. Louis Park High School (USHS, Minnesota)

1993

Round 1, Pick 7: C Jason Arnott, Oshawa Generals (OHL)

Round 1, Pick 16: D Nick Stadjuhar, London Knights (OHL)

Round 2, Pick 33: RW David Vyborny, Sparta Praha (Czech)

Round 3, Pick 59: LW Kevin Paden, Detroit Jr. Red Wings (OHL)

Round 3, Pick 60: LW Alexander Kerch, Dynamo Riga (Latvia)

Round 5, Pick 111: LW Miroslav Satan, Trencin Dukla (Czech)

Round 7, Pick 163: D Alex Zhurik, Dynamo Minsk (RSL)

Round 8, Pick 189: D Martin Bakula, University of Alaska-Anchorage (NCAA)

Round 9, Pick 215: D Brad Norton, Cushing Academy (USHS, Massachusetts)

Round 10, Pick 241: LW Oleg Maltsev, Chelyabinsk Traktor (RSL)

Round 11, Pick 267: D Ilya Byakin, Landschut (DEL)

1994

Round 1, Pick 4: C Jason Bonsignore, Niagara Falls Thunder (OHL)

Round 1, Pick 6: LW Ryan Smyth, Moose Jaw Warriors (WHL)

Round 2, Pick 32: LW Mike Watt, Stratford Cullitons (MOJHL)

Round 3, Pick 53: D Corey Neilson, North Bay Centennials (OHL)

Round 3, Pick 60: D Brad Symes, Portland Winterhawks (WHL)

Round 4, Pick 79: RW Adam Copeland, Burlington Cougars (OPJHL)

Round 4, Pick 95: RW Jussi Tarvainen, KalPa (Liiga)

Round 5, Pick 110: LW Jon Gaskins, Dubuque Fighting Saints (USHL)

Round 6, Pick 136: C Terry Marchant, Niagara Scenics (NAHL)

Round 7, Pick 160: D Curtis Sheptak, Olds Grizzlys (AJHL)

Round 7, Pick 162: RW Dmitri Shulga, Tivali Minsk (Russia)

Round 7, Pick 179: G Chris Wickenheiser, Red Deer Rebels (WHL)

Round 8, Pick 185: D Rob Guinn, Newmarket Royals (OHL)

Round 8, Pick 188: D Jason Reid, St. Andrew's College (Ontario HS)

Round 9, Pick 214: G Jeremy Jablonski, Victoria Cougars (WHL)

Round 11, Pick 266: D Ladislav Benysek, Olomouc (Czech)

1995

Round 1, Pick 6: C Steve Kelly, Prince Albert Raiders (WHL)

Round 2, Pick 31: RW Georges Laraque, St. Jean Lynx (QMJHL)

Round 3, Pick 57: D Lukas Zib, Ceske Budejovice HC (Czech)

Round 4, Pick 83: G Mike Minard, Chilliwack Chiefs (BCJHL)

Round 5, Pick 109: D Jan Snopek, Oshawa Generals (OHL)

Round 7, Pick 161: C Martin Cerven, Trencin Dukla (Slovak)

Round 8, Pick 187: D Stephen Douglas, Niagara Falls Thunder (OHL)

Round 9, Pick 213: D Jiri Antonin, Pardubice HC (Czech)

1996

Round 1, Pick 6: C Boyd Devereaux, Kitchener Rangers (OHL)

Round 1, Pick 19: D Matthieu Descoteaux, Shawinigan Cataractes (QMJHL)

Round 2, Pick 32: D Chris Hajt, Guelph Storm (OHL)

Round 3, Pick 59: D Tom Poti, Cushing Academy (USHS, Massachusetts)

Round 5, Pick 114: RW Brian Urick, Notre Dame (NCAA)

Round 6, Pick 141: RW Bryan Randall, Medicine Hat Tigers (WHL)

Round 7, Pick 168: RW David Bernier, St. Hyacinthe Lasers (QMJHL)

Round 7, Pick 170: RW Brandon LaFrance, Ohio State University (NCAA)

Round 8, Pick 195: RW Fernando Pisani, St. Albert Saints (AJHL)

Round 9, Pick 221: G John Hultberg, Kingston Frontenacs (OHL)

1997

Round 1, Pick 14: LW Michael Riesen, Biel HC (Swiss-B)

Round 2, Pick 41: G Patrick Dovigi, Erie Otters (OHL)

Round 3, Pick 68: D Sergei Yerkovich, Las Vegas Thunder (IHL)

Round 4, Pick 94: D Jonas Elofsson, Farjestads BK (SEL)

Round 5, Pick 121: LW Jason Chimera, Medicine Hat Tigers (WHL)

Round 6, Pick 141: C Peter Sarno, Windsor Spitfires (OHL)

Round 7, Pick 176: D Kevin Bolibruck, Peterborough Petes (OHL)

Round 7, Pick 187: C Chad Hinz, Moose Jaw Warriors (WHL)

Round 8, Pick 205: D Chris Kerr, Sudbury Wolves (OHL)

Round 9, Pick 231: G Alexander Fomitchev, St. Albert Saints (AJHL)

1998

Round 1, Pick 13: RW Michael Henrich, Barrie Colts (OHL)

Round 3, Pick 67: D Alex Henry, London Knights (OHL)

Round 4, Pick 99: C Shawn Horcoff, Michigan State University (NCAA)

Round 4, Pick 113: G Kristian Antila, Ilves Jr. (Finland)

Round 5, Pick 128: D Paul Elliott, Lethbridge Hurricanes (WHL)

Round 5, Pick 144: LW Oleg Smirnov, Elektrostal Kristall (WPHL)

Round 6, Pick 159: D Trevor Ettinger, Cape Breton Screaming Eagles (QMJHL)

Round 7, Pick 186: G Mike Morrison, Exeter High School (USHS, New Hampshire)

Round 8, Pick 213: D Christian Lefebvre, Baie-Comeau Drakker (QMJHL)

Round 9, Pick 241: RW Maxim Spiridonov, London Knights (OHL)

1999

Round 1, Pick 13: LW Jani Rita, Jokerit (Liiga)

Round 2, Pick 36: LD Alexei Semenov, Sudbury Wolves (OHL)

Round 2, Pick 41: LW Tony Salmelainen, HIFK Helsinki (Liiga)

Round 3, Pick 81: G Adam Hauser, Minnesota (NCAA)

Round 4, Pick 91: LC Mike Comrie, Michigan (NCAA)

Round 5, Pick 139: RD Jonathan Fauteux, Val d'Or Foreurs (QMJHL)

Round 6, Pick 171: F Chris Legg, London Nationals (WJBHL)

Round 7, Pick 199: LD Christian Chartier, Saskatoon Blades (WHL)

Round 9, Pick 256: LW Tomas Groschl, Leksands (SEL)

2000

Round 1, Pick 17: LW Alexei Mikhnov, Yaroslavl Torpedo (Russia 3)

Round 2, Pick 35: LW Brad Winchester, Wisconsin (NCAA)

Round 3, Pick 83: LD Alexender Ljobimov, Samara CSK (Russia)

Round 4, Pick 113: LC Lou Dickenson, Mississauga Ice Dogs (OHL)

Round 5, Pick 152: LD Paul Flache, Brampton Bitallion (OHL)

Round 6, Pick 184: RW Shaun Norrie, Calgary Hitmen (WHL)

Round 7, Pick 211: C Joe Cullen, Colorado College (NCAA)

Round 7, Pick 215: C Matthew Lombardi, Victoriaville Tigres (QMJHL)

Round 8, Pick 247: LD Jason Platt, Omaha Lancers (USHL)

Round 9, Pick 274: RW Evgeny Muratov, Neftekhimik (RSL)

2001

Round 1, Pick 13: RW Ales Hemsky, Hull Olympiques (QMJHL)

Round 2, Pick 43: LD Doug Lynch, Red Deer Rebels (WHL)

Round 2, Pick 52: LC Eddie Caron, Phillips-Exeter Academy (USHS, New Hampshire)

Round 3, Pick 84: LD Kenny Smith, Harvard (NCAA)

Round 5, Pick 133: G Jussi Markkanen, Tappara Tampere (Liiga)

Round 5, Pick 154: RW Jake Brenk, Breck High School (USHS, Minnesota)

Round 6, Pick 185: RD Michael Svensk, Vastra Frolunda (Sweden Jr.)

Round 7, Pick 215: LW Dan Baum, Prince George Cougars (WHL)

Round 8, Pick 248: LD Karl Haakana, Jokerit Helsinki (Liiga)

Round 9, Pick 272: RD Ales Pisa, Pardubice (Czech)

Round 9, Pick 278: LW Shay Stephenson, Red Deer Rebels (WHL)

2002

Round 1, Pick 15: LC Jesse Niinimaki, Ilves Tampere (Liiga)

Round 2, Pick 31: G Jeff Drouin-Deslauriers, Chicoutimi Sagueneens (QMJHL)

Round 2, Pick 36: RC Jarret Stoll, Kootenay Ice (WHL)

Round 2, Pick 44: RD Matt Greene, Green Bay Gamblers (USHL)

Round 3, Pick 79: LW Brock Radunske, Michigan State University (NCAA)

Round 4, Pick 106: LD Ivan Koltsov, Cherepovets (Russia Jr.)

Round 4, Pick 111: LC Jonas Almtorp, MoDo (Sweden Jr.)

Round 4, Pick 123: RD Robin Kovar, Vancouver Giants (WHL)

Round 5, Pick 148: G Glenn Fisher, Ft. Saskatchewan Traders (AJHL)

Round 6, Pick 181: LD Mikko Luoma, Tappara Tampere (Liiga)

Round 7, Pick 205: LW Jean-Francois Dufort, Cape Breton Screaming Eagles (QMJHL)

Round 7, Pick 211: LW Patrick Murphy, Newmarket Hurricanes (OPJHL)

Round 8, Pick 244: LC Dwight Helminen, Michigan (NCAA)

Round 8, Pick 245: LW Tomas Micka, Slava Praha (Czech)

Round 9, Pick 274: LC Fredrik Johansson, Frolunda (Sweden Jr.)

2003

Round 1, Pick 22: RC Marc-Antoine Pouliot, Rimouski Oceanic (QMJHL)

Round 2, Pick 51: RW Colin McDonald, New England Jr. Coyotes (EJHL)

Round 2, Pick 68: LW Jean-Francois Jacques, Baie-Comeau Drakkar (QMJHL)

Round 3, Pick 72: LC Mikhail Zhukov, Arbola (Sweden)

Round 3, Pick 94: RW Zack Stortini, Sudbury Wolves (OHL)

Round 5, Pick 147: RW Kalle Olsson, Frolunda (Sweden Jr.)

Round 5, Pick 154: RD David Rohlfs, Detroit Compuware (NAHL)

Round 6, Pick 184: RW Dragan Umicevic, Sodertalje SK (SEL)

Round 7, Pick 214: RC Kyle Brodziak, Moose Jaw Warriors (WHL)

Round 7, Pick 215: RD Mathieu Roy, Val d'Or Foreurs (QMJHL)

Round 8, Pick 248: LD Josef Hrabal, Vsetin (Czech Jr.)

Round 9, Pick 278: RW Troy Bodie, Kelowna Rockets (WHL)

2004

Round 1, Pick 14: G Devan Dubnyk, Kamloops Blazers (WHL)

Round 1, Pick 25: LC Rob Schremp, London Knights (OHL)

Round 2, Pick 44: RD Roman Tesliuk, Kamloops Blazers (WHL)

Round 2, Pick 57: LW Geoff Paukovich, U.S. National U-18 Team (NAHL)

Round 4, Pick 112: LW Liam Reddox, Peterborough Petes (OHL)

Round 5, Pick 146: LD Bryan Young, Peterborough Petes (OHL)

Round 6, Pick 177: RD Max Gordichuk, Kamloops Blazers (WHL)

Round 7, Pick 208: RW Stephane Goulet, Quebec Remparts (QMJHL)
Round 8, Pick 242: LC Tyler Spurgeon, Kelowna Rockets (WHL)
Round 9, Pick 274: G Bjorn Bjurling, Djurgardens IF Stockholm (SEL)

2005

Round 1, Pick 25: LC Andrew Cogliano, St. Michael's Buzzers (OPJHL)
Round 2, Pick 36: LD Taylor Chorney, Shattuck St. Mary's High School (USHS, Michigan)
Round 3, Pick 81: LD Danny Syvret, London Knights (OHL)
Round 3, Pick 86: LC Robby Dee, Breck High School (USHS, Minnesota)
Round 4, Pick 97: LC Chris VandeVelde, Moorhead High School (USHS, Minnesota)
Round 4, Pick 120: LW Vyacheslav Trukhno, Prince Edward Island Rocket (QMJHL)
Round 5, Pick 157: LW Fredrik Pettersson, Frolunda (Sweden Jr.)
Round 7, Pick 220: LW Matthew Glaser, Ft. Saskatchewan Traders (AJHL)

2006

Round 2, Pick 45: RD Jeff Petry, Des Moines Buccaneers (USHL)
Round 3, Pick 75: LD Theo Peckham, Owen Sound Attack (OHL)
Round 5, Pick 133: G Bryan Pitton, Brampton Battalion (OHL)
Round 5, Pick 140: LD Cody Wild, Providence College (NCAA)
Round 6, Pick 170: LC Alexander Bumagin, Tolyatti Lada (RSL)

2007

Round 1, Pick 6: RC Sam Gagner, London Knights (OHL)
Round 1, Pick 15: RD Alex Plante, Calgary Hitmen (WHL)
Round 1, Pick 21: RC Riley Nash, Salmon Arm Silverbacks (BCHL)
Round 4, Pick 97: LW Linus Omark, Lulea (SEL)
Round 5, Pick 127: LC Milan Kytnar, Topolcany (Slovakia)
Round 6, Pick 157: LW William Quist, Tingsryds (Sweden Jr.)

2008

Round 1, Pick 22: RW Jordan Eberle, Regina Pats (WHL)
Round 4, Pick 103: RD Johan Motin, Bofors (Swe-1)
Round 5, Pick 133: LW Philippe Cornet, Rimouski Oceanic (QMJHL)
Round 6, Pick 163: LW Teemu Hartikainen, KalPa (Finland Jr.)
Round 7, Pick 193: RD Jordan Bendfeld, Medicine Hat Tigers (WHL)

2009

Round 1, Pick 10: LW Magnus Paajarvi, Timra (SEL)
Round 2, Pick 40: C Anton Lander, Timra (SEL)
Round 3, Pick 71: D Troy Hesketh, Minnetonka High School (USHS, Minnesota)
Round 3, Pick 82: RW Cameron Abney, Everett Silvertips (WHL)
Round 4, Pick 99: D Kyle Bigos, Vernon Vipers (BCHL)
Round 4, Pick 101: RW Toni Rajala, Ilves (Finland Jr.)
Round 5, Pick 133: G Olivier Roy, Cape Breton Screaming Eagles (QMJHL)

2010

Round 1, Pick 1: LW Taylor Hall, Windsor Spitfires (OHL)

Round 2, Pick 31: C Tyler Pitlick, Minnesota State-Mankato (NCAA)

Round 2, Pick 46: LD Martin Marincin, Slovakia U-20 (Slovakia)

Round 2, Pick 48: LW Curtis Hamilton, Saskatoon Blades (WHL)

Round 3, Pick 61: LC Ryan Martindale, Ottawa 67's (OHL)

Round 4, Pick 91: RD Jeremie Blain, Acadie-Bathurst (QMJHL)

Round 5, Pick 121: G Tyler Bunz, Medicine Hat Tigers (WHL)

Round 6, Pick 162: LD Brandon Davidson, Regina Pats (WHL)

Round 6, Pick 166: LW Drew Czerwonka, Kootenay Ice (WHL)

Round 7, Pick 181: LW Kristians Pelss, Dynamo (Belarus Jr.)

Round 7, Pick 202: LW Kellen Jones, Vernon Vipers (BCHL)

2011

Round 1, Pick 1: LC Ryan Nugent-Hopkins, Red Deer Rebels (WHL)

Round 1, Pick 19: LD Oscar Klefbom, Farjestads (SHL)

Round 2, Pick 31: LD David Musil, Vancouver Giants (WHL)

Round 3, Pick 62: G Samu Perhonen, JYP (Finland Jr.)

Round 3, Pick 74: LC Travis Ewanyk, Edmonton Oil Kings (WHL)

Round 4, Pick 92: LD Dillon Simpson, North Dakota (NCAA)

Round 4, Pick 114: LW Tobias Rieder, Kitchener Rangers (OHL)

Round 5, Pick 122: LD Martin Gernat, Kosice (Czech Jr.)

Round 7, Pick 182: G Frans Tuohimaa, Jokerit (Finland Jr.)

2012

Round 1, Pick 1: RW Nail Yakupov, Sarnia Sting (OHL)

Round 2, Pick 32: LW Mithcell Moroz, Edmonton Oil Kings (WHL)

Round 3, Pick 63: LW Jujhar Khaira, Prince George Spruce Kings (BCHL)

Round 3, Pick 91: LW Daniil Zharkov, Belleville Bulls (OHL)

Round 4, Pick 93: LD Erik Gustafsson, Djurgardens (SEL)

Round 5, Pick 123: LD Joey Laleggia, Denver Pioneers (NCAA)

Round 6, Pick 153: RW John McCarron, Cornell (NCAA)

2013

Round 1, Pick 7: LD Darnell Nurse, Soo Greyhounds (WHL)

Round 2, Pick 56: LC Marc-Olivier Roy, Blainville-Boisbriand Armada (QMJHL)

Round 3, Pick 83: LC Bogdan Yakimov, Nizhnekamsk (Russia Jr.)

Round 3, Pick 88: LW Anton Slepyshev, Ufa (KHL)

Round 4, Pick 94: RW Jackson Houck, Vancouver Giants (WHL)

Round 4, Pick 96: RC Kyle Platzer, London Knights (OHL)

Round 4, Pick 113: LW Aidan Muir, Victory Honda Midget (MWEHL)

Round 5, Pick 128: LW Evan Campbell, Langley Riverman (BCHL)

Round 6, Pick 158: LD Ben Betker, Everett Silvertips (WHL)

Round 7, Pick 188: RW Greg Chase, Calgary Hitmen (WHL)

2014

Round 1, Pick 3: LC Leon Draisaitl, Prince Albert Raiders (WHL)

Round 4, Pick 91: LD William Lagesson, Frolunda (Sweden Jr.)

Round 4, Pick 111: G Zach Nagelvoort, Michigan (NCAA)

Round 5, Pick 130: LC Liam Coughlin, Vernon Vipers (BCHL)

Round 6, Pick 153: RW Tyler Vesel, Omaha Lancers (USHL)

Round 7, Pick 183: G Keven Bouchard, Val d'Or Foreurs (QMJHL)

2015

Round 1, Pick 1: LC Connor McDavid, Erie Otters (OHL)

Round 4, Pick 117: LD Caleb Jones, U.S. National Development Team (USHL)

Round 5, Pick 124: LD Ethan Bear, Seattle Thunderbirds (WHL)

Round 6, Pick 154: RD John Marino, South Shore Kings (USPHL-Prep School)

Round 7, Pick 208: G Miroslav Svoboda, Trinec (Czech Jr.)

Round 7, Pick 209: LD Ziyat Paigan, Kazan Ak-Bars (KHL)

2016

Round 1, Pick 4: RW Jesse Puljujarvi, Karpat (Liiga)

Round 2, Pick 32: LW Tyler Benson, Vancouver Gianta (WHL)

Round 3, Pick 63: LD Markus Niemelainen, Saginaw Spirit (OHL

Round 3, Pick 84: LD Matt Cairns, Georgetown Raiders (OJHL)

Round 3, Pick 91: RD Filip Berglund, Skelleftea (Sweden Jr.)

Round 5, Pick 123: G Dylan Wells, Peterborough Petes (OHL)

Round 5, Pick 149: LW Graham McPhee, U.S. National Development Team (USHL)

Round 6, Pick 153: RC Aapeli Rasanen, Tappara (Finland Jr.)

Round 7, Pick 183: RD Vincent Desharnais, Providence (NCAA)

2017

Round 1, Pick 22: RW Kailer Yamamoto, Spokane Chiefs (WHL)
Round 3, Pick 78: G Stuart Skinner, Lethbridge Hurricanes (WHL)
Round 3, Pick 84: LW Dmitri Samorukov, Guelph Storm (OHL)
Round 4, Pick 115: LW Ostap Safin, Sparta (Czech Jr.)
Round 5, Pick 146: RW Kirill Maksimov, Niagara Ice Dogs (OHL)
Round 6, Pick 177: LC Skyler Brind'Amour, U.S. National Development Team (USHL)
Round 7, Pick 208: RD Phil Kemp, U.S. National Development Team (USHL)

2018

Round 1, Pick 10: RD Evan Bouchard, London Knights (OHL)
Round 2, Pick 40: LC Ryan McLeod, Mississauga Steelheads (OHL)
Round 2, Pick 62: G Olivier Rodrigue, Drummondville Voltigeurs (QMJHL)
Round 6, Pick 164: RD Mike Kesselring, New Hampton School (USHS, New Hampshire)
Round 7, Pick 195: LW Patrik Siikanen, Blues (Finland Jr.)

2019

Round 1, Pick 8: LD Philip Broberg, AIK (Allsvenskan)
Round 2, Pick 38: RC Raphael Lavoie, Halifax Mooseheads (QMJHL)
Round 3, Pick 85: G Ilya Konovalov, Yaroslavl Lokomotiv (KHL)
Round 4, Pick 100: LW Matej Blumel, Waterloo Blackhawks (USHL)

Round 6, Pick 162: LC Tomas Mazura, Kimball Union (USHS, New Hampshire)

Round 7, Pick 193: LC Maxim Denezhkin, Yaroslavl (Russia Jr.)

2020

Round 1, Pick 14: LC Dylan Holloway, Wisconsin (NCAA)

Round 4, Pick 100: LW Carter Savoie, Sherwood Park Crusaders (AJHL)

Round 5, Pick 126: RW Tyler Tullio, Oshawa Generals (OHL)

Round 5, Pick 138: LW Maxim Berezkin, Yaroslavl (Russia Jr.)

Round 6, Pick 169: RC Filip Engaras, New Hampshire (NCAA)

2021

Round 1, Pick 22: RC Xavier Bourgault, Shawinigan Cataractes (QMJHL)

Round 3, Pick 90: LD Luca Munzenberger, Cologne (Germany Jr.)

Round 4, Pick 116: RC Jake Chiasson, Brandon Wheat Kings (WHL)

Round 6, Pick 180: RW Matvei Petrov, Krylja Sovetov (Russia 2)

Round 6, Pick 186: LW Shane Lachance, Boston Jr. Bruins (NCDC)

Round 7, Pick 212: RD Maximus Wanner, Moose Jaw Warriors (WHL)

NHL GAMES PLAYED BY DRAFT YEAR
(THROUGH 2020–21)

1979 (4,143 games)

1980 (3,841 games)

1993 (3,025 games)

1981 (2,215 games)

1996 (1,924 games)

2003 (1,905 games)

1983 (1,810 games)

1991 (1,807 games)

1994 (1,667 games)

1987 (1,602 games)

2002 (1,579 games)

2005 (1,569 games)

2007 (1,554 games)

2011 (1,519 games)

2010 (1,375 games)

1992 (1,251 games)

1998 (1,214 games)

1985 (1,206 games)

1989 (1,137 games)

1988 (1,135 games)

1997 (1,126 games)

2001 (1,043 games)

1999 (937 games)

2000 (928 games)

2006 (895 games)

2012 (858 games)

1995 (845 games)

2008 (834 games)

2004 (773 games)

2015 (740 games)

2009 (682 games)

1984 (607 games)

2013 (509 games)

2014 (505 games)

1982 (394 games)

2016 (201 games)

2017 (106 games)

1986 (50 games)

2018 (31 games)

1990 (0 games)

SOURCES

BOOKS

Gzowski, Peter. *The Game of Our Lives*. McClelland & Stewart, 1981.

Lowe, Kevin, and Stan Fischler. *Champions: The Making of the Edmonton Oilers*. Prentice-Hall Canada, 1988.

NEWSPAPERS AND PERIODICALS

Edmonton Journal

Tampa Bay Times

Toronto Star

Washington Post

WEBSITES

boysonthebus.com

cbc.ca

darkhorseanalytics.com

hockeydraftcentral.com

hockeysfuture.com

hockey-reference.com

nhl.com

puckiq.com

sportsnet.ca

theathletic.com

youtube.com